ALWAYS THE
QUEEN

MUSIC IN AMERICAN LIFE

A list of books in the series appears at the end of this book.

ALWAYS THE
QUEEN

The Denise LaSalle Story

Denise LaSalle
with David Whiteis

**UNIVERSITY OF
ILLINOIS PRESS**
Urbana, Chicago, and Springfield

Library of Congress Cataloging-in-Publication Data
Names: LaSalle, Denise, author. | Whiteis, David, author.
Title: Always the queen: the Denise LaSalle story / Denise
   LaSalle with David Whiteis.
Description: Urbana: University of Illinois Press, 2020. |
   Series: Music in American life | Includes bibliographical
   references and index.
Identifiers: LCCN 2019049761 (print) | LCCN 2019049762
   (ebook) | ISBN 9780252043079 (cloth) | ISBN
   9780252084942 (paperback) | ISBN 9780252051937 (ebook)
Subjects: LCSH: LaSalle, Denise. | Singers—United States—
   Biography. | Blues musicians—United States--Biography.
   | Soul musicians—United States—Biography. | LCGFT:
   Autobiographies.
Classification: LCC ML421.L3715 A3 2020 (print) | LCC ML421.
   L3715 (ebook) | DDC 782.421643092 [B]—-dc23
LC record available at https://lccn.loc.gov/2019049761
LC ebook record available at https://lccn.loc.gov/2019049762

In loving memory of our parents:
Nancy Cooper Allen and Nathaniel Allen Sr.
and
Helen Luby Whiteis and Ulysses Edward Whiteis

Contents

Acknowledgments

NOTE: Denise LaSalle passed away before she had the opportunity to contribute to this section. I know that if she were here, she would first want to give praise to God and to her Lord and Savior, Jesus Christ. She would also want to thank her husband, James Wolfe, and her children, Bridgette Wolfe-Edwards and Kenny Ray Kight Jr. for their love and support through the years. The myriad other people, both within and outside the music industry, who touched and enriched her life are acknowledged and praised over the course of her narrative.

* * *

As always, I thank Laurie Matheson, Julianne Laut, and their colleagues at University of Illinois Press for their support and assistance throughout this project. Thanks also to the readers whose critiques and comments greatly facilitated the editing and fact-checking of the manuscript.

This book is drawn primarily from transcriptions of interviews and discussions between Denise LaSalle and me that took place between January and December of 2017, as well as earlier interviews in 2010 and numerous follow-up telephone conversations in the intervening years. Excerpts from some of these earlier interviews were originally incorporated into articles for *Living Blues* magazine and my book *Southern Soul-Blues*, published by University of Illinois Press in 2013.

Special thanks to Steve Cagle and Linda Higgins for their kindness in sharing recorded interviews they conducted with Denise LaSalle in the early 2000s; these recordings were invaluable in supplying further detail and factual confirmation concerning Ms. LaSalle's narrative. The Rev. Morris Allen, the Rev. Preston Allen Jr., Loretta "Jazzii A." Anderson, Bill Jones, Kenny Ray Kight Sr., Christopher Pruitt, Naomi "Sutter" Pruitt, James E. Wolfe, Karen Wolfe, and Bridgette Wolfe-Edwards made themselves available for extensive conversations during which important clarifications concerning dates and timelines were confirmed. Special thanks to Ms. Pruitt for sharing her written narrative, which included vivid reminiscences of the Allen family's years in rural Mississippi and Belzoni. Ms. Vernetta Washington of the Humphreys County Circuit Clerk's Office in Belzoni, Mississippi, provided vital documentation concerning Denise LaSalle's first two marriages, as explained in "A Note on the Text" at the conclusion of this book. I would also like to thank Ms. Angela Cork, whose YouTube video of Denise LaSalle's performance at the 2017 Delta Heritage Blues & Heritage Festival in Greenville, Mississippi, was invaluable in corroborating Ms. LaSalle's recollection of the event. I thank and commend Peter M. Hurley for his excellent photography and unflagging collegial enthusiasm.

Those whose friendship, collegiality, and support have been invaluable in helping to see this project to fruition include Dee Alexander, the late J. Blackfoot, Cicero Blake, Anna Neal Coday, Larry Chambers, the late Otis Clay, Tommy Couch Jr., Daddy B. Nice (Bruno Nicewanger), Bill Dahl, Dylann DeAnna ("Blues Critic"), Vertie Joann Delapaz (Ms. Jody), Jonathan Ellison—you're a lifesaver and a superb driver!—Toni Green, Queen Ann Hines, Millie Jackson, the late Star Johnson, Benny Latimore, Charles Mitchell, Mr. Sam (Sam Fallie), Ms. Nickki (Nicole Whitlock), Mzz Reese, Jim O'Neal, Bettie Payton-White, Judy Peiser, Sheba Potts-Wright, Joe Pratt, Bob Pruter, Bobby Rush, Howard Scott, Joewaun Scott, Kenneth "Hollywood" Scott, Sir Walter Scott, Helen Sims, Mable Starks, Joyce "Cookie" Threatt, John Ward, the late Artie "Blues Boy" White, and Gary Wolfe.

My deepest thanks, appreciation, and undying love, of course, go to the Queen herself, my beloved friend, Denise LaSalle: "I still feel your presence in everything that I do. . . ."

David Whiteis
Chicago, July 2019

ALWAYS THE
QUEEN

Prelude

"Far Away Places"

> *"Far away places with strange sounding names,*
> *far away over the sea;*
> *Those far away places with the strange sounding names*
> *are calling, calling me . . ."*

Three schoolgirls, about thirteen or fourteen years old, strolling along a dusty street in Belzoni, Mississippi, all hugged up, arms around each other's shoulders. I might have been the girl in the middle; I can't remember after all these years. But I do remember the song I was singing:

> *"Going to China or maybe Siam*
> *I want to see for myself*
> *Those far away places I've been reading about*
> *in a book that I took from a shelf . . ."*

I'd been singing for years, but almost no one knew about it. In the country, first on the plantation where we lived and worked, then later, after we'd moved to Belzoni but still hired ourselves out during harvest time, I'd trudge down the rows lugging my cotton sack, stooped over, raising my voice in song, sweating and toiling under the hot Delta sun.

In those days, I'd sing whatever was on the radio. A lot of it was country, Grand Ole Opry stuff, because that's basically all we listened to. And then on weekends, we had WLAC from Nashville. A guy named John R used to be the DJ, and Hoss Allen, and they'd play blues and R&B. And of course we all sang gospel, because we all went to church. So that's what we would be singing in the fields every day.

On this day, though, I was singing a different song. I'm sure I must have heard it on the radio, too, probably at home. To me, the words felt like a dream:

> *"I feel kind of lonely whenever I hear*
> *the whistle of a train;*
> *I pray for the day I can get underway*
> *And look for those castles in Spain . . ."*

All of a sudden, a white woman stepped off her porch. "Hey singer! Come here!" Said, "What's that you're singing? Sing for me!"

And I sang it for her, and she paid me fifty cents. That was the first time I ever got paid for singing, and that was the first song I got paid for.

I used to dream about standing on stage, singing. To me, it looked like an ocean. It just looked like there's an ocean in front of me, as far as I can see is water, but when I look out over that water, it had faces. I thought it was a sea of faces, that's what it looked like to me. I didn't have actual knowledge of what auditoriums or audiences looked like; I didn't know about that. No, there was no big auditorium. I didn't see walls; there were no walls, it was just an ocean, but it was all people. That's all I could see. And I would dream that I was singing. I don't know what I was singing, but I knew I was up there because I was singing.

When that lady gave me fifty cents for singing that song, of course, I had no way of knowing what was in store for me, that the sea of faces would someday become real, that my songs really would take me far away, to places I couldn't have even imagined then. No, for the time being, the thrill of being heard and appreciated—and paid!—was enough. But still, in the back of my mind, I wondered . . .

> *"They call me a dreamer, well maybe I am*
> *But I know that I'm burning to see*
> *Those far away places with the strange sounding names*
> *Calling, calling me . . ."*

Could dreams come true? Here is one woman's story of how they did.

Chapter One
Mississippi Girl

"A House with a Hole in It"

That's my earliest memory.

Years ago, out in the country, they used to make duplexes, houses for two families to live in. The house had a hallway straight down the middle with rooms on one side and rooms on another side. You could stand in front, look down the front porch, and look straight through the house. And that's the first memory I had; the first thing I remember was a house with a hole in it. That's what I called it.

It didn't come to me until we had moved out of that house. My mama and them, in our new house, now we had both sides; just walk across the hall and go in this room or that room, from one bedroom to another. One day I asked her, "Mama, didn't we used to live in a house with a hole in it?" And she couldn't imagine what I was talking about. But I kept telling her, "There was a hole in the house! You could look straight through it."

I guess I had grown up a little bit, maybe three or four years old by then, and I described it to her. She said, "You don't remember that! We lived in that house when you was a baby. You couldn't possibly remember."

I said, "Well, I remember seeing a house with a hole in it."

And she finally had to admit I must remember it, because nobody talked about it when we moved from there, and I could just see it in my head. I remember crawling around, going on the floor, looking at that hole in the house. And that's the first thing I can remember. So my mother finally said, "Well yes, we used to live in a house like that in The Island."

They called it The Island because from every direction you had to cross water to get there. On one side was the Yazoo River, then on the other side was Catfish Lake. It was over near Sidon, Mississippi, just west of town. The plantation we lived on then was called Phillipston's. That was the name of the white man who had bought the land.

My parents were farmers—dirt farmers. Cotton, corn, and everything. Hogs and cows. They always worked on somebody else's farm, working as sharecroppers, what they called the "third and fourth." For every four bales of cotton they picked, three went to "Mister Ludlow." That's what we called all white folk that used to own farms, "Mister Ludlow." The fourth bale would be my mom and dad's money. Corn, the same way; one out of every three wagon loads went to us.

When we moved from The Island, we moved onto Mister Yaeger's plantation. I don't remember much about Mister Yaeger; we really didn't see him that often. On the plantations in those days, the white man who owned the land would pick him somebody to oversee the property. That overseer was always a black man. I don't know if it was because black folk related better to other black folk or what the reason was, but it was always a black man, and nine times out of ten, it would be someone who was lighter-skinned. He was the one who got on his horse and rode around to all the black folks' farms and see that everything was okay. And then he went back and told Mister Yaeger how things were. Anything my mama or daddy wanted, they had to go tell the black man; the black man take it to the white man, and he ended up getting what they wanted.

The overseer on our plantation was Mister Hunter Southworth. We didn't know who his daddy was; Mister Hunter looked white, but he wasn't white. I think maybe his father or his grandfather was Ol' Massa during slavery times. Because, you know, that happened a lot then. They could do whatever they wanted with us, and a lot of them had children by us. And a lot of times those children were still favored, even later, after all those years, when my siblings and I were coming up.

When my family was working there and we children were coming along, the overseer had this big barn where everybody living on the plantation would come and get mules or whatever they needed, plows and things like that. That's what my daddy was doing at first. But then they made an arrangement where he could purchase his own mules and things. It was pretty much like buying something on credit. They'd give him a price, and then he owed the money, whatever it was, and they'd take it out of his earnings when they paid off at the end of the year. Of course, that meant he never really owned any of it; he just kept paying, little by little, but none of it was ever really his. But he could use it like it was his, and it was probably better than having to go up to the overseer's barn and fetch everything every time he had to go out in the field and work. My daddy got his own mules, and they let him have his own little area that he could farm for himself.

I remember we had a pear tree in the front yard, and we had an apple tree, and there was a little peach orchard down the side, with maybe about eight peach trees out there. And we had a black walnut tree. My daddy had it all fenced in, and that little area was called a truck patch. We didn't actually own it, of course. All the property belonged to the bossman. But he'd let us fence it off and use it if we did the work to keep it up and take care of it. And later on we had—I can't call it a garage because it wasn't a garage; it was a car shed. Four posts sticking up with some tin built over it. That's where the car was. And I think my daddy had a T-Model Ford, or A-Model Ford, something like that.

Our kitchen was attached to the house. It was a four-room house, and it looked like somebody had said, "Well, I need these rooms here, but I want a kitchen, too." And so they went and got a cotton shed, and they brought it up to the back of the house. Then they built a little walkway and put a roof over it. In the wintertime you'd like to freeze to death going out through there, but walk about three steps and you were in the kitchen.

That little walkway to the kitchen came right out of the dining room. My daddy built a big old wooden table to seat all of us, eight children and two adults. We'd walk right out of that dining room up this little walkway, into the kitchen. Didn't have kitchen cabinets; they had what you call a safe. You put your dishes in it, and lard. Grease for cooking was bought in a five-gallon lard can, a big old tall lard can, about five gallons. Those are some of the first things I remember details about.

A lot of people today have no idea how folk lived in Mississippi when I was growing up. But these are my roots, and if you want to know who I am, you need to know who I was and where I came from. I'm going to share some of those memories first.

My Family

My parents were Nathaniel and Nancy Allen. Cooper was my mother's maiden name. There were eight children. My mama had four boys in succession before she had any girls. Albert James was my oldest brother; we called him A.J. The second brother's name was John Quincy. I think John Quincy Adams is what made them name him that; he became John Quincy Allen, instead of John Quincy Adams. His nickname was Buddy, but when they were growing up, the boys all named themselves after cowboys, so he became Hoppy, for Hopalong Cassidy. The next brother, who died in 2017, his name was Frank; we called him Shine. He smiled all the time, so we called him Sunshine. And then my fourth older brother was named John Preston; we called him Pres. He was named after my grandfather, my mother's daddy, who was named John Preston Cooper. The cowboy name for him was Gabby Hayes.

A.J. and Frank had cowboy names, too, but they didn't stick. A.J. was Tucson for a while. That's because my Uncle Bo, Daddy's baby brother, used to go to the movies with A.J. when they went to town. They saw this movie called *The Three Mesquiteers*, and the two lead characters were named Tucson Smith and Stony Brooke. A.J. became Tucson, and Uncle Bo was Stony. And then Frank was Don "Red" Berry for a while, for the actor who played Red Ryder in the movies. But Shine was the name he kept.

In 1930, my mother got pregnant again, and out come my oldest sister. Her name is Naomi, but we call her Sutter because Preston was so young, and he talked with kind of a lisp at that time; he couldn't say "Sister" when she was born. He'd say "Tuh-Tuh" or "Thutta" or something, which turned into "Sutter," and that name stuck. She's Sutter to this day. Even her nieces and nephews call her Aunt Sutter.

Then about two years later came my sister Luberta; we called her Doll, Baby Doll. I guess they thought she was pretty like a doll. And about two years after that, here I come! They named me Ora Dee. There was a lady who lived around us named Miss Ora Dee Nellum, went to our church, and they named me after her.

My nickname, by the way, was O.D. I never did like that "Ora." Hated that name! But you know the way brothers and sisters kid each other? All through my life, my brother Frank, when he'd call me, the minute I pick up the phone:

"Ohh-Deeee!"

"Hey, Shine!"

And J.Q. stayed "Hoppy" until the end of his life. I have a picture of him giving me away at my wedding in 1977, and he was still Hoppy, even then.

My baby brother, Nathaniel Jr., was born a little over two years after me. I was too young to remember this, but later they told me the circus had come to town, Ringling Brothers, and my brothers and my Grandpapa were at the circus when Nate was born. Come home, here's your new baby brother! He didn't have a cowboy nickname. We called him Mike. We had a radio by then, and on one of the programs Mama used to listen to, one of the performers was named Mike. She'd be listening, and sometimes then she'd turn to Nate and say, "Okay, Mike!" So that became his nickname; before that, we called him Junior. Finally, though, he just became Nate.

My first real recollection of him is when my granddaddy, my mother's daddy, was dying. He was crazy about Nate. And I remember Grandpapa was so good to Nate; even when he was laying in the bed dying, he had his hand out of the bed, trying to play with him. Nate was crawling under the bed around Grandpapa's hand. That's my first memory of him, a little baby boy crawling around that bed when Grandpapa died.

In those days, you understand, black people usually died at home because they didn't have any hospitals they felt welcome to go to, and they didn't have any money. Nobody had a birth certificate either. Women gave birth at home, and the family kept the birth records in the back of a Bible. When my brother made the army, that's the first time we ever heard of a birth certificate; they went through some changes to get my brother a birth certificate so he could go into the army. That's when I knew it was important. Before that, going to school or whatever we did, whenever Mama said we were born, that's what they accepted. Four older brothers, two sisters, me, and the baby brother. That was the family. And all my mama's children were born at home.

Toys, Love, Chicken, and Clabber Milk

We were a fun family. We loved each other, and we had a lot of fun. What did we do for fun? Oooh, lordy, it was more fun then than now! We played with each other! My daddy could make toys that we played with. He would take hay wire and bend it into a little small wheel, and we could throw it on the ground and run behind it with a stick. Run all up and down the road with it, make it flip, turn, do anything you want with it. And then my daddy would take a board and he'd fix wheels on it, like from wagons and things like that, for my brothers to play with. And we'd run out and find berries and different things, go out and pick some berries—"He caught a frog!"— run away from snakes, scare us, stuff like that. Oh, we had some fun, now!

Eight children. That's a lot of milk to be had, a lot of hogs to kill. They always killed the hogs and kept the fresh meat. My mom would put salt on the pork and bury it down. Daddy made big wooden boxes. They'd put salt in the bottom of the box, put a slab of meat on top of the salt, then pour some more salt on top of that, put another slab in there, salt that down, and fill that box up with salted meat. When they get ready to fry it, they would boil the salt out of it first. And that's what we had for breakfast almost every day. Salt meat, syrup, and biscuits.

On weekends, we'd have chicken. Every Sunday morning we could count on my mom: She'd send my brothers out to pick the chickens up and wring their necks and pop 'em and pull the head off. I remember seeing one of my brothers pop a chicken, and before he pulled the head off, he threw it. Chicken got up and started running! "Cluck! Cluck! Cluck! Cluck! Cluck!" Like he's laughing at him. The ones who were too little to do that, they'd put the head up on a piece of wood and chop it off with an axe. And that was Sunday morning breakfast. Fried chicken with gravy, country biscuits, syrup, milk. We drank buttermilk or sweet milk, didn't matter which one. Or clabber milk. You know what clabber milk is? That's when milk has to set up and spoil, and when it spoils, all the cream comes to the top. You skim the cream off, and you churn it up in a churn, and it makes clabber milk. Looks like cottage cheese.

For Christmas, they would always buy a gallon or a half gallon of home-made whiskey, what they call "moonshine." They would bring it to the house, and every child in the house could have a little shot-glass of liquor. We thought that was something! Neighbors would come by, "Mama! Want a little something! Got a little nip?" Everybody go in back, give all the neighbors a little nip.

That's the only time we ever had alcohol in our house. The only one in the family I knew who really drank was Uncle Bubba, my mother's brother. Oh, Uncle Bubba! Now that's a story in itself. I mean, I'm talking about a *drunk*! And he lived that way until he died. He died laughing at God; that's how crazy he was.

Someone tell him, "Uncle Bubba, say your prayers."

"I hanged them dang things on the head of the bed! He can get 'em if He want 'em!" That's his answer!

But we were a Christian family. Church, always. *Always*! Mount Carmel Missionary Baptist Church, Rev. J. H. Thompson, that was our church. And Uncle Bubba, he'd clown right there in church. That's right! They had a bench they called a moaners' bench. You go to church, you get down and pray, and they'd be praying for you. And we'd see Uncle Bubba, he'd be down on his knees with his face in his hands, like he's praying. But he's got his fingers spread a little bit and he's looking through his fingers at us. See his teeth, his eyes, shining in the dark behind his hands. Uncle Bubba was something else!

Like I told you, Sundays were special at our house, not only because we went to church, but because that was the day we had our best breakfast of the week. But one Sunday morning, something had happened to our chickens. The chickens were dying of a disease they called the "limber-neck"; they'd have a hard time standing, almost like they were dizzy, they wouldn't be able to eat, and their heads would flop around on their necks like they were looking backwards or staring up at the sky. We call it "botu-lism" today; you can't eat chickens when they have that. So our chickens had gotten infected somehow, and we were sitting down to a syrup and biscuit breakfast on a Sunday morning, and my brother Preston—Gabby Hayes!—he was sitting there at the table and saw this great big flock of birds, flew over, swarmed and lit out in the field. He said, "Wait! Wait! Wait! Wait! Wait! Wait! Wait a minute! Wait a minute! Hold breakfast, Mama! Hold breakfast!"

He got the shotgun with the bird-shots in it, ran out there, threw him a rock, and when the birds flew up, he let down about thirteen, fourteen birds. Change the menu! Mama put on the hot water, scald 'em in there and pull the feathers out, just split 'em down the back, open 'em and get the intestines out and all that stuff, and fry them, just like that. Get 'em open, fry 'em fat, make gravy. Succulent breakfast!

You know how to churn milk? They'd milk the cows, and my daddy had the wooden churn he made by hand, and that's how you made your butter. See the yellow butter floating to the top, take a spoon, go down in there and take it out. When you get it out, squeeze all the milk out of it and put it in little bowls, however you might want it to look. You might want it to look square, you might want it to look like a star. Anything you want to do. Then you just let it sit up there. If it was hot, in the summertime, it wouldn't make hard butter. If it's wintertime, you set it out there in the window. Take it out, you got butter.

We made our own syrup, too. We raised sugar cane and sorghum. My daddy'd take it to the mill and grind all the juice out of it, put it in a big old iron vat and cook it. It would sit there and cook to syrup. It'd keep sitting there, just cooking, and you'd go out there and feed it wood all day long. Didn't ever let the fire go out. Cook it, get a wooden paddle, climb up on the ladder and stir it. It would start getting thicker and thicker. After a while it would get real sticky and they'd know when to pour it out. They had a little spigot thing at the bottom of the vat; they'd open that up and pour it into big gallon buckets. Put tops on those buckets, and all of a sudden you got syrup.

So we never knew what a hungry day was. We were really poor, I mean, poor as you can get, but we didn't know it. We children didn't know how poor we were. Only after I got grown, I realized: We were destitute! We didn't have nothin'! But we never knew what hunger was, not really. My daddy would go hunting, kill possums and coons and rabbits and stuff, come back and put on a feast for us. And we would have fish, galore. Set nets out, catch all the fish we wanted.

So we kids, we didn't know. To us, we were rich. We thought we had it made.

They Were Some Enterprising People

That's probably where I got it from, because I've been that way all my life, and I'm still that way today. When I look at how people nowadays go through these changes, talkin' 'bout welfare and stuff—we didn't have no welfare.

Flour used to come in pretty printed flour sacks, twenty-five-pound sacks of flour. My mother used to wash those sacks and make us dresses out of them. She'd take those flour sacks and pull the thread out. If they had writing on them or anything, she'd bleach them, and then she used lots of dye. She'd dye those sacks, and then she'd go to her sewing machine. Where she got it from, I don't know, but ever since I've known her, she had a sewing machine, and she would make us clothes out of them. And they were pretty. Then those old burlap sacks they used to pick cotton in, the bottom part had tar to keep it from wearing out from being dragged down the cotton rows. When those got too old to use, she would cut that tar off and bleach them, make my brothers shirts and jumpers to wear.

That's the kind of person she was. She was a thrifty woman. We had clothes when other kids were wearing rags. And she made clothes for other people, too. A neighbor would come to her and bring some material and say, "Miss Sis, I want you to make me a dress." And they'd get a catalog, show her which dress she want it to look like, and then Mama would make it.

I still remember the time when my mother went into town, must have been on a Saturday evening—what we call "afternoon" now, we called it "evening" in the country then. That's when the country folk were finished with their work in the fields, and they'd come to town to do their shopping and their errands and things. She'd sell some butter, or maybe some of the syrup or something else she'd made, and this day she took that money and bought me a pair of shoes.

Like I said, they were some enterprising people.

Some of our neighbors were, I don't know any other way to put this, they were what I'd call lazy. Oh, they worked. In those days you had to work; the white folks wouldn't have it any other way, 'cause you worked for *them*. But they did just as much work as they had to, just to get by, and that was all. And then they'd come by us, "Oh, Sis Allen has some food," or "Sis Allen has this," or "Sis Allen has that." And we always had some eggs or something put up, and my mother and father would feed some of those families or help them out if they needed it.

Again, when I think about it now, I realize that times were really hard back then, but I didn't know anything else but to be happy. We didn't live in town; we lived in the country. We didn't know what was supposed to be living good and what was living bad. We'd never been anywhere else. So as far as we were concerned, we were living better than the people around us. Because my daddy was, as some people would say today, an entrepreneur. He was the kind of man who, whatever he had, he made it work. He'd have more cotton, more corn—he had eight children, and five were boys. They were hustlers. Whatever there was, they made it work. Some of the other people around us, we laughed at them for coming to church with funny-looking clothes on, shoes tore up. We had good shoes. Like I told you, my mother was a seamstress, and of course we grew our own food.

Because we were hard workers. My mama and daddy told us, "You *will* go out there and pick cotton, chop cotton," and we did it. We made as big a crop as we could, every year. Every child Mama and them had, we had to go to the field. It's one of my earliest memories, riding that cotton sack. They had those nine-foot cotton sacks wrapped around their shoulder, and that baby'd get back there and sit on it and just ride. They'd drag those sacks up and down the rows, put the cotton in there, and just keep on dragging. I don't know how old I was, but when you're big enough to walk, you went to the field. There were no babysitters in the house. You followed all the other folk out in the field, even if you had to ride their cotton sacks.

When we were real young, we didn't use the hoe and chop cotton. But we'd be out there in the field with them when they were chopping. Sometimes we might run off and play, pick berries and catch frogs, run around and stuff, but we had to be out there with them. Then, when you get big enough to hold a hoe in your hand, you chopped. They had to teach you how to hold it, how to use it, what not to chop down on and what to chop down on, but you were out there doing it, just like them.

And when it came time to pick, we were walking down those rows and picking that cotton right alongside them. We'd have what they call a croker sack made out of burlap or some coarse material like that. My mom used to take a strap and put it on a little croker sack and hang that around our neck, and we'd pull cotton out of the boll, get our hands all cut and bloody on those sharp cotton bolls just like the grown folks, toss the cotton in the sack, keep going. I look at my little two-year-old grandson, right now. At that age, at two years old, if he was with us and we were picking cotton, they'd have on him a little bitty ol' sack about the size of a pillowcase, put a strap on it and hang it on his shoulder. And he would be pulling that cotton out of the bolls, put it in his little sack, walk those rows just like the grown folk.

By the time I was ten years old, same age as my granddaughter, I could pick a hundred and some pounds of cotton. One day, I'll never forget, my daddy talked me into picking two hundred pounds by putting up fifty cents. "First one of y'all pick two hundred pounds, you got fifty cents." So we hustled and got that fifty cents. Then after that, he said, "Now I know you can do it! Now I know y'all can pick me two hundred every day, or I'm gonna whup your butt!"

That was a trick! He tricked me into two hundred. But two hundred twenty-five is as high as I ever picked. That was enough. It was hard, backbreaking work, and even though I still considered myself a happy child, I was beginning to learn some things about life, and about myself, that would soon make me realize I couldn't stay in that place and be that person for long. I guess you could say my dreams were calling me.

Chapter Two
Music and Life Lessons

Music

In church in the country, they used to sing those old hymns, like "I Love the Lord, He Heard My Cry." That's the way they opened the service every Sunday morning, with those kind of songs. The congregation would sing them with no musical accompaniment. Then, after they'd get through with prayer, the choir would march in, and they'd sing choir songs with music. Piano and church choir, that's all it was. Then the pastor would go on with the sermon.

Sometimes they might have a soloist. One lady, I never will forget, the first lady I remember playing for our church was named Miss Hattie Patterson. And she could sing pretty good, or so I thought! When I was little, she sounded good to me. But then later, after we moved to Belzoni and I grew up a little, they came down to do something in our church, and I heard her sing again, and I said, "Wooo! Did I think she could sing? My god! If she sang like that years ago, where was my head?" Years had passed, so she may have lost her voice, I don't know. But I also realized what I had thought was playing piano so great—she played by ear, whatever she did was "clump-de clump-de clump," but I never knew she couldn't play very well. After I got to Belzoni, these people were reading notes, playing from notes the same songs that Miss Hattie Patterson used to play, and it was just shocking to me that it could be so different.

At home, my mom had a record player. They called it a Grafonola. Had a big horn for the music to come out of. Remember that RCA logo with the dog sitting there with the horn from the record player in his face? It looked just like that. We didn't have any electricity, of course; you had to wind it up, and you put this big old platter on there, a 78. A 78 record in those days was made of shellac; it was as hard as a rock, but it was brittle; hit it, it'll break. Plugs would get knocked out of them, they'd crack—they were stiff but fragile.

I remember Mama had Bessie Smith's records, and I also remember another song:

> I never will forget that floating bridge
> I don't know how many times under water I hid,
> When I was going down I threw up my hands,
> Crying "please, Lord, take me to dry land . . ."

I didn't know who was singing it, but that was one of the very first songs I ever heard on a record. Since then, people have told me it was Sleepy John Estes, but you know, someone played his version for me a little while ago, and it didn't sound like the same one. But maybe it was; that was a long time ago. But it was a blues, what they call country blues. He fell in that river and almost drowned.

My mama didn't let us sing blues, but she had those records. But hear us singing it, we got a spanking! If we wanted to sing those kind of songs, we had to get behind their back and sing. But we did. All of us did that, the same way. "They shouldn't have been playing 'em if we couldn't sing 'em!"

Now when I say "blues," my family called anything that was not gospel music, anything secular, they called it "blues." I grew up with country music, and that was "blues" too, to my mama and daddy; they called that blues. If it wasn't gospel, it was blues to them, and sometimes they'd also refer to the songs as "reels."

My family were perpetual singers; I come from a long line of singers, to be honest with you. My father had a voice, sounded like Muddy Waters. I mean he could sound just like him! He used to sing the blues, but he would never let us knowingly hear him. If he was out in the fields working by himself, he would be out there whoopin' the blues. But if we walked up, or if he saw any of us coming, he would stop. He always was religious and kind of undercover with his blues singing.

Now my mother, she couldn't sing a lick; she had one of those kinds of voices where she was laughable! My brother Preston didn't sound good, either. And my oldest sister, Sutter, she didn't sound good. My brother Frank could sing; my oldest brother A.J. sang bass for a quartet group later on, after he moved to Chicago. My other sister, Doll, she sang. She sang in church; my sister and I used to sing duets in church. Then my baby brother, Nate, he sang his way through college with a band. He eventually became a recording artist, too; he recorded under the name Na Allen; I'll tell you more about him later. After he stopped recording, he still sang, and he stayed a good singer until he died in 2017, just a few months after Frank passed away.

Mississippi Flood

Some of the most fun we had as kids was actually when something pretty bad would happen. The Mississippi and Yazoo Rivers would overflow, and we would have to step off our porch into a boat.

When the ice and snow melted up north, like from Canada and all up there, it would come down and fill our waterways. The levees would over-run, and the water would flood all around and under our house. My mom and dad would be almost crying. "What are we going to do? All this is gone! Look what we've got left!" Here's my daddy tilling the soil, planting corn and cotton, and then just as he gets everything planted in the ground, and all the gardens and everything, here come all this water. Flood out all the lowland. Kill the chickens, kill the hogs sometimes, sometimes they had pens that were built up off the ground and they would raise them up, but so much of the time our little chickens and things would be dead, and the ducks and geese and turkeys, everything else. They had coops they would put them in when they knew this was going to happen, put them up off the ground and try to save them that way, but it was still bad, and a lot of times nothing much got saved, and our house would be sitting in the water.

Really, I should say it was more like sitting *on* the water. In the country, they didn't build houses on the ground. The houses were built on concrete blocks, big old concrete slabs at least three or four feet tall, take them big old slabs and erect your house on that. That's why so many houses got blown away in storms, because they were sitting there propped up on those slabs. But then they fixed it so it wasn't easy to blow off. They put a board down there on each side of the block, far back enough so the block was secured up under the house, holding it. So it'd have to really blow hard to bring that up off the ground. It wasn't easy to blow the house down. They would blow down sometimes, but a storm would take the roof off more often than it would blow the house down. So the water wouldn't hardly hurt the house itself; it would just be up under the house. The house would be built way up off the ground.

So while my mom and dad were pulling their hair out, it was fun to us. My daddy kept a boat sitting in our yard. When there was a flood and we would go to school, my daddy or my brothers would have to get in that boat, paddle all the way over to the high ground, pick up the kids, bring us across, go back—that was fun to us. And then we'd catch fish out of the ditch, because the water would spill over in there, and you could be standing out on our porch and see fish out there; it's flooded in the garden, in the yard and the cotton rows, go out there and just pick up a fish. Had fish in our yard! Take it in the house and cook it. And of course my mom was good at everything in the country; she canned fruit, she canned vegetables and everything. We had one of these attics in the dining room of our house where she would store all this stuff in jars up there, and when things like that would happen, we would at least be able to go up there and get food.

Things like that didn't happen every year; sometimes the workers could pack enough sandbags on the levee and stop it before it overflowed. But a lot of the time it'd break through anyway. And it wasn't just the river, either. At one point in time, we were living in a house with a big valley right in front of us, like a big sink, where if it rained real hard, we had to go across in the boat. Living up on this hill area, the school was up on the hill on the other side, we had to step off our porch into that boat, and my older brothers would paddle us across to dry land. And then we'd walk on over to the school.

But when all that wasn't going on, my daddy would plant a corn crop in that valley area. That was another thing he had to sharecrop with the man. Whatever loads of corn they pulled, every third wagon load was my daddy's, to do what he wanted to do with. And the rest went to the man. They'd take that corn to the mill, what they called a grist mill, put the whole cobs in there, and it would shuck the corn. The corn get scraped, the big kernels come off, and then go to the grinder and grind it up into corn meal. And the cotton, of course, they'd bring the cotton to the gin, put it in the gin and it would separate the cotton; the seeds go one way, the cotton go another way—soft, pretty cotton. And then they'd bale that cotton up and take it away by the wagon loads.

Ora Dee Speaks Her Mind

I need to tell you a little more about my mother. She was a country woman, and she raised her children the old country way. My mother used to tear our butts up! And I always thought she treated the others better than she did me.

She said my mouth got me in trouble, and I think she was right. I think it did. Because my granddaughter talks to me just like I used to talk to my mama. And even worse—the kids nowadays are worse than I was, because I was scared to go too far. But I was always like this. You couldn't accuse me, tell me I did something, if I didn't do it. I'm sorry, I got to come back at you. And my mother used to have a habit. I was bad, I guess, so whenever something happened, she'd just assume I did it. She'd say, "Didn't nobody do that but ol' Corner-Head!" She called me "Corner-Head," said I got corners on my head. "Ol' Corner-Head Ora Dee!"

And I would just stand up for myself and say, "No, I didn't do it."

She say, "I guess I'm a lie, huh?"

I said, "I guess so, 'cause I didn't do it!"

And that got me a whuppin' right there. She say I called her a lie. I didn't! She called herself a lie! I know I didn't do it! I'm not gonna stand up there and admit I did something I didn't do.

It got so she was whuppin' me every day for something. Every day, I'm talkin' about now, when we were in the country. Whup me every single day. I had a smart mouth, she said, and I rolled my eyes at her. She tell me to go do something, say, "Don't say another word!" And I'd walk off, and as soon as I get where I think I'm out of hearing, call myself talking under my breath: "That ol' Mama! Make me sick!"

Soon as I said that—"What you say?!"

"I ain't said nothin'!"

"Bring your ass back here!"

My daddy eventually had to take her aside and tell her to ease up, stop whuppin' me so much. But I brought it on myself. I realize that now. When I was a child, it made me hate her, but after I grew up, I knew I'd brought it on myself. Because I would just say whatever was on my mind, and no child has any business talking to their mama like that, or any grown folks. I look at these kids now, how they disobey and don't listen when you talk to them—no wonder Mama beat my butt so.

A lot of times, though, I felt really hurt because of how she treated me. I thought she didn't love me. I never will forget—I'm trying to be helpful, to get a praise out of her. I'm gonna wash the dishes. I'm gonna put the dishes up, I'm gonna put the plates up, I'm gonna make her so proud of me! I'm gonna put the glasses on the shelves they're supposed to be on, the plates on the shelves, the bowls, wherever they're supposed to be, the cups and everything.

So I'm standing on top of this lard can. They had lard cans, five-gallon lard cans that they get all this old grease in, and I went to go up there with something in my hand, and I stepped up on the thing, and the whole thing caved in. And my feet were dirty because we'd go barefooted all the time out there in the country. And my big old footprint was down there on the floor because I had lard sticking to my feet.

Ain't no such thing as hot water, unless you boil it; there was nothing but a pump outside. I go out to the pump and try to wash this stuff off my feet, but when I got out there, I'm walking in nothing but dust and dirt; didn't do anything but stick to my feet a little more, and the cold water wasn't getting it off. Mama went to cook and saw that footprint on the floor. I didn't say anything; I thought I'd cleaned it up enough, but she got so mad about it she came out looking. She didn't say a word. She just looked, looked at my feet, and one foot had all that dirt on it. She knew she had me! And she tore my butt up for that.

And I remember I said to myself, even when you're trying to make her praise you, it just look like something happens. Trying to make her love me! I really thought she didn't. I thought she hated my guts. I just wanted her to say something nice about me. Because she never did, the whole time I was growing up. I never heard her brag on me once. She'd bring up my older sister, "Now Sutter, that's my good child. That's mama's baby, yeah! Sutter-Baby do anything I tell her to do." She didn't say too much about Doll, but she didn't talk about Doll like she did me. Doll was more obedient, I think, than I was.

But, honey, when it come down to me, nothin' but "Ol' Corner-Head Ora!" Said I rolled my eyes at her, lookin' doglike, or like some cow. I can laugh about it now, but that used to hurt my feelings so bad. It made me hate her. I couldn't get her to say I was anything but bad. And ooh, that just hurt me. But I know one thing, it sure taught me to be more loving to my kids, my godchildren and grandkids. The things she used to say hurt my feelings so bad, I could never say something like that to my children. Never.

I know that some of the things she did, today they'd call it abuse. But I don't hold it against her; she was from the country, she was raised that way, and that's all she knew. And she taught me right, yes she did. Wasn't anything wrong with her; what was wrong was me. And then I'm thankful in another way, too, because that helped make me who I am today. She'd always say, like, "You never gon' be nothing!" "You never gon' amount to nothin!'" And I just said to myself, she can't tell me that. I *will* be something; don't make no difference what she say, I'm gonna do what I want to do, and I *will* be someone, I *will* be something in life just because she told me I couldn't do it.

And that's followed me all through life, even to this day. Tell me I can't, I'm gonna turn around and do it. The very first thing you tell me I can't do, you just got your "anti" serum going. Don't tell me what I "can't" do. No, lordy! I ain't never had no one, no man or anyone else, didn't "let" me do something. 'Cause I make up my mind, I might do wrong just because he told me don't do it. That's just my way, and she put that in me.

Later on, when I started making some money, I was able to buy my mother things. I bought her some nice furniture, filled her house with the best furniture I could find. And then now she's proud of me, bragging on me, now I'm so successful, "Look what my daughter did! Look at what she bought me!"

But, you know, I still felt bad, because I didn't do it for the reason I wanted. I did it to prove something; I wanted her praise. I just wanted to hear her praise me; I wanted to hear her say something about, "My baby, she did this, she did that," like she bragged on Sutter and them when I was younger. And she did, too. I got a chance to hear all that junk, she's telling someone, "My baby came home last night; she brought me so-and-so, and she did this and she did that!" And I'd lay up in the bed and just glory: "*Now* you're braggin' on me!"

But I still didn't like it. I didn't want to have to do it for that. I wanted to do it because I loved my mother. The way I felt, all the things I did for my mother, trying to get her to praise me, all that didn't satisfy me and it didn't make me feel good. It was not out of love. I wanted to do it because I loved my mother, but in my heart I knew that wasn't my true feelings; I was doing it because I wanted her to praise me, like I still had to prove something to her. And I always felt bad about that, even to this day.

But anyway, it's all right. She did right by me, the only way she knew. I know I'm the person I am because of her, her and my daddy both. She did love me, even if I had to get grown before I really understood that, and I know her prayers have sustained me and protected me all my life. She passed away on January 27, 1984.

A Few More Country Memories

The war came in 1941. They called for all able-bodied men and boys, eighteen and up, to come and serve. My oldest brother, A.J., took the test but he got turned down, some kind of physical issue; he was 4-F. But then my next brother, Hoppy, that was John Quincy, he had just turned nineteen, and he passed his test. The next year, Frank got called. Hoppy was in Europe with the 92nd Infantry, the famous "Buffalo Soldiers" unit; he was driving a tank. Frank, in the Navy, ended up on a ship in the South Pacific. And Preston was going to turn eighteen in a year or two, so we knew it was only a matter of time for him.

I can't even begin to tell you how heartbroken Mama was. She cried constantly. She'd cook a meal for the family and sit down with us, and she couldn't even eat; she just cried and cried and cried all through the meal. Daddy tried to be strong for her, for all of us. He was such a good man, but we knew it was resting heavy on his mind, too.

Then one day, Mama and them were out in the field or getting something out of the garden, and my sister and I were inside playing, taking sticks and sticking them in the fireplace, making them into little torches. All of a sudden we heard this noise, like a loud motor: "M-m-m-m-m-mmmmmm!" And then a backfire: "Pow! Pow! Pow!" It sounded like it was directly over the house. And Mama came running up to the house: "It's an airplane! It looks funny up there!"

So we jumped up and ran out there. We didn't actually see it hit the ground. But we heard that big loud pop, and by the time we got out there, we saw all this smoke and dust coming up like it was coming out of the ground. And we knew what had happened. It crashed over by Mister Hunter

Southworth, the overseer, it crashed right near his house. So we ran behind Mama, and by the time we got there a lot of other folk had gotten there, too, and they started picking up pieces, scraps from the airplane. We got there in time to see the man's teeth, gums, brains, pieces of him laying out on the ground. And my brothers and all of them, they started picking those pieces up, looking at them. They didn't know what it was until they picked it up and saw that it was flesh.

I was still pretty young then, but later on I was told that Mama almost went crazy when that happened. She had prayed to the Lord for a sign, "Lord, show me, if my sons are going to come home, show me an airplane falling from the sky." I don't know where she got that from, but she prayed it. And now she saw this, and she remembered her prayer, and I think she was afraid that somehow her prayer had caused that man to die. So she started crying and praying even more. She cried so hard that her eyes began to hurt, almost as if she'd cried out her tears, and now her eyes were going to dry up and she'd go blind. Everyone got really scared for her. I think she finally just decided to put it all in God's hands, and she slowly came back to who she was. But that was a terrible time, and a terrible thing that happened.

By the time Pres got drafted, the war was over, but the other boys still weren't home. Pres got in the Navy, too, and they called him to Great Lakes, Illinois, so now there was no one left at home but us girls and my baby brother Nate. I know my daddy tried hard not to show it, but it was resting on his mind, just like it was on Mama's. One time he had to go out and cut some wood, the first time in years he had to go out there and do that all by himself. He went to chop down a tree, and a limb broke and hit him in the eye. He was still blessed, because it didn't puncture the eye, but it put something like a scar or a cataract across it, so he was blind in that eye. He said he could see down, and he could see a little bit up, but he couldn't see out front of that eye. He was in a lot of pain from that, and it made everyone feel even worse about everything that was going on. He was so lonely without his sons, and we were all lonely too.

Well, Pres had been the last grown boy at home with Mom and Dad, and he saw how that was tearing them apart. So he got up there to Great Lakes, and he put on a big act like he was crazy. And they discharged him. That's what he said; that's his story. He tried it, and it worked! I think they kept him about a month, and next thing we know, he was coming home.

He got home in the middle of the night. Everybody was in the bed, and there's a knock on the front door, two o'clock in the morning. He had taken a train down from Illinois, and somebody had driven him out to the house. We didn't know he was coming, so naturally nobody was up waiting for him. Then that knock on the door, and it was Pres! Coming home! Oooh, the whole house woke up. Everybody's jumpin' and hollerin', screamin' and cryin', my mom and dad were so glad to see him, and Daddy was laughing and saying, "Oooh, my eye just got better!" That was one of the happiest times, I think, we ever had in that house.

And then, of course, my other brothers eventually came home, too, and every time one arrived, Daddy just started smiling even more, he was so happy, and he said it again: "Look at my eye! It's getting better all the time!" So we were a family again.

There was at least one thing that happened during the war years, though, that was funny. My brother and I made some German soldiers very happy one day.

In about 1943 or 1944, the government started bringing captured Germans to the United States, and they put them in big P.O.W. camps at some of the military bases in Mississippi. Then from there, they'd send them out to smaller camps. There were some that weren't too far from us. They'd take those soldiers out from those camps into the country, and they'd make them pick and chop cotton. They'd parade them up and down the road, and they'd pass by our house.

Pres and I were out in the yard. I don't know what he was trying to make me do, but I wouldn't do what he said. So I was fighting him. Preston was trying to make me do something or go somewhere, and I kicked at him. Then when I kicked, he grabbed my foot. And he held my foot up in the air and had me hoppin' while he's walking backwards, had me hopping on one leg. And the Germans were passing by the house, and they saw us, and they laughed so hard they were almost rolling! They were laughing at me so hard it was embarrassing. So I always said if those Germans didn't get another laugh being prisoners in the United States, they got this one. They sure got a laugh from me.

A year or two after the war ended, my daddy decided he didn't want to live in the country anymore. The older boys were grown, getting married, starting families; A.J., in fact, had actually gotten married a few years earlier. My sisters were doing some serious courting, and we knew they'd be getting married soon. It was getting harder to make a living, too; machines were doing a lot of the things farmers used to do, and a lot of people were moving to town, trying to find a way to make a better living. So my parents decided it was time to come off the farm. We moved to Belzoni in 1947. That's really how it began for me. Things changed a lot after we moved, and it wasn't but a few years later that I would begin to follow my dreams and move to the big city for the first time.

Chapter Three

"There's Got to Be a Better World Somewhere"

The Town and the Country

When we first moved to Belzoni, we lived on the north side of town on Hayden Street, up around the area they called Hog Town. Hayden Street was one of Belzoni's major black thoroughfares; it ran from our little neighborhood directly downtown. Sutter got married that year, so there weren't but three of us kids left at home: Doll, myself, and my baby brother. And then Doll got married pretty soon after that, so only Nate and I were left. We had a two-room house on Hayden, and both rooms did double-duty. My bedroom was also the living room; the room in the back was the kitchen, and that was also Mama and Daddy's bedroom. Not far from us lived the Reverend George Lee, who would become famous as one of the early Civil Rights martyrs—a tragic incident that had a lot to do with my final decision to never again live in Mississippi. I'll tell that story in a little while. After a couple years, the family moved to Cain Street, a block west of Hayden. It's Jodie Thurman Street now, named for the Rev. J. D. Thurman, one of Belzoni's most beloved pastors, who died in 2005 at the age of 104. My brother Preston and his family had a house next door, so the Allens pretty much had Cain Street locked down!

Daddy got a job as a city street worker, a maintenance man. He made twenty, twenty-one dollars a week, something like that. It was money to live on in those days, and a lot more than he'd made in the country. My mother started out trying to work as what they called a domestic, working in white people's homes, cleaning and cooking, ironing clothes, that kind of thing. But she was a proud woman, and she never liked that kind of job. Then, when people found out she was a seamstress, she would take in sewing.

During harvest season, we still did fieldwork, too. We would hire ourselves out. Trucks would come to town early in the morning before daybreak, pick up the workers, and take them out to "Mister Ludlow's" farm. Mama was always out there on that corner, early in the morning, waiting for the truck to come in to get the hired hands, go out and pick cotton and chop cotton. And me and my brother Nate went right along with her.

Picking cotton as a hired hand like that, they'd pay you $2.50 per hundred pounds, or $3.00 or maybe $4.00 or $5.00. It depended on if the cotton was fresh and thick; then they'd pay less. When it got so you're what they call scrappin'—all the bolls don't get ripe at the same time, you'd be picking, and you have some bolls that haven't even opened up, so you'd have to go back and get a second picking, and all that kind of thing, where you're scrappin' cotton—they paid more for a hundred because it took you so much longer to get a hundred pounds.

Living in town was a big change from living in the country. We didn't have to maintain a farm, for one thing; any farm work we did was on someone's plantation, and we had to ride out on that truck to do it. I also could go to school without having to walk a mile to get there, and I didn't have to take a rowboat when there was a flood or there was too much water in the front yard!

The school in Belzoni was McNair. It had grammar school, middle school, and high school. The old plantation school I went to was called Shell Bluff School. It went from primary to the eighth grade, and it only had two rooms; primary school was in one room, and middle school was in the other. Sometimes we had two teachers, and sometimes it was just one. She'd go in one room, teach the younger kids, and then she'd go in the other room and teach the older ones. When she did that, she'd have one of the students from the older class come into the other room to keep the class in line.

Black children in those days didn't get as much opportunity to attend school as the white kids did. There were times when it was at least October before we had a chance to go, because we were still trying to get the cotton out of the field before the weather set in and got cold. That didn't happen as much to Nate and me, I don't think, but it happened to my older sisters and brothers. And none of them finished school. None of them. When it got down to graduating from high school, Nate and I are the only two, and I didn't do it right away; I had to get my GED later, after I moved to Chicago. But Nate went right though, and then he was the only one who went on to college.

Even after they moved to town, a lot of families would be so hungry after money to feed their family they'd still make their kids go out and work in the field. I think a law was eventually passed to make the black folk let their kids go to school; they had to almost force them to do it. So all of a sudden, we were allowed to go to school, and we could only go in the fields when school was out at 3:00 in the evening. We could catch a truck, go out there, and still make a few hours. Not on Sunday, though. Sunday was a no-no day for work. We had to go to church on Sunday. My mother and father never made us work on Saturday, either.

So for a while, at least, I was going to school as much as the white children. Of course it was an all-black school, and it didn't have the kinds of facilities and things the white schools had, but they had some good teachers and a lot of really smart kids came out of there; they still have reunions in Belzoni, and ministers and educators and businessmen and all kinds of successful people who graduated from McNair come back to get reacquainted with each other and talk about old times.

I liked learning, anyway; in fact, I wanted to read even before I was able. I was too young to remember this, but my sister Sutter says that when I was about two years old I gave my mama and grandpapa the laugh of their lives. I used to watch Grandpapa read the newspaper; he'd put on his glasses to read, and when he talked to someone he'd look at them over the top of his glasses. So one morning he left his chair for some reason, and when he came back, there I was, sitting in his chair, wearing his glasses on my little face, holding the newspaper up in front of me, just like him. Sutter says when Grandpapa saw that, he stopped in his tracks! He beckoned to Mama; she tiptoed in. I turned to look at them, and I peered out over the top of his glasses just like he would, and I said, all serious-like: "I got to weed!" And without another word, I turned back and started looking at the paper again.

Sutter says my family laughed about that one for a long time.

Birth of a Writer

So I was always a bookworm. I'd read my sisters' schoolbooks, even though they were ahead of me in school, and I got so I could do better with those books than they did. As I got older, if there was a word I didn't understand, I'd find a dictionary or keep inquiring until I found out what it meant. I'd find a way to use it, talking to my mom and my sisters and brothers and everybody. If it was a big word nobody understood, it just make me feel good for them to ask me, "What does that mean?"

But you know how people are. When I would find a roundabout way to put it in a sentence, they'd talk about me. "You think you're better than everybody just because you usin' them words! Why don't you just say this or that?" You know, say it just like they would. But I'd have to use that word, get it in some kind of sentence. That's just the way I was. I felt like a show-off when I'd tell them what the meaning was, but it made me feel good, too.

I can't say any one person inspired this in me. I don't remember a particular teacher or anyone like that. It was just something I wanted to do. I listened to other people talk; I'd listen to their conversations. In Mississippi, black people just talked common. "Ebonics," it's called now; we talked like that. White people used a better way of phrasing things; they had better education than we had, better everything. I wasn't trying to sound like them with that drawl and everything, but I was trying to use the words they used, the words I heard when I listened to them talk.

And of course there was no such thing as television back then, so we didn't have anywhere else to get it from, except maybe a movie. Even when we lived in the country we'd go into town, and maybe a few times a year we'd go to the movies. Romance was my favorite kind of movie. I'd always want to be like Claudette Colbert and those old movie stars back in those days. I wanted to use the words they used and sound just like them. I idolized those people.

I said all that to say this: That was the point of my starting to write. When I began writing, I started off writing stories—life stories, romance stories. I wrote about what I saw, or at least what I thought I saw, in the movies, and also what I read about in romance magazines. In those days I read *True Confessions*, *Modern Romances*, all that stuff. I forget now when

Tan Confessions came out; that was the one for black folks, for black women. But when *Tan Confessions* came out I read that, too. I read all those magazines faithfully; I'd just read and daydream. When I wasn't dreaming about singing on stage in front of a sea of faces, I was daydreaming about love and adventure in a world far away from Belzoni, where, as I was rapidly learning, the possibilities for a young black girl like me were extremely limited.

And if there's one thing you should know by now, it's that little Ora Dee was not about to sit back and accept limitations of any kind.

Music (Again)

We heard a lot of music in town. There were juke joints and cafés, and you'd hear music coming out all hours of the day and night. I used to lay up in the bed and listen to it across the street at Mr. Jimmy Griffin's café. They had a jukebox in there, and I would hear people like Roy Milton, Dinah Washington, Charles Brown, Louis Jordan, people like that, coming into my ears at night. I also remember seeing Elmore James and Sonny Boy Williamson doing a live radio broadcast from the window of the Easy Pay furniture store downtown, across the street from Turner's Drug Store at the corner of Hayden and Jackson. And like I said earlier, we had blues records in the house, even if our parents didn't want us singing those songs. And of course, we sang in church.

We also listened to a lot of radio. We heard mostly country music; we listened to the Grand Ole Opry on Saturday evening, just like everyone else. Oooh, when this country music came on, I would go crazy! I used to love me some Roy Acuff and all them guys. Love 'em hard! Even later, after I moved to Chicago, I went all the way up to Conway Twitty. Conway Twitty was my man! And Charley Pride! I was grown, up North and everything, and I'd still be listening to me some Twitty. But back in Belzoni, there was also blues and R&B on the radio from a big station in Nashville called WLAC. They had disk jockeys like John R and Hoss Allen, playing all this blues—and rhythm and blues, which they called rock & roll in those days—and it was only years later we found out those guys were white. But they sure knew how to talk, and they sure knew their music.

When I was dreaming about singing, I never fancied myself a country singer, as much as I loved it, because I didn't have that whine in my voice. I would always see myself singing Nat King Cole style, or maybe Dinah

Washington. Nat King Cole was my very favorite artist. I would daydream, I mean *daydream*, that I was Mrs. Nat King Cole. He and his wife, Maria, made a record together in 1950, "Get Out and Get Under the Moon." Boy, I was so jealous! In my mind, that was *me* singing that song with him. Maria could have stayed home!

People heard me singing in the field and started telling my mom about it. We'd catch those trucks and go out and work, and they'd hear me singing, and they'd say, "Nancy, you need to give this gal singing lessons. This gal can sing." I'd sing whatever songs I heard on the radio or somewhere, and I guess that's what first made me think I might be able to do it for real one day, when someone heard me singing in the field and told my mom she should get me some lessons and put me out there as a professional vocalist.

That didn't happen then, but there was a lady named Miss Sharpe who used to live right across the street from us, and she was a piano teacher. She taught a lot of the kids around there. I had all this music in my head, so I was thinking about it all the time, and pretty soon my mother let me start taking lessons. I took about two years of piano lessons from Miss Sharpe.

I needed to practice, so after a while, my parents said, "Well, we might as well try to get you a piano." Somebody had a piano for fifty dollars, and they bought it. It was one of those old upright pianos. Nothing fancy, but it was a piano. I paid for as much of it as I could; I would go out into the field, picking and chopping cotton, saving up, because they taught me to try to be self-reliant, put up fifty cents here, fifty cents there, save up some money. Finally they decided to pitch in and help with the rest of it.

I never did progress very far. I can't improvise or play by ear. I know the notes on a keyboard and I can play from children's books, but I can't go any higher than maybe a second-grade book. When you start getting into more advanced key signatures and all that, with all those sharps and flats, I'm limited. A lot of songwriters write their songs at the piano, but I don't. I can hear the melody in my head, I write the words, and then I can go into the studio and tell the different musicians exactly what I want to hear. But I can't play it for them, and I can't write it out.

One day I was coming home from school with two of my girlfriends. One of their names was Irma Dee Wells, and I wish I could remember the other one's name but I can't. We used to walk with our arms around each other's shoulders, you know, the way schoolgirls do, so there we were, walking home from school, all locked up as usual, and I was singing. Bing Crosby put out "Far Away Places" in 1948, and that's the song I was singing that day, so I'm guessing I must have heard it on the radio. That's when that white woman stepped off her porch and called out to me and asked me to sing it for her, and that's when she paid me that fifty cents. So that was my first "paid gig" and my first "request." And I didn't even know it was going to happen until it did.

But I definitely had it in me by then, and it was already making me restless. Hearing that music all around me, and then singing and being encouraged by what people said, that's what really started me out, even if at the time I had no idea where it would eventually lead.

By that time, though, it wasn't just about music. I knew—*I knew*—I had to leave Mississippi. I wouldn't survive if I didn't.

"Is It because I'm Black"

Of course, I was aware of racism and discrimination when I was growing up, but in a sense, I was fortunate. It was all around me, but I didn't encounter it personally too often, at least not then. I'm sure Mama and Daddy experienced it a lot more. In the country, the bossman on our plantation was pretty good to us compared to how a lot of them were, and we really didn't have that much dealing with him anyway. The black overseer, Mister Hunter Southworth, was usually our go-between for that. The white folks all lived far away from where we were.

In Belzoni, everything was still segregated, of course, but even though "they" had their space and "we" had ours, and God help us if we tried to cross the line, we were actually physically pretty close. The neighborhoods weren't miles apart like they are in the big cities up North. We might be on the next block from them, maybe separated from them by railroad tracks, maybe even living on opposite sides of the same street. Some towns had separate black and white downtowns, parallel, only about a block away from each other. So we saw each other, we encountered each other all the time, we worked for them, but we were still separated. We didn't cross that line. So I didn't really have too much connection with white folks, even in Belzoni. We just had to go out and pick their cotton. And you'd certainly run across a word like "nigger" sometimes, but we were small and it was probably so common to us we didn't give it much thought until later, when we really began to know what it meant. Now my older brothers, who'd been in the service, they'd probably say different, but I'm talking about what my baby brother Nate and I understood at the time.

I do remember one of my brothers got hit by a white boy on the street one time, said to him, "Nigger, get off the street!" And everybody came home talking about it. My brother was furious. Said, "I'm gon' go back there and kill somebody!"

Mama and Daddy and them cooled him out. "No, you know where you are, son. Leave it alone." They didn't want him to start something that might have gotten us all killed.

But that doesn't mean I was content. I'd certainly had a happy childhood in the country, or at least I thought I did, but by the time we moved to Belzoni I was getting a little bit more up in age and I was looking around, realizing I didn't want to be stuck in a world where someone like me couldn't have much of a future. Remember that time when Daddy tricked me into picking two hundred pounds of cotton? We laughed about it then—"Oooh, he's a clever man! He's slick!"—but that was probably one of the first times I said to myself, "I got to leave here." That was going to be my future? Dragging those sacks around, feeling proud of myself because I could pick two or three hundred pounds of cotton a day? Uh-uh! And I knew a lot of people settled for that, figuring that's all they were ever going to get out of life, but I also knew I could never set my sights so low.

But it was either that or work in some white woman's kitchen, and I knew I couldn't do that, either. I saw what my own mother went through, with them telling black women, "You go ahead and work for me, you gotta say 'Yes, ma'am,' 'no ma'am'," and they ain't nothing! Fourteen-year-old girl! They're cussin' out Mama 'cause she won't tell their fourteen-year-old daughter "Yes, ma'am" and "No, ma'am" and all that kinda shit? And then got to do whatever they say to do? And they ain't no older than we are? Bull*shit*!

I knew I couldn't take what a lot of people took. I would have to be sassy and fight back. Probably end up getting killed. So I just said, "I want out. I can't stay in this part of the country, or I will be dead."

There had to be more to life, and I was determined to find it.

My City Husband

I couldn't have been more than fifteen. My brother A.J. and my sister Sutter were both living in Chicago, and my mother and I had gone up there to visit. I'd been begging her to let me move up there. I could stay with A.J. and finish high school there, I said. Or I could raise up my age. My sister was working at a dry cleaner's; maybe she could help me find a job. I looked older than I was, anyway.

But Mama wasn't having any of it. She said, "Only way I'm gonna let you leave here is if you get married. Or if you have a baby, if you come up pregnant, I'm gonna beat your ass and *put* you out!"

That was the thing that scared me. I was scared of that "havin' a baby" thing. I didn't want her to put me out about having no baby. I wouldn't do that.

"So you just gon' have to get married if you want to go away."

She should never have told me that. We made that trip to Chicago, and now I'm in the city, and now I have this thing about, "I'm gonna marry me a guy, and I'm gonna live here! I'm gonna leave Mississippi! I'm gonna come to Chicago. I'm gonna marry me a city husband!"

And sure enough, I met this guy, did my little flirtin' around and everything, and after I got back to Belzoni we stayed in touch. We wrote letters back and forth, just kept writing, writing, writing. He had some folks who lived down South, so he was coming down to visit some of his people. He kept saying, "Why don't you get your mom to let you come back to Chicago?"

"My mama said only way I'm gonna get out of Mississippi is if I have a baby or be married. Said that's when she'll consider me grown. 'Til I'm grown, I ain't leaving."

So he said, "I'm gonna come over there, we're gonna get married, and I'm taking you back to Chicago with me."

"Good!"

So he came down to Belzoni. My daddy wasn't too happy about it, but by then I think he and Mama both knew what I'd do anyway if I was really determined to do it. So Daddy ended up giving his consent, and we got married. And you know how I said I was going to put my age up? In those days I could put my age up to go anywhere and do anything. I could fix my hair to look like an older girl, and I grew up—let's just say I was really developed for my age. And who was selling you the marriage license? Who was working at the County Clerk's Office where they filled out the paperwork? They were all white. Nobody questioned a black child about how old they were.

They didn't have to show IDs or anything like they do now. So that's what I did. I put my age up, got married, and took off for Chicago with my new city husband.

But he wasn't going to be that for long. When I got to Chicago, I didn't tarry. Took me about two or three days to manage to get away from him. Two or three days! You know, manufacture something to be mad about, and leave. I never even considered that "married." Far as I was concerned, it didn't happen. He ain't even worth talkin' about; I won't even call his name. Just a means to an end. I only did that for one reason: so I could get the hell out of Mississippi. So I left, went over to my brother's house on Langley Ave. and moved in with him.

And that was the end of it. I was where I wanted to be. Just like Dr. King said: Free at last! Free at last! Thank God almighty, I was free at last!

Bright Lights, Big City

That's the way it felt, at least for a while. I didn't get a job at first; I was underage, and I guess they paid a little more attention to that kind of thing in Chicago than they did in Belzoni, even the white folks. But I eventually got a job at a dry cleaner's, just like Sutter. I also started going to school part-time, taking classes, at Wendell Phillips High School. I don't remember now what year that was, maybe it was during this time or maybe it was later, after I'd gone back home for a while and then returned to Chicago, but I did get my GED. Then at some point, I also got that job, making $0.80 an hour, pressing pants in a dry cleaner's.

So I felt grown, like I was really doing all right for myself. And of course, the prejudice wasn't anything like it was back home. Don't get me wrong. Chicago was segregated. The black folk all lived in a certain area of the South Side. We were beginning to move into the West Side, too, but when we did that, all the white folks just up and left, so the neighborhoods never really did get mixed. Even so, the prejudice in Chicago was never bad enough to really affect me personally. I guess I was lucky, or maybe I was just young and didn't know any better. I went everywhere I wanted to go, did anything I wanted to do. And that was important to me. And one thing about it, if somebody said something ugly to you, you could cuss 'em out, talk back to 'em, do anything you wanted to do. Didn't have to worry about what color their skin was. You say your piece, and you gone from there. Wasn't nobody going to challenge you for what you just said. It's just two folk cussin' each other out.

But I'm kind of funny about that stuff, anyway. This may make me sound real funny to you, but if I hear a white person call somebody a nigger, I just laugh. I get a laugh out of 'em. Because that word doesn't bother me. I swear it does not bother me. It used to, years ago, but now it does not bother me. Not one iota.

I call white folk niggers, too. People be hollerin', "He ain't black, Denise!" I say, "That's a *nigger*! You ain't gonna tell me!"

To me, a nigger is a dirty-ass man, a dirty person. Man, woman, anybody. If they're just dirty and lowdown, that's what I call a nigger. I don't call people that because of the color of their skin. God knows that's the way I am. Piss me off, I'll call you a nigger in a minute. Piss me off, you gon' be a nigger to me. I know that sounds crazy, but that's me.

What I really loved about Chicago, though, was the music. I was too young to get into clubs most of the time, but I'd go to the Regal Theater on 47th Street, just about a block north of where I was staying with A.J. Man, I was a Regal Theater freak! Sometimes I'd get up early, like on a Saturday morning if I didn't have to work, I'd go and stay all day. First they'd have a movie, then the stage show, and then another movie, and another show. I'd sit through it all. I'd see the movie two or three times so I could see the show two or three times. I could stay all day and all night if I wanted to. Buy me a ticket, go there, watch it—"Boy, I wish I could do that!"

Or maybe I'd go downtown to the Chicago Theater on State Street. That's where all the big shows came. They had everybody at the Chicago. Sarah Vaughan, Tony Bennett, big bands, you name 'em, they've been there. Ella Fitzgerald, I used to go see her a lot. And Josephine Baker! She was my Number One favorite girl. She'd come out singing in some kind of spectacular costume, then change clothes, and change clothes again, over and over. I think she had a dressing screen somewhere on the stage, with somebody to help her, wearing all that fancy hair, all that glitter and glamor from Paris. She played the Chicago in 1951, if I'm not mistaken, and that's probably when I saw her. I know she played the Regal later on, and I saw her there, too, but that was a big step down for her by then. She'd had trouble with some nightclub in New York; she raised hell at them because their club was segregated, and that got her called a Communist and all kinds of things; it really hurt her career. But before then, when she was still a big international star, she used to play the Chicago. That was prestigious. That was downtown. That's where all the big shows came.

In its earlier years, the Regal brought in the biggest names in black entertainment. We're talking Louis Armstrong, Billie Holiday, Ella Fitzgerald, Duke Ellington, Count Basie, and on down from there. A lot of times, people like that might play the Chicago and then come down and do shows at the Regal, too. I kind of caught the tail end of that when I first came to town. But by the early '60s, when Josephine Baker played there, it was considered, more like, kind of low-class black shows came there, mostly rhythm and blues type things. The glitz and glamor, that was still the Chicago, and they usually had a mostly white audience. But I loved both of 'em! Every time a show came to town, there I was. Just imagine! All these stars I'd been listening to and hearing about all my life, daydreaming and fantasizing about what they looked like, what they wore, how they moved on stage and what they sounded like, and now all of a sudden, here I was, seeing them in person.

So there I was, living in the big city and loving it. But then something happened. I don't know what it was, but something changed inside me. I was staying at my brother's house, and I guess I never quite felt like that was home, or something like that. And then that man I'd married and left, I always knew he was out there somewhere, probably still thinking about me, still mad at me for the way I'd done him. I remember thinking, the only way I'm gonna really get away from this man is go home. I knew he wasn't going to come down there and hurt me. I stay here in Chicago, he might come over and kill me somewhere. You know, for all I knew. I was young, and I guess you could say I was "young and scared," and it got to me after a while.

But anyway, I went back home to Belzoni. I moved back in with my parents on Cain Street. I guess I figured I was just going to mark time until I got a little older and I was ready to do something with my life. I don't know what my plans were. But then over the next few years, some things happened that reminded me why I'd left Mississippi in the first place, and why I knew I could never really stay there again.

"Bloody Belzoni"

A few years earlier, in November of 1949, a white man had been killed on
Ruby Street, in the "colored" section on the southwest side of town. There
were a lot of juke joints and places like that around there, and sometimes
white men would come through, looking for women. They'd usually get a
black man, a pimp or someone, to procure the women for them.

The black man's name was Charlie Holmes. He got these women together
and he took them to the white men down there, and it got to be some kind
of disturbance. Two of the white guys got to fighting over one of the women
or something. One killed the other one, and then he told Charlie Holmes
to take the gun, take it and throw it under the bridge. So, like a fool, he
took the gun and threw it under the bridge. And when they told the police
where the gun was, his prints were on the gun. The white guy told police
that Charlie Holmes had killed his friend. Charlie Holmes didn't have a gun
or anything. He was just there, doing his job. But who they gonna believe?
They believed the white guy.

The woman who knew the real story disappeared. Nobody ever knew
what happened to her. She's the one they were fighting over, and she was
telling it to the law that night, as I understand it. But she never made trial,
and nobody ever knew where she went. They made her leave town, or else
they killed her and buried her somewhere, because she came out and told
them Charlie Holmes didn't do the shooting; the other white guy did. And
honey, when that news hit the fan, nobody ever seen hair nor hide of her
again. We don't know whether she's dead or alive, one way or the other,
but she sure ain't never been seen no more in Belzoni.

So they electrocuted Charlie Holmes because there was no witness except that one woman, and that one woman was gone. It took almost three
years for them to do it; he was electrocuted in 1952. And what they did, they
electrocuted him and opened his casket, came by the funeral home, said,
"Open the casket, 'cause we want all these niggers to see what'll happen
to you if you mess with a white man." They had him layin' up there in the
church like that. This man was burnt black as shoe polish. Had blisters, a
ring of blisters around his head, just like somebody put a hot ring around
it. Just blistered him. And I saw that man, I went down there and looked,
and I couldn't sleep any more after seeing that. I said, "I got to leave the
South. I can't live like this. I can't take this."

But I couldn't leave town just yet. I was still pretty young, and after going back home I was able to cultivate some relationships and friendships that meant a lot to me, and I didn't want to just tear everything apart and have to start over again. Also, I was beginning to think that I could really make it as a writer.

Remember I told you I had been trying to write stories like the ones in *True Confessions, Tan, Tan Confessions*, and all those magazines? After writing and writing and writing for so long, I finally came up with a whole story, and I sent it in to *Tan* magazine. I named it "My City Husband." Sound familiar? I changed it some; I changed it from the real truth, because a lot of the things I put in there were not really what had happened to me. One thing that's different, I didn't come back home and get married right away, but I said I did in the story, and I used a real person's name when I wrote that. A boy from my childhood, McNeal; that's the "Neal" that I got in the story; I said I came back home, and Neal said he loved me, and so I married Neal. That's the way I told that story, but it didn't really happen like that.

So that was my first story. I sent it off, but I never heard anything back from them. They didn't know I was a faithful reader of the magazine; bought it every month. So one day, I was sitting down reading *Tan*, and there it was! It didn't even have my name on it, and they'd retitled it "I Played with Fire." But there it was, the whole story.

"That's my story! That's me!" Oh, it felt so good to be published! But then I realized: "They haven't paid me nothing!" They were just taking advantage of a country girl. So I wrote them a letter, said I read this article and it's the same story I wrote, but you changed the name of it. And they sent me a check for fifty dollars. Back then, that was a lot of money to me.

That was in October of 1953, and I really thought I was on my way. So I kept writing and writing and writing. *True Confessions, Tan Confessions*, you name it, every magazine they had out there that had stories like that, I sent my stories in. I didn't hear back from any of them either, but I didn't get discouraged, at least not yet.

I was very discouraged, though, by what was going on around me in Belzoni. A few years after they electrocuted Charlie Holmes, the Rev. George Lee was killed while driving home from a meeting of the RCNL, the Regional Council of Negro Leadership, an organization doing voter registration, trying to sign up Black folks to vote. He was very involved in that, and he was also the head of the NAACP in Belzoni, so a lot of white folks didn't like him. I knew Rev. Lee very well. Our family had lived close to him on Hayden Street, and my girlfriends and I used to go into his store. He was very friendly to us.

Just before they killed him, he had made a big speech in Mound Bayou, Mississippi. There was a huge crowd there, and he really got them going. I think that brought too much attention on him; white folks at that time couldn't stand a nigger who was getting what they called "uppity." Someone pulled up alongside his car while he was driving and shot him in the face.

The sheriff tried to call it just a traffic accident that killed Rev. Lee, said all those pieces of metal in his face were just fillings from his teeth. So Medgar Evers and some other people came down and demanded an investigation. But the FBI investigation didn't pan out either. Some people said the witnesses were too scared to talk, which was probably true. No one was ever charged. But as word got around, everyone had a pretty good idea of who did it. The FBI even named them in their report, but they said they couldn't get enough evidence against them, so they closed the case.

Rev. Lee's church, White Star Missionary Baptist, is still standing. The street it's on has been renamed George E. Lee Street in his honor. It isn't too far from Ruby Street, where Charlie Holmes was killed. That church wasn't big enough to handle the crowds that were going to come to Rev. Lee's funeral, so they moved it to Green Grove Missionary Baptist on Church Street, not far from where he was killed, and just a block east of Hayden Street, where he lived and had his store. Over a thousand people attended his service.

My nephew Morris Allen is now the pastor of Green Grove; he was young when that happened, and he's the pastor now. Rev. Lee is buried in the cemetery behind the church. His widow, Rosebud, decided to have an open casket so people could see his face with all those scars on it, see the damage they'd done to him. This was just a few months before Emmett Till's mother did the same thing in Chicago, after Emmett was lynched in Money, Mississippi. After Rev. Lee got killed, and with everything else that was happening there, people started calling the town "Bloody Belzoni." It developed one of the worst reputations in that part of the South. And that's really saying something.

For myself, I had no choice. I had to leave Mississippi, and this time I had to stay away. My brother was still living in Chicago; I was older now, and I knew I could find some kind of job there. I really had no idea what was in store for me, but it had to be better than what I was leaving behind.

Pretty soon, though, I found a new family, new opportunities, and then, within a few years, a new answer to my old question: Could dreams really come true?

Chapter Four

"That Was God Talking to You!"

A Godmother, a New Life—and Songs Waiting to Be Sung

My brother A.J. and I loved each other very much, but after living with
him and his wife for a while, I could kind of tell they wanted me to move
out from there. There was a lady named Eloise Aikens who lived nearby at
4823 S. Langley, and she was looking for a tenant. My brother and his wife
kept talking about it, and I kind of took the hint. I don't know whether
they meant it like that or not, but I said, "Take me on over. Let me see it."

Ms. Aikens told me she'd charge me eight dollars a week for a room. She
and her youngest son stayed on the first floor, and that's where my little
room was. Her daughter and her family lived on the second floor, and her
oldest son and his family lived on the third floor.

She was a beautiful woman, very light complexion, sort of Indian-looking
and long hair, soft and long with big waves in it. When I first moved in,
she had broken her leg and couldn't work; I would cook for her and bring
her food and do all kinds of little things for her. So we just became mama
and daughter. I started calling her "Mama Weese." She called me one of her
children; she introduced me to everybody: "This is my other daughter." And
her sons were my brothers.

Mama Weese became the mother that I left in Mississippi, my Chicago
mother, and we just stayed locked in until the day she died. I stayed in that

apartment for quite a few years. Later I moved out for a while, because at her house I respected her enough not to be letting men come in, and I was at the age now where I wanted somebody to be able to visit me. I got me a little efficiency apartment, a kitchen and a bedroom and a bathroom, a few blocks west of there at 4719 S. Wabash. But I moved back in again after Mama Weese remarried and left to live with her new husband, and in 1971, when she put the house on the market, I bought it; I used my first royalty check from Westbound Records for "Trapped By a Thing Called Love." She didn't charge me but $15,000 for that three-flat building with a basement apartment, good shape, good condition. I paid her down on it, and then I paid her by the month. And then finally I got another royalty check and paid her off. I stayed in that house until I moved to Memphis in 1974.

Mama Weese's grandchildren are my godchildren, and we talk all the time. We never lost that. And her sons, always my brothers. I mean, I just had another family there, I really did. When Mama Weese died in 1994, her obituary named me as one of her "adopted daughters."

I had several different jobs during this time. I was working at a dry cleaner's again, and then one of Mama Weese's sons opened up a bakery and he actually developed a little franchise; he had about five or six around the city. I went to work at one of his bakeries, learned how to decorate birthday cakes, wedding cakes, things like that. I still thought about being a singer—always! I never stopped thinking about that. But I just never thought I had what it took to get out on my own and do it.

There's something else about this time I never will forget. It was the only thing my father and I ever disagreed on. And it used to hurt my feelings so bad, because my father was such a good man. I mean, he was a *good* man. Uneducated, couldn't write his own name, but strong. And very wise in almost every way, except one. And that's just because he was a product of his time, but times were changing, especially for black folk.

My daddy was trying to make my brother Nate drop out of school and get a job. I would let Nate come to Chicago, stay with me all summer, and work. Didn't have to buy food, nothing. Just work, save his money for school. There used to be a store on 47th Street; I think it was called Max's Men's Store or something like that. I would take Nate up there to buy him suits and things, and then I'd take him anywhere else he wanted to go, Sears and Roebuck, anywhere, to buy his everyday clothes. "Save your money! Go back to school and finish college."

I did that for Nate every year. He died in 2017, but if he were here, he'd sit there and tell you that, right now. But my daddy really resisted that. He'd say, "You need to get him a job."

I said, "Well, Daddy, he needs an education."

Daddy said, "I'm doing all right. I ain't got no education; I'm doing all right."

"Doing all right?!" He'd never had anything, so he considered he was doing all right. And here we were, the poorest thing you ever want to see. He's out there working on the garbage truck after we moved to town, dumping garbage off, picking up garbage, putting it on that truck. But he's "doing all right!" We had that little two-room house on Hayden when we first moved to Belzoni, then Daddy and them moved into the house on Cain Street that had four rooms and a kitchen. And that was the house they were living in at this time.

But Daddy said he was doing fine. I said, "Well, I don't care what you say; Nathan's staying in school. I'll help him." And Daddy and them didn't want to pay his tuition, they didn't want to do this, didn't want to do that. I told Nate, "Don't worry about it. Go to school. I'm going to help you."

So I helped Nate get through college. And then he still did a lot of it on his own, because Nate was a strong person. He was a good singer. He got him a band when he was at Mississippi Valley State, and he made his own money on weekends. Didn't have to worry Mama and Daddy for anything. And he sure wasn't out there picking and chopping cotton! And I liked that about him. A strong man, and he did it with class. I liked that.

In Chicago, my church was Zion Temple, at 48th and Langley, just about half a block from where I was living. Reverend F. D. Johnson was the pastor. I started singing with the choir, and then I started singing tenor for an all-female gospel quartet called the Sacred Five. I didn't have the nerve to get out there and sing by myself, but we sang on programs at various churches and functions, and I got to meet a lot of well-known people in the gospel field. A lot of them became rhythm and blues stars later on. The Staple Singers sang at our group's anniversary. I knew Johnnie Taylor even before he was with the Soul Stirrers, when he was still singing with the Highway QCs after Sam Cooke left. He was always a wonderful singer, everybody loved him, but Johnnie, in those days, Johnnie wouldn't talk to me. Johnnie was snotty. He was snotty back then.

I never will forget one time in particular, I said something to Johnnie, and I forget what it was we were talking about, but the way he turned me off made me want to cuss him out right there. Oh, he thought he was some doo-doo on a stick! Then he left the QCs and went with the Soul Stirrers, and naturally I didn't see him that much then because he was always gone somewhere. But I'd see him almost every Sunday in Chicago when he was with the QCs, because I was following the quartets around. And not only that, I was in one, so I was out there singing, too. I knew Otis Clay, too; he was singing gospel in those days. These days most people know him as one of the great soul men of all time, but Otis was always a fine gospel singer, and he kept singing gospel and inspirational songs until the day he died.

Another singer, James Phelps, had a hit with "Love Is a Five-Letter Word" in 1965, but before that he was a gospel singer. He was with the Soul Stirrers for a while with Sam Cooke. I knew James really well; matter of fact, before he joined the Stirrers, James Phelps and I had a little thing going on in there; he was my boyfriend for a minute. I met Sam, too; I had the opportunity to be on some programs with him when he was with the Stirrers. But I just met him as a "shake your hand, Sam Cooke" kind of thing; he didn't know me from Adam. Like everyone else, though, I just loved Sam Cooke. Our lead singer in the Sacred Five was named Ida, and Ida could mimic Sam; she was a female Sam Cooke. She idolized him, sang just like him, do anything Sam Cooke could do with his voice. She'd do all that "Whoa-ah, whoa-ah, whoa-ah," that "yodel" just like Sam. I mean, she was bad!

It wasn't just gospel singers I met. I went to Roberts Show Lounge down at 66th and South Park, that's Martin Luther King Jr. Drive now, to see Dinah Washington and Brook Benton, and I got to meet Dinah. She was a big star, of course, and we never got to know each other very well. But it was always a thrill to meet someone like that.

I knew Marshall Thompson of the Chi-Lites when I was working at the bakery. Marshall used to come in there and eat donuts, and we'd drink coffee and talk. The Chi-Lites were called the Hi-Lites at first; they were around for a long time before they started having hits, but they eventually became one of the biggest groups in history. Marshall is the only original member still living, and he's the only one I knew really well.

I also kept writing stories, but as time went on I began to change my focus. After selling that first story, I'd gone out and bought me a typewriter. "Woooh, I'm a hunt-and-peck typist now!" At least they'll be clearer to read, I thought.

That didn't help much. I came home one day and found all these manuscripts laying in the vestibule. They'd all gotten returned on the same day, all of them just layin' down there at the same time. "All that time I wasted!" It really hurt my feelings when I saw those things.

So I said, I'm not wasting any more time trying to write these stories. Ideas come to me to write, I'll just put 'em down rhyming, and I called myself makin' me a book of poems. But then as I'd be writing, it'd come to me with a melody. "This sounds like Jerry Butler could sing this one!" "This one sounds like Aretha!" "This one sounds like Gloria Lynne!" And whoever I thought it sounded like, I would style it to match those people. I didn't know any of them; I just did it because that's what I felt.

I think the first song I ever wrote was called "Tears." I still remember some of it: "I can't see the clock for the tears"; then it said, "Maybe I'll walk in the night, dear, a night I have no fears / But why should I walk in the dark, dear? I can't see the stars for the tears." And when I wrote it, you know who I wrote it for? I wrote that song with Jerry Butler in mind. When I heard it in my head, I phrased it for Jerry Butler. That's the first song I remember writing as a whole song.

I was always writing, even at work. At the dry cleaner's, I always kept a pencil and pad right there beside me; I would write awhile, then I'd sing. The steam would shoot out—*Pssssst!*—then, *Clack-a psshhht-clunk-boom! Clack-a psshhht-clunk-boom!* It had a little rhythm to it. I'd hear that rhythm, and I'd be making that song right along with it.

Finally one girl came over to me and said, "Are you crazy?"

I said, "What you mean?"

She said, "What is all of this you're doin', all of this stoppin', writin', and doin' this and that? Everybody in here talkin' 'bout you. Even the bossman."

So I ended up finally just telling them what I was doing.

They kind of laughed about it. "Well, what you gonna do with your songs?"

"I don't know."

And I really didn't, not for a long time.

"You Oughta Show Your Songs to The Whip!"

One of the first things I did when I got back to Chicago was to start going to the Regal again. By this time all the rhythm and blues people were appearing there. Mitty Collier, Solomon Burke, LaVern Baker. Oooh, I loved LaVern Baker! She was one of the sassiest women I'd ever seen on stage, talk more shit than anybody. I just loved her to death. Some folks used to take off their shoes on stage. Etta James would take hers off, and another woman, can't remember who it was now, but another woman used to take her shoes off all the time, too. She'd kick them shoes off, and then she'd go for it! Dancing and everything. I'd go to the Regal and I'd watch it, idolize it—"Boy, imagine if that was *me* up there!"

But those audiences could be pretty rough sometimes. I know the Apollo in New York had a reputation for that, but the Regal could be that way, too. I remember they laughed at Solomon Burke, made fun of him because he was so fat. And Mitty Collier, that's one of the ugliest women I ever saw standing on a stage in my life. I loved her song, "I Had a Talk with My Man," but she came out there on the stage, I went, "Woooh!" I couldn't even look at her. And the whole audience just gasped; I mean, you could hear people gasping all over the audience.

So there I was, singing gospel with the Sacred Five, going to the Regal, writing those poems, dreaming that someday, somehow, some famous singer might get a hold of one of them and record it. Then, one day my godbrother and I got into a disagreement at the bakery, and I walked out and quit. There was a club around the corner, near 51st Street between Prairie and Calumet, called Mix's Lounge. I used to go there to socialize, have a few drinks—I drank some in those days—so I went over to Mix's, sat down talking to my friends, and I told them I was out of a job. And Mix, the owner, suggested I come in and work there as a barmaid. "A fine-looking girl like you, all the men gon' be just lined up at the bar!" That's what he said.

So I got the job at Mix's. They made me the barmaid in the morning, from ten to three or eleven to four, something like that. I never did work nights. He said I was too young to work the night shift because that's when all the hullabaloo came in. On my quiet time, when nobody was bothering me behind that bar, I was still writing and singing to myself. I'd be walking around, singing, writing songs all the time.

And everybody's still saying, "Well, what are you going to do with all those songs you're writing?"

And I'm still saying, "I don't know. I'm writing this song for so-and-so, and I'm writing this for so-and-so."

Finally, someone said, "You oughta show your songs to The Whip!"

His name was Billy "The Kid" Emerson, but they also called him "The Whip" because of a new record he had out. He'd been on the Sun label in

Memphis, but now he was in Chicago on a label called M-Pac, and he had this dance record called "The Whip," singing, "If you make the trip, I'll pop the whip." It was on the jukebox, and I played it all the time.

Finally one day I hung around until he got there. I remember exactly what day it was: November 22, 1963, the day President Kennedy was assassinated. We were all sitting there watching the news, when he came in. Someone introduced me to Billy, and I told him about my songs.

"Can you sing them?"

I said, "Yes."

"Well, if you can sing the songs, I'll play the piano or the organ and let you make a tape, and I'll take it to Chess Records."

A friend of his, Wayne Bennett, the boy who played guitar for Bobby "Blue" Bland, had an organ. So we went over to Wayne Bennett's, Billy played the keyboard, and we taped it. The song was "Tears," the one I just told you about. That's the one he took down and played for Chess. They listened, they liked it, said they wanted to meet me. I was young and I guess kinda cute in those days, and they saw something or they heard something they liked. In fact, I think they were more interested in me than the song! But they took some tracks by a singer called Little Miss Cornshucks; her real name was Mildred Cummings. They took some of her tracks and pulled the vocals off. And I think they erased Etta James's voice off a song, too, or maybe they just mixed her down real low. I learned those songs, they brought me back down there, and I put the songs on tape with those backing tracks. Chess liked what they heard, and they asked me to sign a contract with them.

You probably won't believe what happened next: I froze. I would not sign the contract. I was scared to death. I went home, and I was just scared. I had never sung by myself; I had always sung with a group. And then I talked to my mom about it, and she went right down my throat with that "God" thing, you know, so that scared me even more. So I was laying in the bed, just thinking about it, thinking about how scared I was and how I didn't want to do it. I was in my bed, right there in that little basement apartment in my godmother's house. And this might sound crazy to you, but it's the truth as ever I've told: Suddenly I felt a weight on the side of the bed, as though somebody had sat down. And a voice said to me, "You asked me for a better way to make a living. Now I've shown you, and you won't take it."

Now I'm struggling, trying to wake up and see who is this talking to me? I couldn't wake up fully, almost like somebody was holding me down. But then the minute I felt the weight get up off the bed, and that voice stopped talking, my eyes flew wide open. I bolted up, tore through the house, nobody there but me. And then I started thinking, evaluating the words that were said to me. And I started to wonder.

I'd been having problems from standing on my feet working at all those jobs I'd had, working on concrete, standing on hard floors, pains and problems down in my stomach and my back all the time. I'd been running back and forth to the doctor, and I'd been praying about that.

So next day, when I went to work at Mix's, there was a young man, his name was Josh Halfacre. He was a very devout Christian, and he used to come in and we'd talk all the time. So I told him about that dream, or whatever it was, and he said, "You need to think about that."

I said, "But I'm scared to do that. I've never sung by myself; I've always had someone on the stage with me."

Then he said, "That was God talking to you! Who did you ask to show you? Who were you asking for a way?"

"I asked God."

"Well, don't you think that was God talking to you?"

"I don't know."

"Well, you think about it. If I were you, I'd do it. That was God talking to you last night."

He gave me a couple of books to read; he gave me Norman Vincent Peale's *The Power of Positive Thinking* and another book by Napoleon Hill. I read those books. I thought about what Josh had said to me, and what that voice had said. I called Billy: "Take me down to Chess."

I was ready to sign.

Chapter Five

"Mama Says It's in My Blood"

Breaking In: Learning the Ropes from Billy Emerson

Even after I signed that contract, I was still scared and nervous about getting out there and singing on my own. So the people at Chess told Billy, "Well, if she's afraid to sing by herself, why don't you take her under your wings and let her get some experience singing?" Billy started taking me around to different jam sessions and amateur-night contests, and I began to meet some of the musicians who were working around town.

Chicago at that time was full of lounges, clubs, little hole-in-the-wall places, all kinds of nightspots, and they all had entertainment. If it was big enough to hold fifty people, there was a band there. And most times, there was music six and seven nights a week. Monday was called Blue Monday, and everybody who had any type of club going had a Blue Monday party. It usually started around 10:00 in the morning and went on all day long. You'd see musicians walking with their axe in their hand, going from one place to the other to sit in and play, bring their guitars or horns or whatever they played. The club might have drums and keyboards set up, and whatever instrument you played, or if you sang, you could come in and work. Nobody's getting paid, but everybody's jamming.

The most famous one to go to was at a place called the Trocadero, at 47th and Indiana. And then, right down the street, Buddy Guy and Junior Wells were at a little place in the basement called Theresa's. Monday was an all-day jam session at the Trocadero, with the talent show that night; Tuesday night was Theresa's. And then they had one out at 64th and Cottage Grove at one of the hotels; I think it was the Pershing.

Billy would take me around to all these places. At first, I couldn't keep time with the music very well, and I had problems with staying in key and all; I didn't know one key from another. But I knew a lot of songs because I was always listening, always trying to sing along with the jukebox or the radio or whatever it was.

Some of the guys didn't want to work with me at first, say, "Aw, man, she can't sing. Get away from here!" But I just kept trying, kept going. The first time I ever sang on my own in front of an audience was at a club called Lonnie's Skyway Lounge on 75th Street. They had a band called the Eddie Buster Band. It was two brothers, Eddie and Bobby Buster. I think Bobby played bass, and the keyboard was Eddie. And at that time, their guitar player was Philip Upchurch, who was considered one of Chicago's best. Played on everybody's sessions, did a lot of work over at Chess, had records out on his own, too.

Billy went up and asked them to let me sing, and Philip Upchurch, I have to say, was very nice to me. He took time when other guys didn't want to do that. Here's a young lady who doesn't even know what key she sings in, doesn't know how to stay in time or anything, but Philip was very gracious:

"You don't know your key, baby? Well, hum or sing a little of it for me."

And I'd sing, and he'd find the key—"Okay, that's the key of so-and-so"—and if I started singing and it turned out to be too high for me, he'd bring it down to a lower key. He was always there for me.

So on this night, my first night ever, they asked me what song I wanted to sing.

"'Drown in My Own Tears.'"

"What key?"

"I don't know."

Philip said, "Holler a little of it for me." And I started singing, and he found the key, and we did the song. First time I was ever on stage with a band. Oooh, I was scared to death! Heart pounding! But I got through it. I wasn't great, it wasn't enough to make anybody jump up or anything, but I got decent applause. That was my beginning.

Usually, when Billy took me around to these places, he'd play a little first, and then he'd say, "I got a girl I want to sing something." And then we'd do a song that we had rehearsed around the house. I would be doing the Supremes, the Marvelettes, all those girl singers and groups that were popular then. And finally, I started moving up from the jam sessions to the talent shows. And when I got in the talent shows, I started placing, coming up second place and all that. And then all of a sudden, I started winning. First prize, fifty dollars. That was real money to me at that time. That was great! And that inspired me. "Hey, there must be something to this thing. I can do it!"

Of course there was some jealousy. I was the new kid on the block, and they had some really great talent who'd come through there, jazz singers and everything. Some of them would laugh at me, say, "She didn't win! She can't sing! Them red pants won! Those tight pants she had on won!" They'd laugh at me like that. They'd say I won because of the sex appeal, not because I sang so good. But Billy had taught me how to put myself over, how to sell myself. So it worked for me.

In fact, I have to give Billy a lot of credit. He really taught me everything I know about a stage. He taught me how to captivate an audience. He'd teach me to watch other performers, how to learn from what they were doing, how to learn what *not* to do by watching them:

See how they're frowning? See how they won't look at the audience and they got their eyes closed? Don't be that kind of artist. Stare your audience in the face. Look 'em in the face; talk to 'em. Get to know them, get out there with 'em. Come off that stage, walk out there and challenge 'em! This is what the audience wants; they want to feel you, they want to feel personal to you. They don't want to feel like you're isolated up there on the stage, all in a world of your own and stuff like that. They want to feel you like they know you.

And so he taught me those things. "All this turning your back to the audience, messing with the band, arguing with the band, never do that." He said, "If somebody plays a wrong note behind you, sing your way around to them. Say, for instance, the drummer loses his foot pedal, or his stick breaks, or anything. You miss that sound, right? But you don't whirl around and let the audience know this; sing your way around to it. Just keep on singing, turn your body all around until you see what's going on, and nine times out of ten, by the time you get back there, he's corrected it anyway.

But just don't make the audience notice. 'Cause a lot of time a whole lot of things go unnoticed if you will just keep your cool."

He also taught me, even if you have to reach down deep and get that gut emotion, growl in that bluesy style or sing a song about feeling bad or being angry, always come out of it with a smile. Always remember to smile at your audience and make them a part of your show. He taught me that if a fight breaks out in the audience, don't start staring at the fight and stop singing. If you keep singing and crack some jokes and make something funny happen to keep the public's attention, the fight nine times out of ten goes unnoticed. And then security can get there, take 'em out, and half the people in the place never know it happened.

He taught me all these little things. But he also said, "If you ever see a chair coming at you, or you see a gun, run like hell! See somebody fixin' to throw a bottle, get out. But as long as people are just tussling or arguing or fighting, stand right there and make as much light of it as you can, and try to keep that audience entertained."

And I've kept those things he taught me, down through the years. I've cherished it, I've kept it with me, and I've used it, and it works. I also learned about copyrights and publishing; I learned all that from Billy. I learned that you don't put your songs out there 'til you get them copyrighted. He told me, "Don't never give nobody nothing until you have 'em copyrighted. Always make sure it's written down right there on the record, or if there's sheet music made, put it there, too. Make sure they see it's copyrighted. And what you can do, if you want to copyright something and you ain't got the money to send it off to Washington and do it, put it in an envelope, put the date on it, and mail it back to yourself. You mail it back to yourself, and it's copyrighted. It's yours."

He said, "Never write a song and give all your rights away to somebody else. Always keep your rights to your song. Start your own publishing company." He had his own label, too, so later on, when I had labels of my own, I had been taught by an expert. I knew everything it takes to keep in business and keep control of my songs, rather than getting them stolen. I named my publishing company Ordena, for Ora Dee Allen. Many years later, I published a booklet called *How to Be a Successful Songwriter*; I used to sell copies of it at my shows. It included a section on copyrights, publishing, and royalties, with information on the performing rights organizations, BMI and ASCAP. All of that stems from what Billy Emerson taught me.

I always give Billy that credit; he's the one who really put me out here. I found all those things out from him. I've always had control of my career. I've had people, like my good friend Don Dortch, who have helped me in what you might call a managerial capacity, but I have never signed a contract with anybody as management. My contract has always been just to record for a company, but I kept my rights to me. So even though later on Billy and I parted under the worst conditions possible—I'll tell you all about that in a little while—I've always cherished the knowledge and the things he taught me.

"Denise LaSalle Is My Name!"

So Billy groomed me, and I started working with him and his band. But first, I had to find a new name for myself. And I guess this means I'll have to do what I've been putting off: tell you just a little bit about the man I'd married and left, years earlier. This man's name was Artic Craig. Everybody called him "Artie," but his first name was Artic. Don't ask me what it means; I don't know where he'd get a name like that. My brother A.J. worked at Campbell Soup, and Artic Craig was working there. That's how I came to know him. So even though I didn't stay with him very long, my legal name was Ora D. Craig for many years after that.

You'll see that name, or some version of it, in the credits on a lot of my early records. Usually it will say something like "O. Denise Craig." I had already changed my name to Denise when I left Mississippi. I never liked that name "Ora," so I dropped the whole "Ora" and used Denise instead of "Dee," which was my real middle name, or at least that's the way it was pronounced. Remember, I didn't have a birth certificate, so after they named me, my name might get spelled "Ora Dee" or "Ora D.," either way. But I liked the sound of "Denise." It sounded French, and I liked that. Eventually, I changed my name legally to Ora Denise. But I didn't want nobody callin' me no Ora, so I dropped the Ora and just went with Denise.

But that wasn't enough. After I signed with Chess, I had made up my mind that my name was not going to be "Ora"-Anything, but it wasn't going to be Denise Craig either, and it wasn't going to be Denise Allen. I wanted a French name to go with my other French name. I almost named myself Denise Darcel, after the actress, but then I realized, no, I can't do that. She's a big movie star, and I'm not going to copy her name. There was a comic strip in the newspaper called *Mary Worth*, and it was a girl who came from France or somewhere, in the comic, called Buffy LaSalle. "Denise LaSalle!" I loved the sound of that! So I chose that name. Everybody thinks it came from LaSalle Street in Chicago, but it came from Buffy LaSalle.

My first actual gig on my own was in 1964, at the Trocadero. Cicero Blake, the soul-blues singer who had that hit "Dip My Dipper" many years later, was working there, too, and he's a dear friend of mine to this day. I had won the talent show there, so I got the chance to do three nights, Friday, Saturday, and Sunday, for fifteen dollars a night. Forty-five dollar weekend. That was my first pay. At that time, forty-five dollars for a weekend was great. And then I had a day job at Spiegel's doing clerical work, so that was a steady income. I felt like I was doin' fine!

At Chess, though, things weren't fine at all. After acting so eager to sign me, and then after asking Billy to train me and get me ready, they never recorded me. They had these great songwriters over there writing for Etta James and everybody; I asked 'em to write me some songs, and I'll have you know, one of those guys said he didn't want an "unknown singer" doing his songs! Jackie Ross, Mitty Collier, Etta, all those people were with Chess, but they wouldn't have a song written for me.

They kept me under contract for a whole year. They'd tell me to come down there and listen to some songs, pick out some songs, and then I'd go there and all they would do was talk. I don't know what their deal was, but I had some pretty strong suspicions. See, I wouldn't go there alone. I'd heard too many stories about how the men in the record industry, like label owners or whoever, they would try to become sexually involved with you in order to "help" you, so I'd never go down there without Billy. I'm not going to accuse them directly, because nobody ever came right out and said, "Come on and lay down on the couch." But the conversation would always be different from what I wanted. I wanted them to say, "Let's go in the studio and record, there's a band here." They never got around to anything like that for a solid year.

They'd always be asking me things like, "Do you have to bring Billy with you?"

"Why not? Billy's my manager."

"I don't understand why you have to bring him with you all the time."

So that told me something right there. What you trying to do to me that Billy can't know about? He's supposed to be my manager.

I honestly think I could have recorded in that first year with Chess Records, had I been the kind that they could take advantage of. But I just stayed out of that position, never let them get me in that predicament, so the year went by and I never cut anything. I always felt that this was probably the reason.

And I'll say this right now, too: When I say I don't play that, I don't play that. Nobody, not an agent, not a record company owner, not a promoter anywhere in the world, can ever say he laid a hand on me. Can't none of 'em tell a lie and say they ever touched me. None of 'em. And none of 'em tried to put pressure on me, either; I got them suckers off me before they could get started. I'm sure they would have, but I just happen to be one of them no-nonsense people. When I said something to 'em, I meant it, and they knew it. Because I ain't never bit my tongue about nothing.

That could be one reason why I'm not further along than I am, even today. Because I never let anybody rule me. I've always been my own woman. I always had the contracts written where I could call my own shots. And if they didn't like it, they didn't get me. Because I've seen too much other stuff go down. I've seen other women out here, screwin' the bossman, and all he does, when she don't cut a hit record, throw her aside. And I wasn't layin' down on no couch with none of them guys that own a record company. And I was young and fine and all that shit, but I didn't let them do that to me. And who knows? Some of those people might've been able to push me all the way to stardom. But if I had to get it that way, forget it. I didn't want that.

After a year being signed with Chess and them not doing anything to record me or further my career, I wrote them a letter, asking for a release from the contract. Then they want me to come down there and record!

"You stay with us. In two weeks, we promise we'll have your record."

I said, "I've been here one year. You didn't cut nothing on me. I'm gone."

Building My Name on the Chicago Club Circuit

I guess you could say I did break my rule at least once about not letting an agent or a manager get next to me. That was at the very beginning. When Billy Emerson started helping me sing, when he got me off in the business, he was in his late '30s, and I was a young lady who didn't know any better. You know, gullible, didn't have a steady boyfriend or anything like that. So

Billy and I became intimate, say he's gonna be my manager and my man. We never signed a contract, never had any kind of legal agreement, but that was the way it was. I didn't realize my mistake at the time, but I found out later, and I found out the hard way. It was one of the most painful lessons I ever learned in my life. I'll get to that later on, and I'll tell it all, because it's a big part of the reason why I'm the way I am today.

But for a while, it felt like a good arrangement, and it seemed to be getting me closer to where I wanted to go. He taught me a lot, as I've said, and he definitely introduced me to the club circuit in Chicago. He's the main reason I gained the confidence to get out there and sing by myself. Eventually I began working actual shows with him. Billy worked in white clubs a lot of the time. He worked Gary and Hammond, Indiana; Rockford, Illinois; and up toward Milwaukee, all those white clubs, all up in there. I didn't always work with him; Billy had a girl that worked with him at most of the white clubs. I only worked with Billy at the black clubs at first. After I cut my first record, "A Love Reputation," he started taking me up there to some of those other places.

We'd do about five shows a night. Forty and twenty: Do forty minutes, take a twenty-minute break. Forty, twenty; forty, twenty. Every time the band came on, I would go up and I'd do three songs. Then Billy would come on. And I kept getting better and more confident—1965, I got a little bit better and '66, I got a little bit better. At first, I was just with Billy's own band; but then I got good enough that other people started asking me to come and play, work with another band in a club somewhere. I also started meeting other entertainers. Some, like me, were just starting out; others were well known, and I was thrilled to have the opportunity to meet them. A lot of times, we ended up being lifelong friends.

Billy introduced me to Lonnie Brooks early on. Lonnie's real name was Lee Baker, but he was using the name "Guitar Junior" when he first started. There was another guitar player in Chicago already calling himself that. His real name was Luther Johnson; he got famous later on when he joined Muddy Waters. So Lonnie didn't want to keep using that name, and I was the one who came up with Lonnie Brooks. I used his initials, the L.B., for Lee Baker, and I named him Lonnie Brooks.

Billy and I wrote a song called "Figure Head" and produced it on him; it came out on the U.S.A. label in 1964, and if you have the 45 you can see Billy's name and mine, "Emerson" and "Craig," as the songwriters. "Figure

Head" was the first record he ever made under Lonnie Brooks. The name stuck, and he eventually became an internationally famous blues man. Played blues festivals around the country, in Europe, all over the world. He was one of those who never came into prominence in the black market; white folk, mostly, knew him, the blues lovers. I knew his wife, Jeannine, too. Lonnie came to the Memphis Blues Awards a few years ago, and I asked about Jeannine, and he told me they had separated. That really surprised the hell out of me; they'd been together for a long, long time. She was a white woman, and he'd married her back in the '60s when that was still rare and could really be dangerous. They stayed together through all that, and I never thought they would separate. And I don't know, but some people said Lonnie was never the same after that. I know he didn't record or perform very much during the last few years of his life. He died in Chicago in 2017.

You know Gene Barge, the tenor sax player they call Daddy G? After Billy, he was the director of the first band I ever worked with. Like I said, as I got better and more confident, I would just sing with whoever I could; when a club owner liked me, saw that I could draw the people and keep a crowd, he would hire me and put me with a band. And Gene Barge was the first band I worked with after Billy Emerson.

I also worked some more with Eddie and Bobby Buster, Matt "Guitar" Murphy, anybody. And there was another singer, called himself Singing Sam; his name was Sam Chatmon. Sam had a girl vocalist with him who was also his girlfriend, and he was having problems with her. Anytime they'd have a spat, she wouldn't make the gig. So he'd call me; I was his standby. He worked a lot in the white clubs on the North Side of Chicago. And that's when I really got over good up there, because over on the South Side, you had to learn how to belt out them blues; up there with the whites, you had an easier music. They liked you to sing like the Supremes and Mary Wells, things like that; you didn't have to do that hardcore stuff. But go back here, work in a black club, you got to learn how to please them, do more of that "black ethnic" kind of music, you know? Everybody had their own sound; it's more "pop" over there, and it's more "bluesy" over here. That's what I had to learn to do—be versatile. And I was holding down both of 'em, doing my thing.

Sometimes it was a problem for us in those white clubs, but mostly for the men. They didn't want the fellas to be out in the club; afraid they might socialize with the white women. They wanted the men to stay in the dressing room or somewhere, keep themselves apart. I could go out, sit at the bar, drink all I wanted to do, and nobody never said anything to me about it, but I just didn't do that. If my guys couldn't go out there, I'm not going either. We never had any real bad episodes about that, but I did hear stories where guys would get in trouble, even get beaten up, for fraternizing in white clubs in those days.

Another one who started out in Chicago as a soul singer but went on to become popular with blues fans is Holly Maxwell. I met her when I first started singing; she hadn't even cut a record yet. She had classical training, and when I met her she still sounded classical but she was trying to sing R&B. That was at the Trocadero. I think Billy Emerson's band used to play for her sometimes, and by him taking me around with him, I got a chance to see her. I admired her, but her voice always sounded too pretty for her to be a blues singer. A local label in Chicago, Constellation, had a song someone had written called "Happiness Will Only Cost You One Thin Dime." They wanted me to sing it; I heard the demo and I tried to sing it, but I couldn't hit those high notes. So Billy said, "I tell you what. I know a girl can hit them high notes. I'll bring her down here." And he took Holly down there, and she cut that. That was her first record, in 1965.

But to me she still didn't sound that good singing it, because she really wasn't that kind of singer. She had that high trill, and it sounded too classical. The record sold a little bit for her, and I know she cut some more, but I never heard any of the others. Later on she moved to California, and she sang with Ike Turner for a few years after Tina left, but I never saw her again until recently. I went to Chicago to do a show, and she showed up. She looks so different from the way she looked back then! She's singing the blues now, and she calls herself "Holle Thee Maxwell, the Original Black Blonde Bombshell." She has a lot of young white folks who really like her. But I knew her when her voice couldn't handle the kind of thing she's doing now.

I got to know a lot of other people, too. Billy and I would go out, like to the Regal, and he was already well known of course, so I had the chance to go backstage, shake everybody's hand—that was like heaven to me. You want to know who else I idolized? Aretha Franklin! Now, she was singing before I was; she had made it before I started as a professional. And I idolized her; I thought she had the best voice ever. And when I started recording, if you listen at some of my early records when my voice was young and fresh and all that, you'll hear Aretha in all my stuff. So Billy Emerson knew her; he introduced us. But then Aretha shook my hand so ugly—her hand was so limp, like it was dead. That really hurt my feelings. She could've at least held it with some warmth or something. But it was like she was telling me, "You're just a newcomer doing this!" And I said to myself, "You bitch!" I like her songs, but the only time we met, I had that experience, and I never really cared to meet her again.

I got to know Gene Chandler pretty well, though. He used to come by my house and eat all the time. He was going with my girlfriend. I had a white girlfriend, Mary Catherine Mouradick, who lived in California. And she'd come to Chicago, and she and Gene would hang out. I also used to love to hear Major Lance sing, but I didn't really get to know him well. He became a big star with records like "Monkey Time" and "Um, Um, Um, Um, Um, Um." Took him up a ladder I hadn't reached in those days. But he and I never got cool like Gene Chandler and I did. For one thing, Gene was a nice-looking man. Dressed nice and everything. Major Lance just looked like a little rat, you know what I'm saying? He just didn't appeal to me. He was nobody I wanted to know, really. He just did his little crazy song and skated around on stage, looked like he had on skates, just turn his little self around. Everybody laughed at him, everybody talked about him. You couldn't help but like his records, but he just wasn't cool, to me. He just wasn't my kind of man.

McKinley Mitchell, though, that was my boy. I was crazy about McKinley. "The Town I Live In," his first hit back in the early '60s, that's my favorite. I loved "The End of the Rainbow" later on, and I guess that's the one most people remember him for, but "The Town I Live In" is the one. That's my song.

Part of McKinley's appeal to me was that he was pretty. I'm just being honest and saying the truth! McKinley didn't have the great voice like the other guys did, but it was different, that little funny scattered voice. I always tried to describe him, and I called his voice "scattered." Scattered, with all that vibrato in it. That made it good, because he didn't sound like anybody else. And then he was pretty when he was young. Oooh! When he was young? That was a pretty boy! But then as he got older, he got fatter and didn't look as good anymore. But he was pretty 'til then. And Dee Clark? Oooh, yeah! I loved me some Dee Clark. He was cute, too. And I used to love his songs. "Raindrops," that was in the early '60s before I met Billy, but Dee had hits going back before that. I think the biggest one was "Hey

Little Girl." I didn't get to know him too well; I met him, but I didn't really know him.

So after the thing with Chess didn't pan out, I just worked and worked and worked, mostly with Billy, until finally I got a job at a place on the South Side called the Gayhawk. The owners of the Gayhawk liked my singing, and they asked me, "Why don't you record?" Billy had been wanting to record me, but he didn't have the money to do it. So they told Billy, "We'll give you some money to get a track for her and record." So Billy went to a guy named Bill Sheppard. Everybody called him Bunky; he had a record company called Constellation, the same one Holly recorded for. He had quite a few singers under contract, and he had a lot of tracks he'd recorded on them. Billy bought one of those tracks from Bunky Sheppard.

And before I knew it, I was finally cutting a record under my own name.

"A Love Reputation"

The track Billy bought from Bunky Sheppard was one Gene Chandler had recorded on first. But that didn't turn out, so they cut another singer, Nolan Chance, singing "Just Like the Weather," over that same track Gene had used. When I got this opportunity to record, Lonnie Brooks had written a song. He'd be singing, "I have a love reputation, known all over the world." I think he wanted to cut it himself. But we asked for it, and Lonnie gave it to me. So we sat down, Billy Emerson and I, and we worked on that song. I helped with some of the writing; Billy did some, and I did some. When Billy recorded me doing that song, he used the same backing track as "Just Like the Weather," kept all the original background, even the vocals, the little "Oohs" and "Aahhs," all those little doo-wop things, and I just recorded over it. And you know, as important as that record was in my career and in my life, I don't even remember exactly where we made it. But I sure did sing it:

> I've got a love reputation, known all over this world
> I'm a highjacker, safecracker, I'll steal your man, little girl
> Oooh, yeah, I can't help it 'cause I know how to love
> Mama says it's in my blood!

Billy released "A Love Reputation" on his Tarpon label; that's where he was originally from, Tarpon Springs, Florida. And it took off like a bullet. It almost went to No. 1 in Chicago in 1967, but it came up against some stiff competition. Bettye Swann's "Make Me Yours" was No. 1, and then Aretha Franklin took over with "Respect," and mine was right behind that. "Respect" stayed No. 1 for weeks, and my record stayed No. 2 for five of those weeks, five straight weeks in Chicago. Billy ended up leasing it to Chess; they got the master from him, and they distributed it internationally. When I reached England in 1974, they had "Denise 'A Love Reputation' LaSalle" all over everywhere, advertising me. Same thing when I first went overseas, to Africa, in 1972. And that blew my mind because I never even knew the record went there.

But in Chicago, that tune was so hot, man, I started getting gigs, gigs, gigs, gigs, gigs! I remember when I used to work from Monday all the way through the weekend. And now it was my name, not some bandleader's name, that was drawing the crowds. I had some sexy publicity pictures made and everything, and I went from, like, eighteen dollars a night to $125.00. That was big money then—"Hey, this is as good as it gets!"

I should have seen the warning signs, though. When Billy and I were working together on writing "Love Reputation," there were some things I wanted to change, so I did. And he and Lonnie got kinda huffed up, complaining about splitting the royalties three ways: "There's too many writers! We're payin' too many folk!"

I think I got a little warm with the selfishness of some of the way they were acting about it, so I just told 'em, "I don't want no money. I just want to put some things I want to say in here. You don't have to give me no credit, just let me put what I want to say. You all just take it and go ahead."

So Billy Emerson and "L. Baker," that's Lonnie Brooks, got all the credit for writing it. They didn't steal it from me; I let 'em. I said that's fine, because it never bothered me; I didn't miss anything. But I was finding out. You know how some people are kind of selfish? They want a lot of credit for themselves? Billy was kind of like that with me. I didn't know him that well when we got together, but I found out through the years that he had little funny ways about things. Wanted the spotlight, credit, things like that. He became a takeover control freak. Had to have everything go his way.

Now that I was making a little name for myself, sometimes a club owner or a local promoter might want me as an artist but they didn't want Billy's band. I had worked mostly with Billy's band, bur I had also worked with Singing Sam around Chicago, Bobby and Eddie Buster's band, I had been working back and forth with all these bands. But now I'm getting a little name, starting to make some money, and Billy felt he had the exclusive right to play behind me. He wanted to be my band.

Like I said, I should have seen it coming.

The Big Explosion—and the Beginnings of a Solo Career

At that time Billy lived with a single old widow lady. He had a room at her place, and I had my little three-room basement apartment on Langley with Mama Weese. He had a few things at my house, but not many, so I didn't actually really live with him. But we were together a lot.

He did push my record; I'll give him credit for that. He got it on a station in Gary, Indiana; he got it on a station in Milwaukee; and I worked in those places, so I became a kind of a celebrity in those areas as well as in Chicago. But like I said, he became very possessive of me and of my talent. In those days, a lot of the big shows that came to town were promoted by radio disk jockeys. E. Rodney Jones, who was the program director for WVON, was one of the ones bringing in these shows, and he got me a spot on a Jackie Wilson revue that was coming to the Regal Theater. They were going to pay me $600, I think it was, and you know, it's kind of funny; it wasn't but about a hundred dollars a day, when you get right down to it, $600 for a week at the Regal. But I didn't care. That was an honor to be on a Jackie Wilson show, and to play a theater, especially the Regal, for a weeklong engagement like that. And for me, after all those years sitting in that very theater, staring up at that stage, daydreaming, wondering what it would be like to be up there myself—oooh, this was going to be the biggest night of my life!

So I'm telling everybody, "I'm gonna be on the Jackie Wilson show! I'm gonna be on the Jackie Wilson Show!" Then all of a sudden, I get booted off. I had no idea what happened. First, when I started questioning, I was told, "Well, they just took you off; they were over budget." I didn't know the real reason, and Billy, who was supposed to be acting as my manager, wouldn't tell me.

One night, I was at one of those local shows they used to call platter parties. They were like celebrity showcases; the record companies broke their artists' records that way. They'd send people like Stevie Wonder, the Supremes, Martha and the Vandellas, the record company paid their expense for them to come play a show where they'd lip-synch their latest release.

A radio DJ, who'd advertise it as "his" show, could collect the tickets and keep the proceeds. That was kind of like legal payola, like money under the table; the jocks could book the room, charge five or ten dollars to get in, and that money they collected on the door was theirs.

So I went over to one of those platter parties one night, somewhere on the West Side. And I questioned this disk jockey.

I said, "Can you answer something?"

"What?"

"Why did I get taken off the show at the Regal Theater?"

He said, "You don't know?"

I said, "No. All of a sudden, I just was off the show."

He said, "I didn't take you off."

I said, "Well, how'd I get off the show? What happened?"

He said, "Your man took you off."

"My man?!"

"Yeah. Billy Emerson said if his band couldn't play the Regal behind you, he'd take you off the show."

"What?!"

"That's what he said."

See, the Regal had its own house band, led by a drummer named Red Saunders. Guys like Jackie Wilson would bring their musical director in, along with maybe a rhythm section, but the Red Saunders band had the horns and strings and everything, and the musical director would have charts for them to play. And Billy didn't like that. He wanted himself and his band with me, or nobody. And when I found that out, I went berserk. I just went berserk behind that. I couldn't hardly wait to leave that place, I was so angry. And when I got home and talked to Billy, I don't know if I talked to him that night, or whenever it was, but I went off on him.

And then he started in on me: "I made you! I'm the one that started you! And then they gon' try to put you up there on the stage without me? I'm the one got you this! I'm the one got you that!" And so and so and so and so.

So I just said, "Well, I tell you what. You won't get me nothing else!"

It's like smothering something you're growing, you know? You got a plant, you're growing this plant, and then you gonna turn around and turn all the rain off? All the oxygen off? Let it flower! Let it grow! That's the way he wanted to do. He wanted to smother me.

I told him, "I got to cut this down. Because I can't go along with it. You gonna be one of the two. You gonna be my manager or my man, whichever one you choose to be."

He said he gonna be both.

I said, "Well, not this girl, you're not gonna be both. You're either my manager or my man."

First he said, "Ain't gonna be like that." Then a little later, or maybe a few days later, he said, "Well, I'd rather be your man than your manager."

"Okay, you wanna be my man rather than my manager? That's cool. So as of right now, I'm managing me. And you're my man, okay?"

So that's when I started working with other people really strong. But I could tell he always had it in for me after that. Anything he could find to argue about he did, because he didn't like being where he was with me. I remember one particular night, he told me, "You know what? One of these days, you gonna make me beat you so bad, ain't nobody gon' want you."

So I got a gig at a club on the West Side; Tyrone Davis was a part of that show, and the band was the Busters again, Bobby and Eddie Buster. One of the Buster boys, the one that played the keyboards, I think it was Eddie, had to be out of town or something. They asked me if I would ask Billy to come over and play in his place that night. I had kind of moved on a little bit from him by then. That's what he was really teed off about, because I still wouldn't let him take over my life. I was kind of trying to move out from under his wing. But we needed a keyboard player, so I agreed to bring him along.

By that time, I had gotten me a car. I'd made it that far with that little $125 a night thing; I finally got me a little car. I picked him up, I took him over to do the show, and on my way back to bring him home, he asked me could he stop by my house and pick up some stuff. There was some writing material in a briefcase, stuff he used to use for writing songs. And I told him it was back in the basement, and he could come get it.

So we stopped by my apartment and he went down in the back of the basement and found it, and when he came back, I heard him in the kitchen, doing something, fumbling around in the kitchen. Turns out he had gone in one of my kitchen drawers and took out a knife, a big butcher knife, and laid it on the table. But I didn't know that. Came back in and started talking to me about our relationship, and how we were growing apart, and I should let him back in my life.

I said, "Billy, I don't think we need to really be together, period. The vibes I'm getting from our relationship, it's not gonna work." Because even though he wasn't managing my career, he was still trying to be dominant and controlling. So I told him, "I don't think that's right. I just think we need to just let it go."

Then he started going off again about what all he'd done for me to get me here and all that. "And now you're being ungrateful to me! And you doin' this! And you doin' that! I made you a star! I got you out of the ghetto! I got you started! And now you wanna drop me?!"

I was just sitting there on my couch. He was pacing the floor, pacing the floor, walking like a big old turkey, this way in front of me and that way back. I was letting him vent because I knew I didn't want him anymore and that was that, but I remembered what he'd said about beating me, so I didn't give him no backtalk; I just let him talk.

Then he came out with it: "Well, if I can't have you, nobody will!"

Oooh, lordy . . . I had a big ashtray on my coffee table that was made with a little curved shape on the end, and he picked this ashtray up and hit me in the face with it. Blood started gushing out, he raised his hand to hit me again, I lifted my arm and knocked that thing out of his hand. It hit the tile floor and just smashed into small pieces. He came lunging over the coffee table, pulled me off the couch by my hair, took his fist and beat me all the way to the floor. I had blood running all in my eyes and everything, couldn't see, and now he's kicking me and stomping on me, trying to break my ribs. He put his foot on my chest; I bit him on the leg or somewhere to get him off me, but I didn't have the ghost of a chance to fight, because he caught me so much by surprise. He stomped me all over my body, bruised all over, face and eyes all swollen, blood everywhere, I'm lying there helpless, just begging him, pleading, "Please don't kill me! Don't kill me! Don't kill me!"

And then, while I was lying on the floor, he picked up the keys to my car—my car!—and walked out the door. My brother A.J. lived next door, so I picked up the phone and called him to come and get me. But what I didn't know was that Billy had driven to the 48th Street police station in my car and was signing a complaint against me, saying I drew a knife on him and he had to beat me up. And that knife was still sitting on my kitchen table, where he'd planted it. Smart old man, I'm telling you; had his shit together. Knew what he want, set up anything. So while my brother was there, the police knocked on the door. I'm sitting there bleeding, crying, and going on, holding an ice pack to my face because my brother had brought ice over, and the police came in, said, "He's at the station right now filing a complaint against you." But they didn't arrest me; they called for an ambulance and got me to the Michael Reese Hospital emergency room. Nine stitches on the bridge of my nose, right next to my eye. And that scar is still there.

The police found the knife, but it had both my fingerprints and Billy's on it, so it didn't prove anything either way. I had to go down and sign a peace bond on him, where he wasn't allowed on my block or anywhere near me. He did come by the house once, though, maybe about a week later. At first I didn't know it was him; he had another boy knock on the door, say, "Billy told me to come get his stuff." I didn't open my screen; I had a storm door there, and I kept the storm door locked. Went back and got his stuff; when I got back to the door, Billy was standing there. And I said, "Be there when I get back."

By then I had bought a pistol from a lady across the street. I went back in and grabbed that pistol. When I got back to the door, he saw it, turned around, started running. So I opened the door and shot up in the air—POW! POW!—behind him. He was gone! And he never did get his stuff back. I ended up throwing it in the garbage.

I didn't have anything else to do with him after that, but one night I was back in the club. I went back to work about two weeks later, after the swelling and bleeding in my face went down, and they said, "You got even with Billy, didn't you?"

I said, "Like what?"

"Yeah, we heard about him beating you up. You sent somebody to work him over, huh?"

"I sent somebody over?"

"Yeah, Billy was in here last night. He was all beat up with his eye black and his nose all bruised."

Somebody had beat him up. I had a nephew, my brother's son, who also lived next door. He's dead now, they called him Junior, Albert Allen Junior, he and his friends, they wanted to find Billy and hurt him; they walked the street looking for him. And I often wonder did they do that. I know somebody did. Somebody caught him and beat him to a pulp. He came in the club one night, still had a swollen face, and I said, "Hmm?! You lookin' like I was lookin' a few weeks ago, huh?"

"You oughta see the other guy! They tried to rob me! You oughta see the other guy!"

So I've always wondered, but my nephew always said he didn't do anything. It could have been someone else; Billy was kind of an antagonizing person in those days, rubbed a lot of people the wrong way. A lot of people didn't like him very much. From that point on, though, whenever I was around him I was always kind of hesitant to relax.

But you know, it's a funny thing about him. He became an Apostolic minister later, and he's a different person. We're friends now, on the phone. I haven't seen him, talked to him in person, in years, but he just changed so completely. I told him, "I guess you repented for that, didn't you? For God to call you into the ministry, you had to repent."

But we talk now; he calls me every once in a while, wishes me well, so we're cool, as far as conversation's concerned. When you talk to him on the phone, he's humble, and he's all those things that you would expect a Christian to be.

In 1981, Z.Z. Hill had a record, "When It Rains, It Pours." Billy had a song by that name; it was one of his famous ones. Elvis even recorded it. So he told me he was going to collect his royalties from Malaco, Z.Z.'s label, and sign them over to me. I think after all these years, he felt like he still had to atone for what he'd done. I said, "Billy, that's not your song. It's a different song with the same name." You see, by him being a minister, Billy didn't listen to the blues anymore, so he'd never heard Z.Z.'s song. But he was talking about suing them because they didn't have his publishing company named on there. He wanted to get the money, but then he was going to give it to me.

It's just like God just went through him and just changed him all around. So I've forgiven him. You know, young folks do a lot of stuff, but Billy has come out of that, and I've forgiven him. That's God's will. God took that man and turned him into something else. And I will always give him credit for what he taught me and how he helped me get my start.

So, exit Billy "The Kid" Emerson out of my life. I was free now to work with anyone I wanted, and I worked all over the city with all kinds of people over the next few years. "A Love Reputation" kept me going for a long time. At one time I was working steadily with Otis Rush. Eddie Shaw played saxophone with Otis then. Eddie was always very dramatic with his playing; he was all out in the audience, people sticking money in his horn as he'd walk around and play. Years later I was surprised and delighted to find out he'd made a name for himself as a band leader. He's another one of those who became popular in Europe and other places while he was still struggling to be known back home.

One place I worked with Otis Rush was called the Avenue Lounge on West Madison. I used to love to hear Otis sing and play them blues! And he could do a lot of other styles, too, soul music, whatever was called for. Like I said, in those days you had to be versatile, give the people whatever they wanted to hear.

Jimmy Johnson was another one like that. Today, Jimmy is just like Lonnie Brooks. Famous blues man, plays festivals all over the world, white folks just love him to death. He could always sing some blues, but he could also change things around to fit another audience. I worked with Jimmy's band all over Chicago. His brother Syl was the one making records at that time; Jimmy just had a band. I was the featured vocalist with Jimmy at a club over on 22nd Street; I can't remember the name now, but I used to work there with Jimmy every weekend. Back in those days, when you got booked in a place, it wasn't a one-night stand. It was your gig every weekend until you mess up and fall out with the boss. So the people would know who's going to be there every week. Sometimes I had a Monday night gig at a place like the Trocadero, different places like that. But I knew where I was going every weekend. They knew that I'd be there every weekend with Jimmy Johnson's band.

For a while I used to go from that club, jump in the car, leave there, go up and do a show at another club on North Avenue, then flip back down to 22nd Street for my second show. And then go back up to North Avenue and close out. Bobby Rush always talks about he was the one doing that in those days, but I did it, too.

Then there was a place way over on the West Side, out around Pulaski Road, in that area. That's where I first met Tyrone Davis. He hadn't made a big name for himself yet; he was still calling himself Tyrone the Wonder Boy. He started working with me over there, and I remember I was supposed to close the show, because I had built up a following, so they had me closing. But Tyrone, he'd be outside, sitting in his car or something. They'd be waiting on Tyrone, and he wouldn't show up. So I'd have to go up and sing, and while I'm up on stage, here he comes walkin' in! So he got to go on after me and close the show. Do that every week—never come on time.

Meanwhile, I was developing a stage act, working up a persona, getting a professional identity for myself. Not only did that help me get better known, but it also led to my meeting the man who would become my next husband. In partnership with him, I went on to start three record labels and establish myself as a businesswoman, not just an entertainer, in the music field.

And, oh yes—I also landed my first chart hit. It went all the way to No. 1, it sold over a million copies, and it was the beginning of my career as a frontline entertainer. The name of the song was "Trapped By a Thing Called Love."

Chapter Six
The Road to "Trapped"—and Stardom

Developing My Stage Show

I first met Bobby Rush at the High Chaparral, at 77th and Stony Island Avenue in Chicago. A man named Clarence Ludd used to own that place. I used to work there all the time, and that's how I met Bobby. Bobby and I have been friends ever since then; he calls me his sister. Bobby and Latimore, both. Just like that. I mean, like *that*! Take a rubber band around 'em and wrap 'em just like that. Those are my boys. I just love 'em to death. Out of all the people I've met out here, those two are my favorites. There's nothing anybody could ever tell me about either one. I wouldn't believe it if you told me anything bad about either.

But what got me thinking about Bobby is that I used to do what he did before I even met him. At one time in his shows, Bobby would go back and change clothes between almost every song; he'd come running out looking entirely different. But I was doing that before I even met Bobby Rush.

The one who inspired me was Josephine Baker. She'd come out in some elaborate gown or costume, do a few songs, then disappear off stage or behind a dressing screen and come back out looking even more spectacular than before. And she'd keep doing that all night. I wanted to be her! I said, "I'm gonna bring this to the black folk," because she had a mostly white audience at that time. So I got me a lot of clothes, and I also started making some of my own clothes, or having them made. I didn't have any roadies or anyone to help me then, so I began lugging a wardrobe around to my gigs. I usually took two or three gowns or dresses; I'd go on stage, sing four or five songs, run off, then come back and do the rest of the show in another outfit.

I took it for as long as I could, but it got really tiresome. Most of those little places I worked didn't even have a dressing room, or maybe it would be way down yonder somewhere, and I got to go all the way over there, change clothes by myself, then come all the way back. It got so bad I started having the band do a whole song while I was changing, but that wasn't jelling, either. And then, when I finally got back, I'd be almost too tired to sing. So I just quit doing that. I started staying in one outfit, staying on stage, doing my stuff.

But that's not quite true, either. I didn't do very much "staying on stage" once I got out there on my own. I was always flirty in my act anyway, and then I began to pick at the guys, come off and mess with them, go to the bar or one of the tables and sit in a man's lap, play in his hair, all that kind of thing. That was my style. And I'd talk a lot. I'd do narrations, like describing various incidents between men and women. You know, talk to the audience before I sing, ease them into the story: Okay, I got to tell somebody something. What would make me say that? Who would I say it to? So I would do a little monologue.

This really goes back to when I was wanting to sound like Aretha Franklin. Aretha could take a phrase and build these incredible vocal ad-libs around it. But every time I'd try to sing with the power she had when she sang, I fell flat on my face. I still wanted to say those words, though, so I started talking 'em. It was kind of like having church; the ministers did what I wanted to do.

Now Aretha's from that church era, too, where she'd grab that stuff, throw it around. But I couldn't sing it like she could, so I just dropped down to saying it. It wasn't written down; it was just coming off my head, and I got to be really good at that. I was talking and acting the fool on stage before I ever cut a hit. Most of what you hear me say up there now came out on the spot at one time or another. When I found out it worked, I kept it in my act. Same thing with my monologues on my records later on, like on "Snap, Crackle, and Pop," "It Be's That Way Sometimes," "Why Am I Missing You?"

"Down Home Blues," "Someone Else Is Steppin' In," all of them. Came out of me just like that, either during my show or right there in the studio.

It wasn't common, back then when I was doing it. I patterned myself a little after LaVern Baker, but to a lot of people in the clubs it was something new. I wasn't cussing in those days; I started using those words later, after I heard Richard Pryor doing it. I made gestures and motions and all that, and I would talk, but I'd never use the bad words.

I used to open with that Johnnie Taylor song: "Who's makin' love to your old man, while you was out makin' love?" You know, change it around so it's from a woman's point of view. And at the end of it, I'd go into a little spoken-word thing mixed up with the verses, and I might mix another song in there, too. I'd say:

> *I used to have this habit of staying out all night . . . I walked into my*
> *bedroom one morning, and guess what I found?*
> *"Somebody was lovin' my old man / While I was out makin' love!"*
> *But you know what I did? I turned around, looked back over my*
> *shoulder, headed for the door, and I said . . .*
> *"It's yo' thang / do what ya wanna do!"*

That's the kind of thing I'd do. And it got over big.

And then I'd be sashaying around, playing with all the guys, sitting on their laps. Sometimes I had to run off real quick, though, when they tried to reach up under my dress! Oh, they'd try it. They'd try it. You'd just have to know how to get up fast, and at that time I could. I'd just jump straight up and keep on going to some other table, or to some other guy sitting at the bar. And this might surprise you, but most of the time, the women didn't care. Women actually liked for me to mess with their man, or at least some of them did. Some women would be sitting next to their husband or their boyfriend, they'd reach their hand up and point at his head—"Get him!" And they'd be laughing and I'd be laughing, and I'd go sit on that man's lap and do anything I wanted to do, and then get up and go to the next one. And even if he reached for me, tried to pull me back down, the woman wouldn't say anything. Just laugh at him.

I never will forget, though, one night I was working in a place on the West Side. I was sashaying around as usual, sitting in these guys' laps and playing with 'em, and this one guy's wife, or his woman, whoever it was, she hit that man so hard his chair fell over on the floor with him. Had to put them both out of the club, and then they stayed outside fighting until the police came. That was it. I said, "I can't do that no more." That woman knocked the shit out of that man that night.

There were some singers who went a lot further than I did. I remember this one girl, used to work at the Trocadero. She used to put a dildo all in her mouth. She's the first one I ever saw do it, long before Sweet Angel or any of these younger singers. And she got talked about, too.

Then there were the shake dancers, girls like Rose Marie. Dirty gal! She'd have two or three pairs of panties on, and she'd keep dancing around, let one pair drop to the floor, she'd pick 'em up, look at 'em, and sniff 'em. And then she'd go to a man, she'd put those panties to him, throw 'em up in his face. That man be running from her! When I left Chicago, she was still shakin', and I'm told she kept doing it until she died. Billed herself as Rose Marie Black, the World's Oldest Shake Dancer.

But I just said the little things I said, did whatever I did, and I wouldn't go any further.

"Craig" + "Jones" = "Crajon": Married and in the Record Business

I'd gotten myself released from Chess, and I'd never actually had a contract with Billy Emerson, so after I left Billy I was free to do whatever I wanted with my music. As it turned out, though, there was another record, called "Private Property," that Billy had recorded on me. I can't tell you the exact circumstances of how it got cut, but I do remember writing it, and I remember some of the lyrics:

> There's a tag on this heart that says "Fragile—please handle with care"
> There's a sign on his heart that says, "Danger—you'd better beware"
> There's a label on his lips that says "No trespassing here"
> 'Cause he belongs to me—he's private property!

I gave Billy half writing credit on that, and he didn't write one word of it. Not one word did he write. But, you know, to get him to try to get the music done, I put his name on there as one of the writers, and I guess we must have cut it as a demo track or something at some point. Chess put it out in 1968, after "Love Reputation," and I didn't even know it had been released until I went overseas years later. Those record collectors over there have everything, even stuff you had no idea existed! Billy must have leased it to Chess after we broke up or something like that, or maybe Chess already had it lying around somewhere. I really don't know the story behind that one.

So I always had it in my mind to do some more recording, but it was going to have to be on my own terms. I didn't just decide that; like said, I learned it the hard way. When I started, I had nobody; it just was Billy Emerson. And when I left Billy, after the way Billy treated me—I wasn't even signed to Billy, but the way he treated me, I didn't ever want anybody else bossin' me like that. Ever! I just said I will never get in that predicament again. And I never did. I never signed a management contract with anybody, or anything like that. No, lordy! This girl learned her lesson. Denise LaSalle owns Denise LaSalle. That's the way it was gonna be, and that's the way it still is.

So getting together with Bill Jones, the man who became my next husband, had nothing to do with wanting someone to help me in the business. In fact, at first I didn't even want him! I was singing at a place called the Talk of the Town in Phoenix, Illinois, just south of Chicago. He would come in and sit every night and watch me. I'd be doing my thing, strolling around, and every time I'd go over and try to play with him, put my hands in his hair, sit on his knee, he'd turn his back to me and look down at his drink on the bar. But then as soon as I got away from him, he'd turn back around again and stare at me with these wishful eyes. But then, as soon as I start back in his direction, he'd get his drink and turn back to the bar. Really made me mad. "Okay, if that's the way you wanna act, I'll never sing to yo' ass again!"

Well, he sent me a drink one night. I remember the MC that night was a dancer and comedian named Mr. Lee, who later became a promoter and a very dear friend of mine. He and his dancing partner, a man they called Little Willie Parker but his real name was Frankie Newsome, they danced and told jokes, really got the crowd going. They'd be cuttin' up! And on this particular night, if I recall correctly, Matt "Guitar" Murphy was in the band I was working with.

So I was on break, and I was sitting at the bar talking to some friends of mine there. The bartender told me, "The guy down there sent you a drink," I looked up, saw who it was. This man who had been turning his back on me! I looked at him, and boy, I wanted to cuss him out so bad! Because that was so ugly the way he was doing, you know, just trying to play hard-to-get and all that stuff. So I just looked at him like he was nothin'.

So what happened was, when I got up to go back and get ready to go on stage again, he caught my hand as I walked by. He reached out and caught my arm and asked me, "Do you know Otis Redding?"

Well, he said the magic word. Someone must have told him, because I used to be just talking about Otis all the time. I loved—I mean, I *loved!*—me some Otis Redding. Oooh, if I'd met him! I always say I would've been his baby mama. I loved that man! And so when Bill Jones said that to me, I had to answer:

"No, but I sure would like to know him."

"I went to school with Otis Redding."

"You did?!"

Come to find out he was lying. They went to rival high schools, and his team played against Otis's team. But he grew up in Macon, Georgia, and he knew Otis, and that was enough for me. He came in every night after that, wanting to talk to me, and as long as he's talking about Otis Redding, I'd talk with him. He ain't talkin' 'bout Otis, I'd be gone. But eventually, after we kept talking about Otis so long, we started just moving on to general conversation. That's how we got to know each other, and that developed into him becoming my boyfriend. He started coming over to the West Side where I had a gig over at the Avenue Lounge. He was a chef; he worked an afternoon shift at a steakhouse, and after work he'd come to the Avenue Lounge to see me.

After we got to know each other better, he wanted me to meet his family. We had scheduled to go to Macon, Georgia, for the holidays, and he said, "I'm gonna let you meet Otis Redding on New Year's." So he called Otis's wife, Zelma, said, "I'm gonna be in town, and my girlfriend is a real fan of Otis Redding. She wanna meet Otis."

And Zelma said, "Well, he usually comes in for Christmas, and he'll probably stay here through the New Year."

Oh, I just had my head set on it. I'm gonna meet Otis Redding! I'm gonna meet Otis Redding! But then he got killed. I was working at the Avenue Lounge with Otis Rush on December 10, 1967, the day Otis Redding's plane went down in Wisconsin. I didn't know a thing about it until Bill came to the club that night. He sat there in the audience, and when it was time for me to take my break, he said, "I need to talk to you about something."

And I said, "What?"

He said, "Have you heard the news yet?"

"What?"

"Come on out. Let me tell you something."

So I went outside with him.

He said, "Your boy got killed tonight."

"What boy?"

He said, "Otis Redding."

"What?!"

"It's on the radio. It's all you hear."

He told me, said, "His plane crashed. They haven't found his body, but they're looking for it. And they know he gotta be dead, 'cause there ain't nobody floating around out there. They said they pulled the other boy, they pulled the only survivor out, Ben Cauley, but they haven't found Otis."

We went out to the car and listened to the news, and they were talking about how they hadn't found Otis's body yet. By the next morning they had got him out. Yeah, that was terrible. That was a bad night for me. I was really glad my night was almost over; I didn't have but one more show to do. I was just out of it for that last set, I was so hurt about Otis.

Bill and I still went down to Macon. We got on the train in Chicago, went to Atlanta, rented a car, and drove the rest of the way. We went out to the house, that big ranch Otis and Zelma had outside of Macon, with the horses and everything. Zelma had his grave in the yard. She and I ended up becoming pretty good friends, too, long-distance friends. At one point, it was more or less I told her as a joke, but really it was true! We were sitting around talking, and I said, "Girl, you better be glad I didn't know Otis. 'Cause I was gonna take Otis from you. I was game to take Otis from you, honey!" She didn't do anything but laugh.

It couldn't have been too long after I met Bill that I also met Michael Jackson, because I met Michael just before the Jackson Five had their first record, "Big Boy," on that little label out of Gary, Indiana, called Steeltown. He was maybe about eight or nine years old, and he was singing and dancing like James Brown, going down and doing the splits and everything on stage. I was working at a little place in East Chicago, or it might have been Gary, I don't remember now, and the Jackson Five were on the show. After "Big Boy" came out, they'd come to Chicago to appear at some of those platter parties to promote the record and get better known, but at that time I'd never seen or heard of them. I'm telling you, it was really kind of a shock when this little boy came out there dancing and carrying on. He got the house before I even had a chance to come on and do my show.

I remember I came home and told Bill Jones, "There was a little boy named Michael on that show, and he stole the show!" I was kind of upset behind that. He was a child! I didn't know his brothers or his father or any of them. The next time I saw him was after I'd moved to Memphis, and he was a star by then. I was on a show at the Coliseum, and the Jackson Five were head-lining. By that time Michael was about sixteen or seventeen years old.

But what hurt me to my heart was that I had a picture made with Michael out there in Gary, the first show I did with him. I had Michael up, just as if he was my little son, hugging him. They took a beautiful picture of me and Michael; I brought that picture back home, and what I should have done was get a frame and put it in there. But at that time, I didn't know Michael was going to get famous. Nobody did. So I put it in a box full of pictures, just laying there with the rest of them. And heaven knows, the basement flooded one time, and when it flooded, those pictures got damp. When I found that box and pulled those pictures, the whole face of that picture was stuck to the other picture when I pulled it loose. And that's the only picture I had of me and Michael. Never, never again. I said, "Lord, have mercy!" But it still didn't hurt me as bad then as it did later on, after he got real big, I wanted to show somebody, and boy! I wish I still had that picture.

I also used to work with Joe Simon a lot. He was a quick-tempered man in those days, but he was all right if you didn't push him in the wrong way. He used to have a lot of women pulling at him too. I loved his singing, loved his songs. What I liked about Joe—he had a church sound. I asked him about that one time, and he said he never sang with a gospel group.

I was really shocked, because almost every song he did—"Nine Pound Steel," "It Be's That Way Sometimes"—sounded like preaching.

"It Be's That Way Sometimes" was one of his songs that I loved. I couldn't sing it the way he did it, but I liked the words. I finally did my own version of it on my *Rain & Fire* album for Malaco in 1986. I did it real slow, with a long spoken introduction, kind of like a gospel blues. I don't think it ever made the charts, but it was pretty successful for me, a lot of people told me they liked it. And Joe actually did become a minister. He has a church up near Chicago now. He came to the Blues Foundation Awards in Memphis a few years ago. They gave him an award; that's the last time I saw him.

Bill Jones and I dated from 1967 until we got married in '69. Actually, we started living together before we got married; he moved in with me at Mama Weese's on Langley. And like I said, getting together with him initially had nothing to do with my career. He wasn't trying to help me up the ladder. Only thing he did was just produce some money, say, "Hey, we got some money to go ahead on with; we gonna cut a record." It wasn't him trying to make me a star; it was *me* trying to make me a star.

After a while, though, he got interested in that. We decided it would be a good idea to form our own record company; I wanted more control over my business anyway, and that seemed like the best way to go. We ended up with three labels: Crajon (for "Craig" and "Jones"—I didn't get my marriage to Artic Craig formally annulled until just before I married Bill), Parka, and Gold Star. I was busy performing and building my career in Chicago, so Bill ended up taking care of a lot of the business end. I wasn't entirely comfortable with that, and it ended up being a problem, but as long as we were equal partners, I went along with it.

One of our first recording projects together was my "Count Down (and Fly Me to the Moon)," which came out in 1968. Those were the years when space travel and going to the moon were on everybody's mind, with the Apollo program and all that, and that's what I was thinking about when I wrote that song. I still like the lyrics I came up with:

> I'm fed up with two-timing earth men
> I hear there's a man on the moon
> Right now there is no competition
> If I don't get there first, I'm doomed
>
> I'm telling you I've been hurt
> Oooh, I lost my man
> These girls in miniskirts
> were more than the guys could stand
>
> So dear commander of Cape Kennedy
> I know you're a busy man
> Still I hope you'll understand . . .
> Count down and fly me to the moon!

I think we might have recorded "Count Down" at Paul Serrano's studio in Chicago. Our own labels were just getting off the ground, so we leased "Count Down" to Chess. Whatever problems I might have had with them before, I couldn't afford to hold a grudge; Chess had the connections and the ability to promote and distribute records, and that's what we needed.

I was singing really strong by then, the lyrics were good, and the record could have been a hit. The only problem with it, I think, was Eddie Silvers's arrangement. Now Eddie Silvers was a talented man. He was a good saxophone player, he'd worked with a lot of well-known people, and he had a band called the Soul Merchants that had a couple records out. He also wrote "Big Boy," the Jackson Five's first single. But he never really jelled with my stuff. Even though we had musicians like Matt "Guitar" Murphy on some of those sessions, I didn't like the arrangements Eddie did for me.

But then, I never really felt comfortable recording in Chicago anyway. A lot of the musicians had attitudes like, "If you don't know music, then you can't tell me how to play." I'd try to tell them what I wanted, but they'd want to hear me say, "Play A-flat minor over G; do this and do that." And their attitude was, "If you don't know that, I'm not gonna work with you."

That's the ego thing they had. And that bothered me, and it still bothers me, because I know what I'm doing with music. I knew it then, and I know it now. You see my name listed as producer on most of my records, and that's exactly what I am. I write my own songs, and I tell my musicians how I want it to go. I may not know how to do it technically, but I sing my songs and give them an indication how I want them to play, sing like a horn or a guitar part—"I want this right here," or "I want this right there." I'm the one paying for the session, I'm the one telling the musicians what to do, and I'm the one telling the engineer what to do. That's what producing is all about. But those boys in Chicago just couldn't accept that.

Bill and I got married April 1, 1969. Yes, April Fools' Day! By then, though, we were in the record business, and we were determined to make a go of it. Leonard Chess had a reputation for being a ruthless competitor, but he was very helpful to Bill. He helped teach Bill how to carry records around to different cities and towns and bring them to the influential DJs. Along with some payola money, of course! In those days, a lot of record pluggers would just drive through the countryside looking for a radio antenna, walk in, talk to whatever DJ was working there, and "convince" the man that here's a record going to be a hit and he should get on it right away. Bill said Leonard Chess even told him never to carry his records around in the trunk of his car; Leonard did that one time, and when he got where he was going, all he had in the trunk was ashtrays; the heat had curled all those little vinyl records up. Bill and I also ended up signing a contract with a distribution company out of Summit, Illinois, called Summit Records, so as our labels grew, we got at least a little more adept at getting our product out there.

I released a few more sides on Crajon and Parka, including "Heartbreaker of the Year," which later also came out on Westbound. To this day, I think "Heartbreaker of the Year" is one of my best songs. But again, just like "Count Down," they gave it a poor arrangement. Eddie Silvers, as good as he was, just couldn't seem to hear what I heard when I brought him a song. I was really getting frustrated, trying to find someone who could make a record come out sounding the way I wanted it to.

But that was about to change.

Memphis, Royal Studios, and Willie Mitchell: Now This Is More Like It!

There was a disk jockey at WJLB in Detroit named Al Perkins. His sister Velma married my brother Nathan; she's also a singer, and she's a very dear friend of mine. After she married Nate, she began recording under the name Vee Allen. One of her records, "Can I," was a pretty big hit in 1973. That's how I got to meet Al, through Nathan and Vee.

Al and I got to be good friends, too; he started coming over to my house, and we'd sit up and try to write songs, talk, and have a little fun. I never did go with him. No, we never had anything like that going on, but he'd come to visit, and sometimes he'd sit in my house all night. Matter of fact, sometimes he slept there, stayed up so long, be drinking, and he'd crawl up in the bed behind me. Both of us got our clothes on!

So we got to be really good buddies. But he couldn't sing a lick. Couldn't sing worth a quarter. Couldn't keep time with the music, didn't know a thing about singing. Had a beautiful voice, but he just wasn't trained. In 1969, though, he went down to Royal Studios in Memphis, Willie Mitchell's studio, and he cut a smash hit record called "Yes, My Goodness, Yes." They said they had to patch him together, took forever to cut it, but Willie kept working with him until he got it.

When I heard that record, I said, "Now if Willie Mitchell can make Al Perkins sound like this, what could he do for me?" And then Al told me about how it went down there. He said, "Hey, all you got to do is sing a little of your song, and they got it. The musicians in Memphis, if you can sing it, they can play it."

Well, you know that's just what I wanted to hear after working with all those studio musicians in Chicago. I packed up my bags and went to Memphis. Went down there to Papa Willie, walked in that door, and I cut a record, "The Right Track." It was actually an old Billy Butler song. Bill and I put it out on Parka in 1970. We paired it with a song I'd already released on Crajon called "Too Late to Check Your Trap," another one of those Eddie Silvers arrangements. If you listen to both sides of that record, you can really hear the difference.

At Royal, I found just what I was looking for. Papa Willie was a genius, and his musicians were the best. The Hi Rhythm Section, all those guys, they were some of the greatest people you ever want to work with. I loved working with those guys. I'd know how I wanted to sing a song, and they'd just play it according to the way I sang it, start putting chords behind it right away. Papa Willie would tell the horns what to play, mainly, and if the guitar player need to go in there and do some lead stuff, he'd just go in there and do whatever fit. Never any arrangements or anything; they did what they call "head arrangements," put together right there in the studio. And I was usually the one singing the parts to them, letting them know how the song went and how I wanted it to sound.

Of course, Bill Jones and I also had our own labels, and we were looking for other artists to record. While I was working at another club on the South Side called the Black Orchid, I met a singer named Bill Coday. He was calling himself Chicago Willie then, and he was James Brown all over. I mean, if James could do something, he could do it. I finally talked him into cutting a record with me, and I took him down to Royal. The first one we released on him was called "Sixty Minute Teaser," and then "You're Gonna Want Me." They both came out on Crajon, and they were pretty good, but they didn't go too far. Then, in 1971, he hit the charts with "Get Your Lie Straight."

Bill Jones and I finally had a hit on our hands, but sometimes, for a small label, a hit record can run you right out of business. "Get Your Lie Straight" got so hot and so big we didn't have the distributorship for it, and we couldn't keep up with the pressing. The Galaxy label, a subsidiary of Fantasy out in California, asked us for the master, and we leased it to them. And that's where Coday stayed, on Galaxy. His other hit for them was another song I wrote, "When You Find a Fool Bump His Head."

I had to have a parting of the ways with Bill Coday. He got married, and his wife started stepping in, saying, "Don't do what she say do. Do it this way and that way," all like that. Now this wasn't Anna Coday, his wife later on, the woman who owns the Coday label in Memphis; she's one of my best friends. This was a girl he met from Macon, Georgia. And she really got inside his head, had the audacity to tell me that I couldn't sign his contracts anymore or tell him what to do, or if I got an advance from a record company for him, he'd have to have so much of the money, and all that stuff. And as much as I was doing for him, I said, "You really don't tell me how to spend no money, 'cause I'm doing stuff for you, sending you places, and buying you clothes to wear on stage and all this, so don't tell me what I owe you."

No, I wasn't going for that, so I just turned him loose and let him go. And after I did, he went without a hit until he met me again years later. "Cut a record on me! Why don't you cut a record on me?" I took him on the road with me and let him open shows for me, but I wouldn't cut him. I got my own career; I ain't got time to worry about you and yours. If you're not going to work with me and just go along together when I'm trying to do everything I can for you—I got you out here and got you started, so now don't start telling me what I've got to do. Later on he went to Ecko Records and made a few CDs for them; in fact we were on that label together for a few years. But he never had a real chart hit again. But Anna and I got to be really good friends, and we're still that way today. My sister-in-law Karen Wolfe is on her label; Karen was one of my backup singers for a long time, until I told her she needed to get out there and make a name of her own. Now she's one of Coday Records' biggest stars.

Bill Jones and I also had a boy from Flint, Michigan, named Lonnie Polk. He sang in a high, soft voice. We had him, I think, before Coday. He had one little record, "I Can Make You Happy"; the flipside was "I Kiss It and Make It Better." I did the arrangements, along with Willie Mitchell's brother James, and the record came out sounding pretty good, but Bill and I didn't release it on any of our labels. Mercury picked it up. Lonnie couldn't really get a career going, though. He had asthma. He sounded okay on record, but he couldn't hold his notes very well, and he just didn't go anywhere.

And then we had another boy from San Antonio, Texas. I can't even remember his name. He wasn't really our own artist; we were cutting him for somebody else who was a disk jockey and didn't want to say it was his record. I wrote a song, and we cut it. The disk jockey was getting a piece of it, it was his deal, but when it came down to paying for his part of the session, he wouldn't pay. The record was good, but we just never did anything with it because the guy said it was his, but he didn't pay a dime getting it cut, and then he wouldn't put up anything to support it, so we just sat on it.

But the way it went down, Little Milton finally cut that tune, "Packed Up and Took My Mind," in 1975 on Stax. Then later, in 2007, this rapper called Ghostface Killah took that and sampled it on his song "Walk Around." He called me up and told me he had put the song on his album, and he wanted to know where to send the money to. I got royalties like crazy! The first royalty check he sent me was $7,500. Since then, about every three months I've been getting a royalty check. I didn't have to go after him. He called me and told me what was going on, and I give him credit for that; he's not like a lot of them. I don't try to audit his books or anything. I just let him go ahead.

There was also another singer, Al Williams, who we had for a little while. He was a cousin of Sly Stone. I found him at a club in Chicago, I forget which one it was, and we went to Memphis and cut a pretty good record, "The Other Side of Your Love," with "Go 'head on with Your Good Thing" as the B-side. We released it on Crajon in 1971. Al worked with me on some shows around town, sometimes with Bill Coday on the same bill. But the record never went anywhere. My own career took off with "Trapped By a Thing Called Love" right after it came out, and Al didn't stay with us for very long.

The other successful act Bill Jones and I had was the Sequins, a girl group out of Chicago. There were three of them: Ronnie Gonzalez, Linda Jackson, and Dottie Hayes. I was working at a nightclub on 51st Street, I think, or maybe it was 57th, something like that, and they were one of the groups on the bill. That's when I first saw them, and I was immediately impressed. They sang and danced, a Supremes-type thing; they couldn't sing like the Supremes, but they had a lot of showmanship and dancing, and they kept the audience hollering. They were pretty girls, too, prettier than the Supremes or the Emotions, and I fell in love with their little showmanship and asked them could I cut a record on them. I wrote a song for them, "Hey Romeo," we cut it at Royal with Willie Mitchell, and we put it on Gold Star. It turned out to be a pretty big hit in 1970. We did a few more records on them, and I ended up leasing them to Fantasy.

The Sequins never had another hit after "Hey Romeo," and I eventually had to let them go, just like I had to let Bill Coday go. Two of the girls, Ronnie and Linda, were sisters; Dottie was their cousin. Linda was a really strong lead singer, and Ronnie was fair. But Dottie had one of those kind of delicate, shaky voices, which wasn't popular in those days. Now, later on in years, singers like Deniece Williams with voices like that got to be real popular. But she came along before those kinds of voices got popular, and she couldn't make a record that people liked. They were great on stage. I mean, they made the Supremes look like wallflowers, because the Supremes didn't do anything but just stand there and sing. But after we put out "Hey Romeo," some hard feelings came up because I didn't want to cut Dottie singing lead, and then Linda wanted to go, leave the group and go play this place and that place by herself, and my own career was starting to get bigger by this time, so I just said, "Well, y'all want to go? I'm gonna let you." 'Cause I didn't have time to be arguing with them. So at that time, Pervis Staples from the Staple Singers was saying he wanted to branch out into artist management, and they wanted to go with him. So I said, okay, let's see what Pervis Staples can do for 'em. And they went over there with Pervis.

As it turned out, all he was doing was hittin' on the girls, gettin' him some. He never put out a single record on them. Not one. But I know he was gettin' it. They were some pretty girls, fine-looking girls, and you know how men are. Not just in those days, all days! Men gonna look for sex, and that's all Perv was after. See what these little young girls wanna do. But anyway, I was through with them after that, so I just gave 'em their release and let 'em go.

"Denise, You Got a Motherfucker!"

As I said earlier, we originally put out "Heartbreaker of the Year" on Crajon in 1969. Even though I didn't like Eddie Silvers's production on "Heartbreaker" very much, I loved the song, and I still thought it could be a hit. So we released it again in 1970, this time on Parka. The B-side was another song I'd written called "Hung Up, Strung Out." We recorded that in Memphis with Willie Mitchell and them, and once again you can really hear the difference in the sound.

I have to say, though, the only problem Willie Mitchell and I ever had was with that song. He wanted "Hung Up, Strung Out" for Ann Peebles. He told me, "Denise, you gonna fuck that song up. Why don't you let me have that song for Ann?"

I said, "I wrote that song for me."

He reached down into his pocket and pulled out six one-hundred-dollar bills, tried to give 'em to me. "I'll buy it from you."

I said, "Willie, I wrote the song for me. I'm not selling it to nobody." And I wouldn't sell it.

And I believe to this day that Willie messed that song up for a reason. See, I used to leave my stuff in Willie's hands. But the way I had the song, the way I had it going, when Willie mixed it, the mix was not like it should've been. I didn't hear it any more until it was out, and when I heard it again, it hurt my feelings real bad because I felt like he did it deliberately. But he never did anything like that again; he was always cool. In fact, we recut "Hung Up, Strung Out" later on; we did a faster version of it, and it ended up as the B-side of "Here I Am Again" in 1975.

But in 1970, even though it was a B-side and I didn't like the way it sounded that much, "Hung Up, Strung Out" was the one that attracted most of the attention. Al Perkins was in Detroit then, and he had that record going real hot there. But it just didn't get out all over the country like it should have. There was a label in Detroit called Westbound; it was owned by a man named Armen Boladian, and he'd already had some success with acts like the Detroit Emeralds and George Clinton's group Funkadelic, before they became Parliament, but he'd never had a No. 1 hit. Armen heard my record, and it made a believer out of him. He liked it so much he got in touch with Al Perkins, because Al had brought it to him.

Al said, "Man, this is my friend Denise."

Armen asked him, "Well, what's she going to do with it?"

Al told him, "They got their own label."

So Armen said, "I want to buy that record."

Armen purchased the master and released it on Westbound. I signed a one-year contract with him, and he gave me the money to go to Memphis and get back in the studio. That's when I did "Trapped By a Thing Called Love." And I tell you, Willie Mitchell was the kind of man that knew a hit when he heard it. Oh, he knew a record. If he didn't think it had it, tell you in a minute: "That ain't shit! That motherfucker there ain't goin' nowhere!" But on this day I was in the studio with the band, working up the song, letting the band get familiar with the way I'm doing it, and Willie turned the machine on and said, "We gonna get a demo on it."

I got to the second or third line, he said, "Ooooh, wait a minute, y'all. Hold it! Hold it! Hold it!" He stopped everybody. He said, "Girl, you're in good voice today. You're in *good* voice! Hold on, y'all! Just a minute!" And he turned a few knobs, said, "Okay, y'all, go ahead." And he sat there in that seat until we did the whole song. When we got through with the song, Willie said, "Come in here and listen to this."

I went in there and sat down, listened, I said, "You taped that?"

"Yeah."

"Oooh, Willie, I meant to go up on the end there. . . . Do you think we could—"

"I ain't fuckin' with that! I ain't gonna touch it no way. Denise, you got a motherfucker. You got a smash, Denise. It's a smash, right there. I'm not touching it."

First take, and that was it. That's the kind of ear he had, and that's the kind of musicians they were. Teenie Hodges, Leroy Hodges, Charles Hodges, Howard Grimes, that's them. The Hi Rhythm Section. All Willie had to do was add the horns to it. The background vocals, by the way, were done by a trio called Rhodes, Chalmers, and Rhodes. Donna and Sandra Rhodes were a couple of white girls Willie Mitchell had seen singing on a country music program on TV a few years earlier, and Charles Chalmers was a horn player and an arranger at Royal. Willie got him to add his voice to theirs. They did a lot of backup singing with Al Green. Really soulful vocalists, and a lot of people never guessed the truth, that they were white.

In Chicago, Don Cornelius had his first version of *Soul Train*, a little thing on a local television station, WCIU-TV, Channel 26. They'd be dancing and singing, it was just like Dick Clark's show, only it was a black thing. And when "Trapped By a Thing Called Love" was brand new, in fact even before it was released, Don asked me to come on *Soul Train*. I went on *Soul Train* and did it for him. It happened that he didn't have anybody else to book that week, so for three days straight, they played back that show. And that record just hit off like a bullet. People were calling for records, they had to press records and ship them to Chicago so fast, everybody panicked. Those folks *had* to get that record in Chicago! And that was a major market. Chicago, Milwaukee, Hammond and Gary, Indiana, all through there, and a few other cities were also carrying *Soul Train* at that point, so it just grew, just spiraled out nationwide. So I give Don Cornelius credit for breaking that record for me.

It came out just before the Fourth of July in 1971. The first time I heard it on the air, I was sitting in the park on the Fourth of July, and I heard it playing. My first hit, and it stayed on the charts for sixteen weeks and went all the way to No. 1. It sold over a million copies, and that was a Gold Record in those days. I gave Westbound their first Gold Record. I still have a picture of E. Rodney Jones presenting me with that beautiful Gold Record plaque at the High Chaparral in Chicago. Denise LaSalle, recording star at last!

So I signed with Westbound, and I have to tell you, I had a year's contract with Armen; that was when I cut my first two records for his label, and they were my biggest hits. When that year's contract was up, the next contract I had, everything I gave him reverted back to me in five years—my masters, everything was mine after five years. Everybody told me after that, "You will never get a deal like that with nobody else." Said, "He had to be a mighty green person to give you a deal like that." I guess I was the only person he had that kind of showed a little knowledge about the business, that's Billy Emerson again, he's the one who taught me those things, and I just went in there and made my deal: "I want my masters back after five years." And all that stuff with Westbound except those first masters, "Trapped By a Thing Called Love" and "Now Run and Tell That," everything else I cut at Westbound belongs to me.

When I went down to Memphis to cut "Trapped," I was still working a day job as a cashier at a supermarket in Chicago called Dell Farms. "Trapped" turned out so big in the studio, with Willie Mitchell and everybody declaring it a smash, I never went back. Instead, I waited for the record to break. Then I hit the road.

Chapter Seven
Dreams Come True

The Sea of Faces Comes Alive

My first big gig after "Trapped" hit was at the Cobo Arena in Detroit. I think it sat about twelve thousand people. I was on the show with the Detroit Emeralds, and the Temptations were headlining. What a feeling! Here I was with a hit record, in the biggest hall I'd ever been in, on a bill with some of the biggest names in the business! I didn't even have to pay the band; the band was paid to play for me. So I took home the whole six hundred dollars I got paid. Six hundred dollars! Ooooh, that was big time to me!

But that was also when I learned how mean David Ruffin was. Bill Jones had a little boy, Lynn, and he was about six years old. Everybody was at the rehearsal that evening. I was sitting out in the audience, waiting; I'm a newcomer, so I have to wait until the other, bigger acts get through. Lynn was playing with David's little boy, and David was trying to make his little boy sit down. But two little boys about the same age, they're going to play together, right? David kept on snatching on his little boy, started pinching him, grabbed him by the ear.

"Oh, Daddy! You're hurting me!"

"Just sit down! Siddown! Come on over here and siddown!"

I never will forget that. It hurt my feelings so bad. I just said, "Lynn, come on over here and sit down." And when David saw it was my child, then he started letting them be together. But he never apologized or anything. He just stopped messing with him and let him play. And I thought it was so dirty; I thought that was so ugly for him to be pinching that little child's ear like that. That made me mad. I never really cared for him because of that. I actually got to know the other Temptations much better. Paul Williams, the one who killed himself, he was there that night. He was already drinking heavily by then; he was drunk that night, drinking backstage. He posed for a picture, him and Lynn, and I kept that picture for years. I wish I knew where it was now.

But it was later that evening, when I walked out on the stage, that it hit me: There it was. That was my dream. I saw nothing but wall-to-wall people out there. My sea of faces. It was more people than I'd ever seen in any one place in my life. And when I saw myself with all those people out there in front of me, it came back to me: This is my dream. This is it. It came true.

So I came on singing "Who's Making Love," that little routine I told you about, and then I did a ballad, a slow song, and believe it or not, I can't remember which one it was now, but I think it was probably a Gloria Lynne song, because I used to love her so hard. Then I moved on and ended with "Trapped." I did my little three songs and sashayed on off that stage with a standing ovation. A standing ovation! Those people, they made me feel so good. Felt like I was wanted, like I was needed. The nicest thing that could've happened to me.

So I always tell people, don't ever tell anybody, and don't let anybody tell you, that dreams don't come true. Because they do. I'm for sure they do. I'm living proof.

"Run and Tell That"—My Career Is Taking Off!

The next big gig I got, I played a week at the Apollo with the Dells and the Main Ingredient; that was Cuba Gooding Sr., he was the Main Ingredient's lead singer. Some other little group, I can't think of their name, opened the show. It was all groups except me. I came on second, and then the Main Ingredient came on after me, and then the Dells. And by the Dells being from Chicago, they knew me, because we had met up at the studios and things like that. They were still working at the steel mill out there in Gary, Indiana, when I met them; they still had their day gigs then. I think they're the ones who got me on that show. They were the headliners, and the people from the Apollo asked them who they wanted on the show with them. And they chose me.

I played with their band behind me, so I just took my little money and went home, whatever the Apollo paid me. I know it wasn't that much. But hey, it wasn't about getting paid. It was about the honor of being at the Apollo Theater, the prestige of it. I didn't care; I'd have worked there free!

At the Apollo, you didn't have to do but three songs a show, but you'd work all day long. They'd play a movie, then you'd do the show, then they'd put in another movie, you'd do another show, and so on. You had an early afternoon show, around one or two o'clock, and you did one that was around four or five in the afternoon, five or six, something like that, and the other one started at ten something that night, and go on until midnight. By the time I got to the last night, I was too hoarse to sing! I couldn't go on for the last show. Marvin Junior, that great baritone singer in the Dells, just told me, "That's okay." He said, "You got Apollo-itis!" He said, "If you don't get Apollo-itis here, you ain't doing nothing. You must be ain't singing." Said, "Everybody gets hoarse here if they're just coming here for the first time."

A few years later, by the way, I wrote a song for the Dells, but very few people know I wrote it. They changed the title of it to "I Wish It Was Me You Loved." It came out in 1974, and someone else got the songwriter's credit. But it wasn't the Dells' fault. They had a manager, and I was told to send this song to the manager, and he'd see that the Dells got it. When I heard it—my words, exactly! "Wait a minute, I heard them words before!" But the title was changed. I asked Chuck Barksdale and them about it, and Chuck said, "I don't know. That's the song we got. People just gave us songs." So I couldn't blame them for that, and I never held it against them.

By this time, Bill Jones had decided he was going to get more deeply in-volved in my career. Bill got hooked up with all them disk jockeys, drinking and whoopin' and hollerin' with them, out there hanging out with them at night, putting fifty dollars and a hundred dollars in their hand, havin' women with 'em and all that. He'd always been a pretty heavy drinker, but he'd had that job as a chef, so only on weekends did he get drunk. The rest of the time, he was pretty cool. But now he started drinking a lot more, and that ended up coming between us pretty hard. For a while, though, it looked like maybe he could handle it.

Bill was the one responsible for breaking Al Green's first major hit in
Chicago. I remember when I first saw Al. Al hadn't made it big then. He'd
had his first record, "Back Up Train," and maybe a few minor hits for Willie
Mitchell by that time, but he wasn't any kind of star. So we were standing
in the studio one day, and Willie said, "You see that little boy goin' right
there?" I didn't know who he was.

He said, "That little nigger goin' right there, that's a bad motherfucker,
Denise."

I said, "Really?"

He said, "Listen. He's a genius. That's a genius goin' there. I'm trying
to get him in that studio; I got him in there, but I haven't found him yet.
We're searching, trying to find him. I got to get the right songs where his
personality comes out. I haven't found it yet. But when I find him, it's gonna
be all over." Said, "That's a motherfuckin' genius."

Then Al came out with "Tired of Being Alone." Willie almost lost that
record; he was getting ready to take it off the air in Chicago, it was doing so
bad. But Bill Jones said, "Man, don't do that. Send Al Green to town, man,
and let me take him around."

Willie sent Al Green to Chicago and put him up in a hotel. Bill Jones
picked him up every day and took him to every radio station in the city,
introduced him, let him talk on the air to these people, you know, do whatever he had to do to get his record played. And that record took off like a
bullet. Al's next record, "Let's Stay Together," went platinum, and after that
they never looked back with Al Green. I give Bill Jones credit for that. If it
hadn't been for him, there's no telling what Al would have gotten to.

Even though we'd had that disagreement over "Hung Up, Strung Out,"
Willie Mitchell never treated me bad or anything; we always got along. But
after "Trapped" became a hit, when I called him to go back in the studio,
there was never any room for me. I had to find me somewhere else to go
because he says he's got too many artists now. He's got Ann Peebles, he's
got Al Green, then he got Otis Clay and Syl Johnson, said he didn't have
time for me to come in there. So that's where Bowlegs Miller came into
the picture. Bowlegs was a good trumpet player; he had played in the horn
section on some of our earlier sessions down there, he'd done a lot of the
horn arrangements, and I knew he was a good producer. Bowlegs was a
nice jolly guy, big ol' fat, crazy guy, talk shit all the time; he was a nice cat.
His wife, Frances, and I were good friends. So I just went on and got with

Bowlegs and went to Mark XVI Studio on Chelsea Avenue. That's the studio that used to be called Universal; in fact, I think it still might have had that name when I did my first sessions there. Later, when Isaac Hayes bought it, he called it Hot Buttered Soul Recording Studio.

I did a lot of work with Bowlegs Miller. When I went to Ardent later on, John Fry's studio, Bowlegs was still doing my sessions. But it wasn't the same quality at those other studios; it was a totally different sound. A lot of the time I couldn't even get Hi Rhythm to work my sessions. They felt loyal to Willie, so they wouldn't come. One good musician who did work with Bowlegs, though, was Larry Lee. He was a guitarist, played a lot of different styles, even worked with Jimi Hendrix for a while. He was Al Green's bandleader on the road for a long time. Most of my records don't emphasize the guitar too much, but I always had a good guitarist to lay down the rhythm, play those chords, keep everything on track. Larry was great at that, almost like Teenie Hodges.

I never did go back to Willie until after Bowlegs had died. After Al Green and all of them left Willie, that's when I went back to Royal. I cut most of my album *This Real Woman* there in 2000, and then two years later I went back there and recorded my first CD for Ecko, *Still the Queen*. By that time, Willie's grandson Archie had come into the picture and was doing most of the engineering.

"Now Run and Tell That" and "Man Sized Job," my next two hits after "Trapped," were both cut at Mark XVI. "Now Run and Tell That" was a phrase I got from Roy Wood, a newsman on WVON in Chicago. During that time, the Civil Rights movement was going on, a lot of meetings where everybody's trying to figure a way how to get out from under this oppression. So this guy would get on the radio and say, "We as a people are going to do this, and we're going to do that; we're going to stick together, we're going to do this and that." Then he'd say: "Now run and tell that!"

He would always end his commentaries on WVON with that phrase. I kept liking to hear it; I liked what it meant, and I just said I'd start working on a song with that phrase in it. That's where "Now Run and Tell That" came from.

"Man Sized Job" came about after the Staple Singers had their hit, "Respect Yourself." You can hear how the melody line of "Man Sized Job" is based on "Respect Yourself," but, of course, the message is entirely different. When I went into songs like "Now Run and Tell That" and "Man Sized

Job," that was a little less serious a message than "Trapped" had been. It was telling a story, but it wasn't a love song; it was telling somebody off. People started accepting me in a sassy bag more than they did in a serious bag, and that's the way it's been ever since.

"Making a Good Thing Better" was another good example of how I could take a phrase or an idea and build a song around it. It's on *On the Loose*, my second Westbound album. I was driving down the street in Memphis one day, and I looked up and I saw a sign that said, "Make a good thing better—Bank at Union Planters Bank." And I started thinking, okay, what would make me say, "That's what I call making a good thing better"? Like, if a situation was going on, I wouldn't accept the situation as it was; I would add to it, and that's what I call making a good thing better. That's how that song was born. A lot of my songs came about that way. Even today, I'll get titles and ideas like that; it just happens.

In February of 1972, I was on *Soul Train* again. Don Cornelius had moved the show out to Los Angeles and taken it nationwide; in fact, I think this was its first season in national syndication. I was on with the Whispers and Al Green. Al sang "Tired of Being Alone" and "Let's Stay Together," his first two big hits, and the Whispers did "Can't Help But Love You" and "Seems Like I Gotta Do Wrong." I sang "Trapped" again, and I also sang "Now Run and Tell That," which had just been released. Then about a month later, I was on Dick Clark's *American Bandstand*, singing those same two songs. I never really felt comfortable lip-synching, but I sure did it then! That was another thrill, to be featured on nationwide broadcasts like that, especially alongside stars like Al Green and the Whispers. I definitely knew I was getting somewhere then.

I was also touring more and more. My first big tour was on a show with Little Milton, the Staple Singers, King Floyd, and Little Johnny Taylor with his crazy self. I remember we went through Texas, New Orleans, Georgia, all through the South. Going around like this, pretty soon I realized I'd need a band of my own to really do it right. At that time, if you couldn't bring your own band you worked with a local band wherever you were booked, and they had to know your material. So I'd get me somebody who could write music, and they'd write down my arrangements. Any place I'd go to, I had to send my charts ahead of time. They either had my charts or my records. They'd learn my music, whatever I was going to do, and when I got to town, if I could I'd go to the club before the show and rehearse with them.

Most of the time I didn't have anybody traveling with me. I probably traveled for about a year by myself. Then I hired a guitar player, a boy from Chicago named Jimmy Pleasant. His daddy used to sing quartet; I used to be out there with his daddy when I was singing with the little quartet group. Jimmy came out on the road with me as my musical director so I didn't have to kill myself rehearsing for all those gigs; he'd go and rehearse with the band while I rested at the hotel. That way I didn't have to sing myself out that afternoon with the band, and then go back that night. By the time I'd go back that night, I'd be hoarse.

So I was taking charts around, playing with whoever the people hired. Then Bill Jones went out and got a van, and we put together a band, called it the Man Sized Job Band. Jimmy stayed on as lead guitar in that band, too. "Man Sized Job" came out in late 1972, so it had to be either then or in early 1973 that we put the Man Sized Job Band together. That meant that I knew I'd have good musicians with me all the time, which was never a guarantee with those pickup bands. The Man Sized Job Band stayed with me until I moved to Memphis in 1974. Then I assembled a new band, Imagination Unlimited. That was the one that had horns. But then, after things began to change with the new technology, keyboards playing the horn parts, it didn't make sense for me to be paying three musicians out there when one could play all those parts. So I did like everybody else, dropped the horns and went that way.

"Baby, You Met Your Match This Time!"

I never got into another really bad situation like I had with Billy Emerson, but there were still a few hard lessons that had to come my way. Being young and new out there, it was hard not to get involved, especially with people you'd admired through the years. How you gonna turn someone like Sam Cooke down? You sat there for years, looking at them on stage, you're sitting there, "Oooh, Lord! Oh, if he was my boyfriend! Oh, God!" Now here he is, the man you idolized all these years, and he's hittin' on you! I never did have that experience with Sam, but I know, like, if Otis Redding had hit on me, I'd have sure gone with him. I would have had to have me some Otis Redding!

I remember one night, I never was so glad my husband showed up. It was down in Georgia somewhere, and Teddy Pendergrass and his group,

Harold Melvin and the Blue Notes, were on the show. When the show was over that night, boy, did Teddy ever crowd me. He was on my case so hard. His room was right down from mine, and he kept knocking on the door. I finally opened the door and talked to him, and he said, "I'll be back. I'm comin' back tonight."

I said, "Now what do I do? How do I do this? I've got to tell him something." I liked him, but I didn't like him that way. My husband was managing Bill Coday at that time; they'd played somewhere in the area, and I knew my husband was going to join me sometime 'fore day that morning. And I was like, "I can't have this man in here, with my husband on his way."

I didn't answer my phone in my room, I didn't open any doors, nothing, until Bill Jones came up there. Whew! Was I glad he showed up! I really was crazy about Teddy and his group; I might have fallen for him, done a little infidelity or something that night. Because I really liked him, but I didn't like him well enough to get caught like that.

There was one singer, though, who sho' 'nuff got me for a while. I won't call his name because his wife is still living; she's become a good friend of mine over the years, and I don't want to hurt anyone with old memories at this late date. But he was a pretty big star, and he got bigger later on. He had a bus and he also had a car, a big old long Cadillac or something, like a limousine. I had met him years earlier through Billy Emerson; he came to my house to eat, because he and Billy were good friends. But I didn't really know him until I got on this tour with him. He insisted that I ride with him in his limousine. He was going with one of his background singers, but he made her sit in the front seat with the driver, and he made me sit in the back with him. She was pretty huffed, really pissed, and I offered to ride in the front, but—"You're sitting back here with me!"

So we were in conversation and talking after that. I forget how many shows we did, but I ended up in bed with him before it was over. Young, gullible, I went for it. And at the beginning, he was great, I mean, total respect. But then the next trip we went on, he took me aside and said to me, "Uh, I want to talk to you about something."

I said, "What?"

"I got a li'l ol' girl coming tonight; she ain't nothing, don't meant nothing to me, but she's the one who gave me all this jewelry and stuff that I wear, she buy me all my jewelry and stuff. So can I get you to just act like there ain't nothing going on between us?"

That's the same thing he did to that band girl! Told her to act like it wasn't nothing going on between 'em, so he could rock with me. And then now he gonna ask me can I move out like that, get on the side and act like we just friends, so he could rock with this bitch!

Well, I wasn't used to men passing me around. I said, "Okay, fine." Let him rock all he wanted to. And then he was also going with a woman in Texas, and when we got down there, he's like, "Uh, let's go to one of my girls' house for dinner."

So we went over there to eat. She just thought I was his friend, and I didn't let on that I had been more to him than that. But I liked her a lot; we hit it off right away; we just became, like, lifelong friends immediately. So I went back to my room, and now here he comes, trying to get in the bed with me.

"No fuckin' way! Uh-uh! I don't play that. I'm gon' go to your girlfriend's house and eat dinner with you, and you tell me that's your woman, and she does this and that for you, and you gon' come back and try to sleep with me? Ain't no way!"

And I just told him to kiss my ass. From that day forward. He'd come to my door after hours, everybody gone, hotel closed, he's knockin' on my door, wanna know, "Can I sleep with you tonight? Can I sleep in your bed?" He had a way of doing things that was so cute; yeah, he was cute down deep, I'll give him credit. But I wasn't gonna take that kinda shit. A woman can't have any pride if she gonna go and let some man do her like that. Hell, no! You don't tell me to stand back for nobody!

He and I stayed friends until the day he died. But he couldn't touch me no more. I was through with that. So I made up my mind, right then and there, just like I said about the promoters and the record company men and all of them: No more entertainers. I would never let another entertainer get next to me that way.

Another dear friend I met during this time was Millie Jackson. The first time I worked with Millie Jackson, I never will forget this. We were in Louisville, Kentucky. Millie was on that show, and she didn't do any talking that night. Nothing. Did a whole show without all that talking. That was when she had her record out, "Child of God." Next time I worked with Millie was somewhere up in Michigan or Ohio, and she was up there talking just like I was. I know a lot of folks thought I got that from her, but I always told them, "You must didn't see me before I met Millie, 'cause I was doing that before I ever cut a hit." Like I told you, going out there, being sassy and sitting up in guys' laps and run off when they tried to reach under my dress.

So after we did that next show, Millie played in Indianapolis, Indiana. When she came off the stage, they told her, "Denise LaSalle is out here; she wants to see you." So I went back there, and—"Oooh! You caught me doing your shit!" First words out of her mouth: "Oooo, girl, you caught me doing your shit!" She was saying some of the same things I'd been saying!

Like I said, Richard Pryor is really the one who got me started with all this cussing and going on. I was talking a lot, but I'd never use the bad words, "fuck," "motherfucker," none of that. And I never called anybody a bitch or anything like that. I was just talking and being sassy. But after Richard Pryor, I saw all those folks laughing, then I started using a little "mother—," and a little "bitch," and it didn't do anything but get me some laughs. And I said, "Okay, all right. I got something here!"

Actually, Millie has toned down a lot, because she used to be some kind of dirty. Went a lot further than I ever did. Take her finger, simulate putting it up her booty, and then stick it to her nose and turn her nose up like it's stinkin'; then I've seen her bend over and spread her legs wide open, and thrust her booty to the audience, and stick her finger back there and tell 'em, "kiss my ass!"

Oooh, that was so gross to me! I have a limit. I'm sorry. I can say dirty words, but it's a limit to how far I'll go. I could be just as dirty as the rest of 'em, but I don't want to be. I don't want to do that. And now, some of these girls coming up, they think they got to outdo us. You know, Denise LaSalle is the woman with the mouth, that does all that talking. Me and Millie, right? So they got to go further than we go. And I think we go a little bit too far sometimes, so I don't think it should be any further, any more explicit than we do. These gals going up onstage with dildos and stuff, that's something neither Millie nor I, neither one, have ever done. That's just ugly. If that's what they want to be, then go ahead, but I don't deal with that.

Millie is one of my best friends in the world, to this day. We don't see each other but a few times a year, but I feel close to her. If anything goes wrong, or if I'm sick or in any kind of trouble, she'll call me in a minute: "Hey, what's up? What's happening?" Her birthday is July 15, just one day before mine. We always talk on her birthday, and she says she makes sure it's right at midnight that we talk, says she wants to get it over with so she doesn't have to call me again the next day and waste her breath! That's my girl. Sassy as ever, still talkin' shit, and I love her to death.

My First Trip Overseas

My first time out of the country was in 1972. Continental Artists were booking me at the time, and they booked me on a tour with Rufus Thomas. Fenoye Lanier was the drummer with a group called the Jacksonians, and that was the band they put together for us. It was wonderful, really a fun trip, because I'd never been out of the country before. Fenoye's group was all a bunch of young men, and we just had a good time.

I was only known over there from "A Love Reputation." "Trapped By a Thing Called Love" was new to them; in those days, it took time for a record to make it that far. But a lot of people there really loved American soul music, and they knew me from "A Love Reputation." They'd have a banner stretched across the street announcing my name, "Denise 'A Love Reputation' LaSalle," along with Rufus's name. I tell you, we really felt loved!

We went to Dakar—Senegal—first, then Freetown in Sierra Leone. The one I enjoyed the most was when we went to the Ivory Coast, to Abidjan. I honestly don't know if they charged people to come to the shows or if they let them in free, because the people there were very poor. Some of the shows were outdoors; I remember they had one in a ballpark, or maybe it was a soccer field, and you could tell that very poor people were there. But they had a ball.

Crowds were mostly in the hundreds; it wasn't thousands like at a big festival here or in Europe. And I have to say, they treated us like royalty. Anywhere we were booked to play, as soon as we arrived they would take us to the finest hotel in the city. When it was time to eat, all of us had a special table we'd go to. They'd have a person standing behind us holding a fan, or sometimes it was a big stalk from a palmetto or something like that, from the floor to the ceiling, and they would stand there and wave it back and forth over the table, wave away the flies and bugs, while we eat. One thing I didn't like, though, was that no matter how nice the hotels were, nine times out of ten they did not have air conditioning. And it's really, really hot, and they have the windows open, curtains flying in and out of the windows, bugs, flies, everything. I didn't like that. But we always stayed in the best hotels they had, and the people were very nice to us—treated us like visiting dignitaries.

I was shocked by the poverty, though. I thought I knew what poverty was; I didn't know what poverty was until I went to Africa. I'd never seen anything like that in my life. Open latrines on the streets, people urinating in a trench and it's running down the street. The stench is terrible; windows open in the buildings, curtains flying out, flies all over little babies, see babies in the street and the ladies are there with their breasts out suckling their babies, flies in the kids' eyes—oh, it was devastating. I was shocked. I'd never seen areas like that, and people like that, in my life. You're staying in this nice hotel, clean and spacious, well-kept, then you leave and go across town to work, and then you see it.

On the streetcorners, they would have our paraphernalia, mine and Rufus Thomas's, all our stuff, be on the streetcorners selling it. They'd sell you anything off those street corners. They were selling food: Get a sandwich here, sauce over there, get this here, get that there. Flies all over everything, the meat lying up there, it's raw now but they cook it for you when you ask for it. And I'm thinking, I'm gonna let them cook me this meat that gotta be maggots in it? Oh, man! I said, "No, lordy! I don't want none of it."

But I was glad to be there. And Rufus, that was my friend. We had a lot of fun. He'd get over there, get him one of them young African women, young women running behind him, and he thought it was something with his ugly self! And of course he did a great show, did his little dance, his comedy routines and everything. Oh, he'd carry on some!

One thing that happened to me, though, I came back home weighing 203 pounds! The way the hotels were, food was hard to find certain times of the day. If you woke up and breakfast was over, you'd have to go out and find a restaurant, like an open-air restaurant down on the beach. But there was no food in the restaurant either unless it was time for a particular meal. When you go down there, it's a basket full of rolls on every table, hard rolls, French rolls, croissants and stuff, and a little basket full of butter packs with a big coffee urn sitting there. Sometimes they'd have a person come through, clean the tables for you or something, but there was nobody in the kitchen. There was nothing cooking. Just that continental breakfast, juices, butter and rolls, a setup of coffee. And then when we'd get back at night after performing wherever we were, get back to the hotel, everything's closed, so it was back to the butter and bread. So I ballooned up to 203 pounds while I was there.

I've had a problem with weight ever since. When I got back, I went on that protein and water diet, the Dr. Atkins diet I think it was, and I lost forty-three pounds in three months. I kept it off until I met James Wolfe. We got married in 1977, I started cooking for him, and both of us started blowing up again!

But I really enjoyed that tour, despite the bad things I saw and some of the inconveniences we had to go through. It made me know I was getting somewhere, to be so recognized and appreciated so far from home. And then from there I began going to Europe and other places, and it's been the same way every time. I'm more popular over there than I am over here. My first time in Europe, when I got off the plane, they sent a bus to pick us up. Riding into town, there it is again: great big banner hanging across the street, "Welcome to Germany, Denise LaSalle!" Stuff like that. Man, I was just shocked! I said, "Whoa! They ain't never done that in Chicago or nowhere else in the States!" Because those people over there cherish you more than they do here. They don't care how old your music is, they don't care if you haven't had a record since I don't know when. If they ever loved you at all, they love you right now.

"I Wish You Well"

I remember the first time I met Bill Withers. I was in Chicago, and he came to town to perform on one of those platter parties I told you about. They'd have these around the city and they would be packed; five or six hundred people sometimes. I was a known name in Chicago by then, and that's how I met Bill. He'd probably heard of me, and someone introduced me to him and we got to be really good friends. The next time he came to town was for an actual gig; he was playing one of those upscale clubs on Rush Street or somewhere, and he invited my friends and me to come to where he was working. We came up there, he did the show that night, and I said, "Y'all want some home cooking tomorrow?"

And he says, "Yeah, I'd like some. You cook like my grandma?"

I said, "I probably do."

"All right, then; I want some good ol' cookin' like my grandma used to do."

So I went home, my girlfriend across the street helped me go out and shop, and I bought up and cooked all this food. And Bill came by with his whole band, and boy, did they slam! I had oxtails and ham hocks and greens and cornbread and all kinds of things, chicken and dressing and everything else. And they sat down and ate and begged me for a plate to take back with them. So I wrapped each one of them up a big pile of food, and they took it back to where they were staying.

We went back to the show that night, and Bill had a thing where they didn't have someone get up on stage and announce, "Ladies and gentlemen, Bill Withers." That's not the way they did it. You're sitting there drinking and talking, and all of a sudden here come four guys walking up to the stage, one go to the drums, one to the piano, one to the bass, and one to the guitar. Bill just comes out, "Good evening, ladies and gentlemen." That's the introduction. Then he said, "I got some guests in the audience tonight." And he started talking about me, and telling about the food he had in our house, and I mean he bragged his ass off! "They cook like my grandma!"

His grandmother had to be something in his life because he never talked about his mom; everything was his grandma. That's what he talked about. And then, of course, he wrote that beautiful song, "Grandma's Hands." So he introduced us to the audience that night, and as time went on, we became very, very close friends. No kind of affair or anything; his wife, Denise Nicholas, was a dear friend of mine also. No, just two people who knew each other well and loved each other very much.

That was knowing Bill Withers. He was the kind of person that if he liked you, he liked you. If he didn't, then no. He was a deeply spiritual man; he was raised up in church, talked about how his grandma made him go to church and things like that, and he talked about religion-type stuff, spiritual stuff, all the time. And his songs always had a message. So we just clicked and got to know each other. He just was a sweet guy. I remember going to his house one time, and they were rehearsing. He and his band were out on the lawn, right out there in the front yard of his house, practicing all those songs, "Lean on Me" and everything. Yeah, that was Bill—just like him to do something like that!

We used to correspond through letters. I used to have a rack up in the kitchen where I had things like that, letters from V.I.P.s, letters from different people. I held onto Bill's letters for years, but I don't know where they are now. Over time, a lot of things have gotten lost or misplaced, and it's hard for me sometimes to talk about the past when I don't have the pictures and letters and things at hand. It's something I feel bad about, but there's nothing I can do about it now.

The last time I worked with Bill was on a festival in New Orleans. O.V. Wright was on the show. O.V. had lost all this weight by then and gotten down to skin and bones. His suits were hanging off him, looked like he had on Solomon Burke's clothes or something. That man looked so bad; drugs had taken him down. O.V. loved him some alcohol, too. He used to get high off cough syrup, bought it by the case, kept it in his car, and everybody knew he was high on that stuff. And the way he looked in New Orleans, I was just shocked, because he'd been a good-looking man. I guess he was spending so much money on drugs and whatever he was doing that he didn't have the money to get his suits taken up. His clothes were just falling off him; he was pitiful looking. When I saw him looking like that, I was shocked. But that was also the last time I ever worked a show with Bill Withers. After he and Denise broke up, I kind of lost contact with him. You know, moving in different circles and all that. But we stayed in contact for a long time, at least four or five years. He was a really nice guy to know. I haven't seen him, though, since the New Orleans date.

But back at home, things weren't going so well. Oh, I kept making hits, even if none of my records hit No. 1 again after "Trapped." I kept touring, and during those years, like I've been telling you, I was blessed to meet and get to know a lot of people who have become my lifelong friends. But things with Bill Jones were getting tense, and it didn't take long for me to realize it was time to make another getaway.

Chapter Eight
Going through Changes

More Treasured Friendships—and a Visit with Ike Turner!

Another really good friend I made during those years was Ann Peebles. She was quiet, sort of an introvert; she wasn't loud and vocal like I am. When I went to Royal, she was already there, on Hi Records with Willie Mitchell. Willie was grooming her to be a star, just like he was doing with Al Green. Ann and I got to know each other through Willie. I had been in Memphis to do some work in the studio, and Pervis Spann, the DJ at WVON in Chicago, was bringing Ann up there to do a show. So Willie called Ann and said, "Listen, Denise and them are ready to go home. Let her go back with you. Is that all right?" So we drove back to Chicago together. She wasn't married to Don Bryant then, but they were going together. Willie Mitchell traveled with them a lot, too.

When they were in Chicago, they always stayed at Roberts Motel, where the famous show lounge was that brought in big stars like Dinah Washington, my old crush Nat King Cole, Sammy Davis Jr., and people like that. Then, after I got to know them, they'd come to my house and eat. When they come to town, everybody came to eat at my house. All roads led to Denise's house for the whole Willie Mitchell clan.

And Koko Taylor? Oh, that's my sister! I first met her in Dayton, Ohio; she was on a show with me there. I can see her right now, the outfit she had on, and everything. See, I had never really met Koko before, even though she was down at Chess Records when I was there. She was there with Willie Dixon and all of them, but I didn't know her. But when we did that show together in Dayton, I got a chance to actually meet her that night, and we kept in touch with each other a lot after that. She would call me and I'd call her, and we'd stay in touch like that. Then I met her daughter Cookie, and we all just became really good friends over the years. Closer than me and Millie, even.

I know Koko had mostly white fans for most of the latter part of her career, but she was highly respected in the black community, too. She made more money with the white audience, true enough, but in her earlier years Koko played the Regal, the Apollo, she played all those black venues. She had that big hit with "Wang Dang Doodle" in 1966, when there weren't a lot of blues singers like her on the R&B charts, and black folk never forgot her, and they never stopped loving her. She'd come out to my shows when I played in Chicago, like at East of the Ryan or someplace like that, and she'd always act like she was just so pleased to see me, see how well I was doing, that I was still out there, still going strong. She was sweet. She was a sweet thing.

I had another girlfriend, a white girl, named Mary Catherine Mouradick. She lived in California. Bill Jones used to call her "Mo-Dick"—"Hey, Mo-Dick! How y'doin'?" She's the one who used to go with Gene Chandler. She'd come to Chicago, hang out with him, come over to my house with him to have dinner and things like that. Later on, she got mixed up with an ex-boyfriend of mine who was a bank robber, a real outlaw, and that's a story I'll tell you in a little while, too.

But she also became good friends with Ike Turner. I went out to California one time, and she introduced me to Ike, took me to his studio. I got out there—that man had so many freaky ideas and crazy shit! I was thinking, how in the world did Tina stay with this crazy man? He's just out there laughing, talking about all the women he's got and the sexual things they do when they come to his place, and then he took me to this big ol' round waterbed he had. His apartment was in the studio, and he had this bed built up on a stand. He was showing me where he had cameras taking folks' pictures, and then he'd sit up and look back at that stuff, naked women, two people in the other room screwing; he'd give them access to his bedroom, they think they're in private, and he's filming it. Now he's up there showing it to us. Come in his place, get naked, he had you on camera!

At one point Mary Catherine and I both had to go to the bathroom, and I told her, "I'm holding mine! I ain't going. I'm not pulling off my clothes here!" I would not use Ike Turner's bathroom. No ma'am. He ain't gonna look at my ass and be showing it to everybody.

Man, Ike was something else. No, let me rephrase that: Ike was *from* somewhere else. He was not of this planet.

I only met Tina once; we were in Memphis, and Don Dortch got us the passes to go over to the place where Ike and Tina were. I saw her perform many times, but that's the only time I actually met her. We got a chance to talk a little bit, and that was it. I know everybody says Ike would beat her up for anything she said if he didn't like it, even if they were in public, so she was steady watching him, and if he gave her that look she'd know to shut up. That's what I heard. But I didn't see them being like that when I met her.

So I can't say for sure what he did or didn't do to her, because I didn't see it and I didn't know her well enough to have that kind of conversation with her. But I do know that a lot of women stay with a man who treats them like that. I honestly don't know why. I think they're afraid of not getting a man, or of not having him. And then sometimes, I hear it said, it starts at home. You see how Mama treated Daddy, you see how she sat there and took whatever Daddy threw out. And some women, when they're starting young in life, they think it looks good for a man to be in control. Only when they grow older and realize they want to control themselves, do they really understand. But when they're young, it looks good to them. I've seen a lot of girls think that's cool. Be sitting up there, "Child, he won't let me do this, he won't let me do that. Oh, I can't do it, honey. He would do this or that to me," and so and so and so.

What the hell you mean, he won't "let" you do this?! How can he stop you? But they think it's cool. And I think it's horrible. Don't ever tell me "You can't go there" or "You can't talk to him" or "you can't" this or "you can't" that. Tell me what you don't *want* me to do, and then let me decide, and maybe we're okay. But tell me what I *can't* do? Mmm-mmm! Better not!

Now, a lot of people ask me if I'm a feminist. Not necessarily. I'm just a woman. I like being a good wife, I like cooking, I like fixing my man's meal, I like bringing it to the bed. But I also consider myself as being my own person. Now, if that's what a feminist is, cool. I'll be it. I've always considered myself my own woman, and couldn't nobody tell me what to do. I wouldn't let nobody rule me. If that's what a feminist is, I'll claim it. If a feminist is a woman who got to have it her own way, and she'll only give in if she thinks the man is right, then call me a feminist. I don't know if that means good or bad, and I don't care whether it means good or bad. If that's what it means, I'm it. 'Cause I'm not gonna be going through changes with no man. I tell no man what he better do, and he better not tell me what I better do. That part of my show, when I say that or sing that on stage, is absolutely sincere; I be meaning exactly that. That sure enough ain't no joke. Don't dare me to do nothing. No, lordy! I just might do it.

"I'd Rather Pack My Bags and Go"

When I separated from Bill Jones in 1974, I knew an important chapter in my life was over. It was with him that I'd launched my record labels and begun my activities as a businesswoman; I'd recorded hits on Bill Coday and the Sequins, I'd gone on to cut my own No. 1 record, and I'd established myself as a touring artist and a recording star. That was a lot of history to walk away from.

But I had coupled all my money with Bill, and he'd just gotten so irresponsible that he spent it all and pretty much ruined us. You see, what happened was, for as long as Bill kept his job as a chef in that restaurant, he couldn't drink during the week, so he held himself together pretty well. But the minute Bill Coday's records started happening, he wanted to drop all that and go out there on the road with him and be his manager. Well, he couldn't live in that environment. He got out there, say he gonna drive Coday all over the country, and sometimes Coday had to do most of the driving because Bill got somewhere and got drunk, hanging with the promoters and the DJs and all those fast-living folk you run into on the road.

He wasn't mean or anything; he wasn't one of these mean drunks. He was lots of fun; all he'd like to do is laugh and talk and tell jokes. But he didn't care how much money he spent. When he was drinking, he'd spend every dime in his pocket. Give everybody in the house a drink until you close the door and have to put him out. They had to close the door on him every night.

And then I struck gold. Gold Record, money coming from everywhere. Things really got worse then, because now he had plenty of money to spend.

He'd go out of town to go and promote records, and all he's doing out there is drinking and spending the money. That's not doing me any good. Then he decided he wanted to come on the road with me as a road manager, got us a van, now he's going to drive us. Well, if he's my road manager, before I go on stage he's supposed to collect my money. But he and the club owner or the promoter get to drinking and talking, they become best of friends, say, "Everything's okay. It's cool. Go on." So I go on stage, still don't have my money. Come off, money's not there and neither is the promoter. He's nowhere to be found. They'd just wait 'til Bill Jones got nice and drunk, then leave and not finish paying him.

So it became a thing where I said, "Look. I don't need you on the road with me 'cause you're drinking so much that somebody else got to do the driving. You're not collecting my money, so I don't need you out there." So I wouldn't take him on the road with me anymore, but by that time, even at home he wasn't doing anything but getting drunk every day. And then what really hurt me, the final time, I went to Memphis and cut a session, and when I got back home, writing checks to the musicians' union to pay off the session, the checks started bouncing, and I didn't realize why. And I called my bank, First State Bank, in Worth, Illinois, to find out why the checks were bouncing. They told me, "You got checks out of sequence. That's why your money's not there."

Our money was in the Crajon account, and we were co-owners of Crajon, so he had as much right to it as I did. Turns out he'd gone in the back of the checkbook and written checks out. Plenty of blank checks up here in the front of the checkbook, but he knows I'm going to see them if they're missing. So he goes back there, and he writes him a check for five hundred dollars, six hundred dollars, something like that, and spends it. So the money's not there.

So I left and went to Memphis. I had to put some miles between us; I had already gone back to him when I knew I shouldn't have, and I was determined not to. I loved living in Chicago. At that time it cost, maybe forty-some dollars to fly to Memphis. I could be in Memphis in a matter of an hour. So there was no problem there. I loved Chicago, but I had to put some miles between me and that man, or I'd've been gone back to him. And I was determined I was not going back.

I didn't say a thing; I just went to Memphis and rented me an apartment. And when they called me back in Chicago, told me my credit had gone through and the apartment was available, I packed a bag and said I'm going to Memphis, going to work in the studio with Papa Willie for a few days, do some tunes; I left, went down there, checked into a hotel first until I got my business together, I got my lights on, my telephone in, got me some furniture, rented furniture, started putting it in that place, and I moved out of the hotel straight into my apartment. It was out by the airport on Winchester Road, a little community area called Winchester Park Court. I had a four-room to begin with; after Bill Jones vacated my house in Chicago, I went back and took my furniture and brought it down, and at that point, I had to get a six-room.

The drama in Chicago wasn't quite over, though. Not long after I'd moved to Memphis, Westbound asked me to do another album, and they sent me some money, I think it was $15,000, but they couldn't send it to me personally. They said, "Well, we have to send it to the company, Crajon." And I never saw a dime of it. Bill Jones took the whole $15,000 and opened him up a record shop up on 47th St. and Langley, just about a block north from where we had been living. I had gone off and left him, he didn't have any chance of getting any more money out of my career, so he took that $15,000, and that was it.

There was nothing to reconcile. He had a right to it, and I didn't get into it with him about it. When we finally got divorced a few years later, before I married James Wolfe in 1977, we split our business interests so I kept Ordena, and he kept Crajon. We're still friends, to this day. He was a good person, really; I understood everything because I understood what he was doing. He just thought it was beneath him to be a chef, with his wife being a star. That's what he felt. And I understood him. I really understood. He was embarrassed that he was a chef, and I kept telling him, let's open up a soul food restaurant. I even tried to get him to move to Memphis and open up a soul food restaurant, and have all the entertainers coming to us. But he didn't want that. He wanted to be in the music business. And he wasn't temperamentally qualified for that.

He got married again, but later on his wife had a serious accident. They were getting ready to open up a barbeque place, and she drove into one of the viaducts in Chicago and was in a coma for ten, twelve years. She just died a few years ago. He never did get the barbeque place open after she got hurt, and he'd already closed the record shop, so he just took care of her. I think they got a large sum of money after the accident; he bought some buildings and had her taken care of at home. Round-the-clock nurses, right at home, until she died. Since then he's moved back to Georgia, near his hometown of Macon, and we stay in touch. I don't hold a grudge, and he doesn't either.

I was glad to get away from the mess in Chicago, but being in Memphis felt, in a way, like being in a small town. Nightclubs stayed open in Chicago, some of them, until three or four in the morning, and then on Sunday morning 'fore day, they'd stay open until five. Memphis, everything cut off at two o'clock; if you didn't leave home at nine or so, you're going to miss half the stuff that's going on. Over in West Memphis, across the river, things were a little looser and the places stayed open later, but I didn't go to West Memphis until later, when I started getting booked over there.

But I was free again, and ready for some new adventures. And honey, what an adventure those next few years turned out to be!

Bad Boy

I first met Nate Johnson in Atlanta when I was doing a show down there. His real name was Nathaniel Doyle, but he went by Nate Johnson. He said he was an ex–pro-football player with Buffalo, big ol' husky thing, supposed to have gotten hurt with Buffalo and wasn't playing anymore. Said he knew O. J. Simpson and everybody. You know, to know about these people all you have to do is watch television and get everybody's name. So he could call names and talk about what happened, like "Oh, yeah, that time we played Baltimore," or "That time we played Green Bay," and everybody would go for it.

He was a guy who would frequent the nightclubs every night. Real friendly, outgoing. When he walked in, everybody started, "Hey, Nate! Come on, man!" You know, like that. He kept plenty of money in his pocket, set up the whole bar, and just everybody loved him because he was so generous. He just had this charisma. He was a Sagittarian, and when he walked into a room, he just lit the room up, one of those people who just take over a room when they walk into it. Now I didn't know jack about football. Nothing. But everybody's saying, "Yeah, he's with Buffalo." "Yeah, he been in the playoffs." All that kind of stuff, and he'd talk like he knew everybody. So I'm sitting there thinking, okay, he got plenty of money, a 1975 El Dorado, brand new, must be somebody. And if everybody's telling me they know him from Buffalo, who am I to dispute? I don't watch. So anyway, I met him, and we just started dating. He started driving up to Memphis to see me, and then he'd meet me at different places I was working. If I tell him I'm going to play at Detroit or Milwaukee or somewhere, he'd meet me there.

So we began dating, back and forth; I'd visit him in Atlanta, and then he started traveling around the country with me. We went on vacations, too, went to the Bahamas, went everywhere. But I still kept wondering how he had all that money; something just wasn't holding together right. So I finally asked him, "Look. You got to tell me the truth. What is it you do? I gotta know. Somethin' wrong."

And he said, "I'm a professional gambler."

So that went around for a while. I'll tell you one thing, too, he certainly was a good gambler. He'd break any game we go to. He just loved to get people in that game, come out of there with all the money. But then one day we were in Chicago, driving down the Outer Drive, and he looked over there at the stadium, the Bears' stadium, Soldier Field, and he said to me, "What's Soldier's Field? What is that? Is that some kind of army thing?"

"I said, 'You don't know what Soldier Field is?!'"

"No."

"Then you ain't no football player."

"Whatcha mean?"

"That's the Bears' football stadium, and if you don't know what that is, and many a time you say you done played the Bears, and you don't know what Soldier Field is? You ain't no football player, so stop lyin' to me. What do you really do? 'Cause I'm not crazy. Things are not panning out the way you say it is, and I know it's got to be something else."

And he was just outdone. He said, "All right. Want me to tell you the truth?"

I said, "Yeah."

"I'm a bank robber."

I said, "I believe that!"

I was halfway joking when I said that, but I thought about how that man had so much money in the glove compartment of that car. He had five or six thousand dollars stuck up in there. Now a man with common sense wouldn't do that. This is somebody hiding his money, because anybody else would have had a bank account.

So I told him, "Now I believe that."

"Why you believe that?"

"'Cause that's the only thing make any sense!"

So I finally found out the real truth. And when I found out the real truth, it kind of scared me a little at first. All the money he's taking me all over the country with, sportin' around with me, that was bank-robber money! This guy was going out on the road with me, and I didn't know he was out there casing banks, and then going back and robbing them. And when I'd be at home, like during the week, he'd say, like, "I'm going over to Ohio"; his people lived in Ohio. Or, "I'm going back to Atlanta a few days" or something like that. And he was robbing banks!

But it was kind of funny, too. Yeah, it was kind of dangerous, but I didn't care. You have to remember, I was still pretty young, and Nate was coming in with two and three thousand dollars stuck up in the glove compartment of his car, giving me half of it. I wasn't worrying about it. I was spending the money, I wasn't out there robbing anybody.

We'd travel together; sometimes he'd even MC my shows. He'd get up there, talk to the people, bring me on, "Ladies and gentlemen, Miss Denise LaSalle!" Wasn't scared of anything. He was smooth, charismatic, really good at it. He just was the nicest, most fun guy I ever met in my life. I never had fun with anybody like I had with him. All the guys who've been in my life, he's the one I had the most fun with. I mean, if I wanted a perfect guy, as far as traveling and all that, he was it. He was everything. He finally moved to Memphis, moved in and lived in my apartment with me.

His lifestyle, if that's what you want to call it, ended up being more than I could handle, and eventually I had to cut him loose. I'll tell you more about that in a minute. First, though, I need to talk about a tragedy that occurred in Memphis during the time Nate and I were together. It would have been bad enough in itself, but it involved people I knew well and considered good friends, and both Nate's name and mine got dragged into it. To make matters worse, the things Nate was doing also ended up spilling over onto me, getting me into trouble with the FBI and doing some serious damage to my reputation.

The Al Jackson Murder: Tragedy and Its Aftermath

Al Jackson Jr. was one of the greatest drummers Memphis ever produced. He was the original drummer for Booker T. and the MGs, and he was on most of those famous sessions at Stax in the 1960s. He'd gotten his start with Willie Mitchell, though, and he always stayed loyal to him; he played on some of the biggest records Willie produced on Al Green.

I knew Al's wife, Barbara, better than I knew him, but I was as shocked as everyone else when he was murdered on October 1, 1975. A policeman found Barbara in front of their house on Central Avenue in Memphis with her hands tied behind her back, hysterical and crying about an intruder who'd broken in and tied her up. She said that as he was ransacking the house, Al showed up at the door, and the burglar shot him dead before running away.

Al and Barbara had been having problems. They'd almost gotten divorced the previous year, and just a few months before he was killed she'd shot him in the chest during a fight. I know Barbara also knew about the other women Al was messing around with, because she was a friend of mine and we used to talk about that. He was going with a woman who worked at Stax, and Barbara knew all about it. But by the time he was killed, she had another boyfriend, too. Al was supposed to go out of town that night, so Barbara didn't expect him to show up at the house. But instead he went to the Mid-South Coliseum in Memphis to watch the Muhammad Ali/Joe Frazier fight on TV.

Nobody in Memphis that I know really knows what happened. Everybody had their theories. One story was that Barbara was at the house with her boyfriend when Al came to the door, and things escalated from there. Then some people said they thought it had something to do with all the problems Stax was having, financial problems and problems with their bank and all that, or maybe somebody at Stax was mixed up in something heavy and Al got caught in the middle somehow. And then some people believed Barbara set him up and had him killed. No one was ever arrested, but at some point they started saying they thought Nate Johnson had something to do with it, probably because he was my boyfriend and everybody knew Barbara and I were friends.

Nate had come to my house that night, said he was going to Atlanta. As far as I knew, that's where he went. He called me back from Atlanta, or at least that's where he said he was, and of course telephones in those days didn't show you where someone was calling from, so wherever they said they were, you had to believe them. I think Bowlegs Miller's wife, Frances Miller, was the one that started that rumor about Nate killing

Al Jackson. She's the one who called me that night and told me Al got killed. She had heard it on the news or something like that. I don't know whether she didn't like Nate or what it was, but it was something I said to her in regards to Nate and Al and Barbara that made her say that. She somehow took it that I said Barbara wanted to get Nate to do something to Al, or something like that. Barbara had said something, and whatever she said, Frances took it in a way I didn't intend, and that's probably what she was talking about when she started saying, "Nate's probably the one who did it."

Frances had a reason to start the rumor. Frances was also going with Al Jackson on the side. She was one of Al's women, along with that woman from Stax I mentioned. But I knew Nate, and Nate would have acted different if he had killed that man. Anyway, Nate didn't even go around Barbara unless I went around her. He wasn't a friend of Al's, and he wasn't a friend of Barbara by herself. He might go with Barbara and me if we went somewhere, but as long as Al Jackson was living in this world, I never went in Barbara's house. I never once went to her house when he was alive. I only started going to her house after he got killed, you know, consoling her; I was one of her friends so I was there for her. So Nate wasn't going there either, even when he was in town. So yes, I think it's Frances Miller who probably started that.

The police came to me and asked me questions. First they wanted to know where was Nate that night. I told them the truth, that Nate said he'd gone back to Atlanta. Then they wanted to know did I know anything about Al's death. And I said, "What do I know about this kinda stuff? What are you talking about? What reason would I have to be involved in something like this? I'll go down and take a lie detector test right now. You want me to take a lie detector test? I'll take it."

They didn't have me do it, but I wanted them to know I was telling the truth; I didn't know anything about it. They sure had my name in there, though, trying to make it like I knew something, but I just said, "Well, I tell you what. Y'all can investigate me from now on. You won't find me having nothing to do with that, because I didn't have nothing to do with it. You can just get my name out if it, 'cause I ain't in that. I don't know nothing."

Evidently, I guess, after I offered to take that lie detector test and everything, they felt that because I'd offered them that, they believed me. But some people still thought I had something to do with it. In fact, it still comes up in different books and articles and things, saying I was somehow associated with Al Jackson's murder. But I know the truth.

By the time all this was going on, though, even being associated with Nate had become a threat to me, both personally and professionally. I remember when I finally realized that this relationship had gotten more dangerous than it was worth. We were in Ohio, outside of Cincinnati, and all of a sudden he decided he's going to leave me in the car—I was driving—and run into this restaurant for a minute. He didn't tell me what he was doing, just said, "Hey, I'll be back in a minute; hold on, sit in here 'til I come back." And when I looked, he was at the back door of this place. They were closing. Somebody came out to take the garbage to the garbage can, and he put a gun on them and went back in with them. But I didn't see all this; I didn't know.

They were standing off in a sort of semidarkness, and here I am, sitting in the parking lot in the car. And then all of a sudden he comes running out of there, jumps in the car, and now he's mad because I'd cut the ignition off.

"I told you don't cut the motor off on this car!"

I said, "So what?"

"Get outta here! Get outta here! Come on! Let's go! Let's go!"

So I start taking off as normal because I still don't know what's going on, and he starts cussin', just going through all these kind of changes:

"Come on, goddam it! Let's go! Go! Go!"

Then, "That motherfucker! Sonofabitch wouldn't open the goddamn safe!"

I said, "WHAT?!"

"Sonofabitch wouldn't open the goddamn safe!"

Well, I'd already figured him out as a bank robber, but now this is two different things. If you rob banks, now you tellin' me you gonna rob a little restaurant?

Oooh, I was so mad at him. I drove back to the hotel, and the next morning I left, packed my clothes, went to the airport in Cincinnati and caught me a flight back home. I said, "I'm not riding back with you. You think I'm gon' sit here and let you get me in jail?" I said, "You can't care nothing for me if you let me sit out there in that car while you go rob something and gon' have somebody, police, chasing me up and down the highway. No, I'm not going for that." And I got on a plane and flew back to Memphis.

When I got to Memphis, I went to my apartment, and I don't know what was wrong with me, but I just couldn't go back and get in that bed and go to sleep. I lay up in my living room, asleep on the couch. And I heard a knock on my door about four or five o'clock that morning. It was him. He had driven all the way from Ohio, coming in to apologize to me and all that kind of stuff. I told him, "I'm not gonna have it; I'm sick of it. I can't do it." And I made him leave, and we stopped being together like we had been. We were still in touch; he'd come back through Memphis and call me from the airport, but that was the beginning of the end.

Sometime around early 1976, the FBI got in touch with me. Nate had robbed another bank, and they were looking for him. He was gone from Memphis by then, told me he had to go to Houston, Texas, but they came to my house looking for him. They thought I'd know where he was, and I wouldn't tell them. I just said, "Look if y'all want him, you catch him. 'Cause he ain't done nothing to me. The man been good to me. That's all I can tell you."

That didn't satisfy them, and they indicted me on January 15 of that year for harboring a fugitive. I had to post a $2,000 security bond. That was in the papers, too, *Jet* magazine and everywhere. But when they took my case to court, I got up there and proved to them motherfuckers I wasn't "harboring" nothing. How in the world are you "harboring a fugitive" when he's everywhere you go, out there in public with you? Even when Al Jackson got killed, Nate was standing right out there at the funeral, with the news people, being interviewed. And my attorney took that to the judge. He had a projector in the courtroom, showing Nate up on stage with me, MC'ing my show. "She's not hiding him. He's wherever she goes. Here's a picture of him on stage, bringing her on; here's a picture of him at the funeral with her; here's a picture of him doing this and doing that. Is that 'harboring'? That's not 'harboring'!"

Now how you gonna knock that? How you gonna convict me? He said, "You can see she ain't 'harboring' nobody. This man ain't trying to hide from nobody." Them folks sat up there looking like fools. Twelve jurors sitting there, wanted to convict me so bad, and it really got them because they couldn't do it. They had to find me not guilty, and they did.

I have to say, though, Nate never slowed down. After I finally put him out, he went to California; he knew my girlfriend out there, Mary Catherine. She used to come visit me in Memphis all the time, so that's how Nate knew her. He went out there, got with her for a minute—and then he robbed her bank! I tell you, that man was bold. It wasn't too long after that that he went up to Seattle and got into a gun fight with the police, and that's when they killed him. This was on July 15, 1976, and he was on the FBI's "Most Wanted" list by then.

The way I found out about his death was kind of shocking, because I had just signed with ABC and was on my way to Detroit to cut *Second Breath*, my first album for them. My birthday was on July sixteenth, so we had my birthday party on the fifteenth at a place in Memphis called the Big M. Everybody at the party that night knew Nate was dead, but Don Dortch, the man who'd been working with me as my booking agent and helping me with my career was there, and he said, "We're not going to tell her because she's going to Detroit tomorrow to do a session." Not only that, my trial for harboring a fugitive was still pending, so the less I had to do with that mess, and with Nate, the better off it would be for me.

So the next morning I left town, went on up to Detroit and stayed there two weeks doing my session, and when I got back home, Nate had been buried and everything. Don called me to come to his office to tell me about it. He gave me all the newspaper clippings and everything for me to read and hold onto, and I was just shocked because it was done. It was over.

But you know that saying, "when God closes one door, He opens another"? My relationship with Nate, as crazy and doomed as it was, had already lit another spark that would soon burst into flame. I was finally ready to settle down, and the Lord made the way for me by allowing me to meet the man who, I discovered, was truly the man of my dreams.

Chapter Nine

"One Life to Live . . . Let's Live It Together"

Dreams Still Come True

When they put me under arrest for harboring a fugitive and it came out in the news, James Wolfe was a DJ on WDXI in Jackson, Tennessee. They called him "Super-Wolf." He was the biggest thing on radio then, and people all over Jackson, me included, still call him "Wolf" or "Wolfe" to this day. But he hadn't met me when he first met Nate. Nate had come through Jackson on his way back home from somewhere; Wolfe used to have a record shop, so Nate went by there and told Wolfe he was Denise LaSalle's man and all this, and he gave him my contact number to book me for some shows. So then when I was indicted and Nate's picture was in the paper, Wolfe put it together: "That's that man who came through here. He said he was Denise LaSalle's boyfriend!"

The FBI was still trying to find Nate through me, and by then I knew my phone was tapped. Every word I said, I could hear it ring back in my ear. So Wolfe called me, talking about "this man I met named Nate," and I was trying to stop him from talking. But he said he wanted to book me for a show. He asked me if I knew Estelle Axton, the woman who had co-founded Stax Records. Yes, I knew Ms. Axton, so I met Wolfe over at her office in Memphis, and he brought me a contract. And the funny thing is, the first check he gave me, I think it was a $200 deposit check, it bounced.

First money he ever gave me, and it was no good. Then he gave me another check, and *it* bounced! So I called him up, and he's like, "Damn! I'm sorry. Tell you what. Meet me back over there and I'll give you the money."

So he came by, and he brought me the cash money this time, so I came up to Jackson and did the show for him. And now he keeps asking me, "You have any girlfriends look like you?"

"Yeah. I got plenty of 'em."

"I want to find me a girl that looks like you. The same kind."

You know, just hinting, wanting me to say, "Well, what's wrong with *me*?" or something, I guess. So when I did the show, I brought a girl with me that everybody used to say we looked like sisters. He came in, and then he ran from her all night! She was chargin', honey—"Super-Wolf! That's Super-Wolf!"—and he was runnin'. He didn't want the "friend like me," he wanted me! But instead of being a man and saying "I like you," he put that "somebody like you" or "one of your friends who looks like you" thing on me. That really rubbed me the wrong way, and it was almost the cause of our falling out before we even got started. If you like me, you like me. Don't ask me to bring somebody else up!

Anyway, when the show was over that night, I was staying at a hotel on Highland Avenue, and we all went back there after we'd been to an after-party in town. I ended up hanging out with Ed "Too Tall" Jones, the old Dallas Cowboys star. He and I and a couple of other people went up to my suite, and we sat there playing records and talked half the night. So when Wolfe got there, Ed and I were talking, sitting real close, and I guess Wolfe said, "I can't beat this. He got more prestige than I got." He turned around and left. But Ed and I never did anything. In fact, I didn't see him again for a long time.

After that, though, Wolfe kept calling me. One day, the Doobie Brothers were playing at the Coliseum in Memphis, and the after-party was going to be on a riverboat. That afternoon, it just so happened that Wolfe called me from Ms. Axton's place:

"Can I come over? Whatcha doing today?"

"I'm going to an event."

"Oh, I was thinking I could come over, maybe we could have a drink together."

"Tell you what. How're you dressed?"

"I got on a suit."

"If you got on a suit, you're dressed good enough to go to a party. I'm going to a party on the river with the Doobie Brothers. Wanna go?"

So he came by where I was, and it was the funniest thing. He was driving a big ol' long limousine Cadillac. Why would anybody want to drive a limousine? A limousine is to lay back and ride and have a chauffeur! But this boy had a big ol' long limousine, he's driving, and I said, "No, I don't want to ride in that." I put him in my car, and we went out to the river and got on the boat, the Memphis Showboat, and we partied all night with the Doobie Brothers and all those guys, danced and had a good time. Our first date.

That was the beginning. We kept dating, kept seeing each other, and we got married the next year. I told him I wanted to get married on the same boat where we had our first date, and we did, on July 16, 1977, my birthday. My band, Imagination Unlimited, played for our wedding. I wrote a song, "One Life to Live," and they played it and I sang it just before James and I walked down the aisle.

You can find that song on my album *The Bitch Is Bad!* on ABC. I started it off with one of those spoken narrations I told you about, immediate and from the heart:

> *Now, honey, we're getting ready to venture off into life together today, and I realize that things are not going to always be easy for us. As a matter of fact, we're going to have our ups, and we're going to have our downs. But if we really, truly love each other, we can make it work. Life can be beautiful for us. So let's try to make it last. Because remember one thing:*

And then I sang:

> *One life, that's all we have to live*
> *So, baby, let's live it together*
> *And if our love is strong enough*
> *We can face anything together*
>
> *And if I should hurt you, and the rain should fall*
> *Dark clouds coming over us*
> *Faith in each other, just like an umbrella*
> *Our love will be a cover over us*
>
> *We've got one life to live*
> *Let's take it, baby, let's make it, baby, what we will*
> *We've got one life to live*
> *Let's take it, baby, come on and let's make it what we will*

One heart, that's all we have to give
And mine will always belong to you
And thanks to you, for giving yours
And I will always be true to you

Now we'll make mistakes, we'll have our fights
But before we decide to break up
Remember before we go to bed each night
Let's take the time out to make up

We've got one life to live
Let's take it, baby, let's make it, baby, what we will
We've got one life to live
Let's take it, baby, come on and let's make it what we will . . .

We've done just that. On July 16, 2017, Wolfe and I celebrated our fortieth anniversary. After all these years, I guess you could say that song is another dream that came true.

Making It Work

I needed to get a few things straight with Wolfe before I married him: "Don't try to run my career, and I'll stay out of yours." That's the conversation we had. Because after everything I'd gone through, first with Billy Emerson, then with Bill Jones, when I met Wolfe, I told him how it had to be. I said, "I don't have anything to do with what you're doing as a disk jockey, and don't tell me how to run my business. If I need help, I'll ask for it. If you see something, got a suggestion you want to make, you can make it. But don't get mad with me if I don't take it. You know your business, and I know mine."

We came to that understanding, and we have always stuck to that. Another thing I told him, I said, "Now, I know women are gonna be running after you, and there are gonna be men chasing after me. If you can't stand it, ain't no use to us getting together. 'Cause men gon' call me, and women gon' call you. So we just have to have that understanding from the git-go." That boy had so many women chasing him, it was funny! But I could live with that; wasn't 'bout nothin', as far as I was concerned.

After we got married, I stayed in Memphis for about six more months; I was flying a lot to gigs then, and when I'd come home, I would go to my apartment in Memphis and stay until daylight, and then I'd drive back up to Jackson. Pretty soon we realized we were wasting money doing it that way, and we ended up buying a ten-room house in Jackson over on Sweetbay Drive. After about two years, we moved to the house on Henderson Road where we still live.

Before we moved, I made a big effort at getting a house on Country Club Lane, just off Plantation Road on the north side of town. The man was going to charge me two hundred and fifty thousand dollars for it, but then he turned around and sold it to Carl Perkins for a hundred thousand and some! That man didn't want no black folks moving into that area. I knew Carl from various events and functions around Jackson, and of course I'd been a fan of his from "Blue Suede Shoes" on up. I actually knew his wife, Valda, better than I knew him. His old drummer, Fluke Holland, had a house on Campbell St. that I also looked at for a minute. Once I got inside, though, I didn't like it that much, so I just let it go.

Wolfe and I never had any problem with having separate careers; as a matter of fact, it's been good for us. When we started dating, sometimes I'd take him with me on road if he was available to go. But most of the time he was busy doing his own thing, and it's been like that all the way through our marriage. As I got to know him better, though, I did get more interested in his career, how he felt about it, and his dreams for the future. I'd go to the radio station with him, sit up with him at night while he was on the air from ten 'til two, and he'd get calls from kids. Should be in the bed sleeping, and they're calling him, asking to hear Earth Wind & Fire, L.T.D., Jeffrey Osborne, those kinds of people. Because other than his show, it was all country music on that station. That was when I realized why he wanted a station of his own so badly, saying they need a black station in Jackson to play black music, so these kids don't have to spend all night long staying up listening to him and requesting music all night.

But he didn't have the resources to do something like that. He made decent money doing what he was doing, like going out, spinning records in clubs, doing little DJ sets. He might make $150 a night. If he did several of those shows a week, along with his regular paycheck from the station, that was pretty good. But he was still working for someone else, and he didn't have any other income. I was making a lot more money than he was then. So in 1983, when we started working on building the station that would become WFKX, I basically put him in business. It was $100,000 to just get the license and get the station going, and I had to pay the biggest portion of that. Then we got some more partners, and they paid the rest. KIX 96 went on the air February 1, 1984.

It wasn't easy, believe me. It's hard for a black man, in the first place, to get the information he needs to go into something like the radio business, and it was ever harder then, because there weren't that many black radio stations. And certainly in the South, there's not a white man out here, hardly, willing to help you get it for yourself unless it's something in it for him. So Wolfe had to align himself with these white people, and they started showing him the ropes, how to go about getting it. But once he got in the door, these people who were supposed to be his partners saw this great big ol' thing, this dumb black boy, they figured, who didn't know anything about it. So they're gonna do this and they're gonna do that and they're gonna end up having it all to themselves.

But he wasn't quite as dumb as they thought! We just got in there and kept hammering away until we finally became sole owners. KIX 96, the first black-owned radio station in west Tennessee. WDIA in Memphis was famous for having an all-black format, but they were still owned by a white corporation. We were it! When we started out, you couldn't own but one station in a market. After that changed, Wolfe bought two more, WZDQ and WJAK. WZDQ was more of a pop station with mostly white jocks; WJAK was gospel. So by the mid-1990s, we had three stations going. I'd say we were some of the leading black entrepreneurs in that area during those years, and we got a lot of respect for what we were doing.

We were quite the socialites in those days, too. We had a big backyard with a swimming pool, and we'd have great big parties out there. Everyone would come out to Henderson Road to have a good time. In those days our basement was almost like a little nightclub; we had a bar and everything, and people like Ed "Too Tall" Jones and his buddies, like Sylvester Hicks from the Kansas City Chiefs, they used to party downstairs in that basement. Rudy Ray Moore, that nasty comedian they called Dolemite, he was a good friend of Wolfe's; he'd even stay over at the house sometimes.

We finally had to put an end to those parties, though. A lot of times I'd go to bed and they'd all still be down there having a good time, and one night I was laying in bed in the dark, couldn't sleep, and I opened my eyes, and there was this dude with his hand on the doorknob, looking in my room! I could see him, but he couldn't tell if my eyes were open or not. I said,

"What do you want?!" and he slammed that door and flew. When Wolfe came upstairs, I told him the parties had to stop, 'cause this man was up in my bedroom, looking in the room at me. And I didn't want any more of that.

Taking Care of Business in Jackson

The first business Wolfe and I went into, even before the radio stations, was a nightclub called the Players Palace. It was out on Airways Boulevard; if you drive out there now, the building is still there. Now it's David White Body Shop, 769 Airways. No one had ever seen a black club anywhere near Jackson, Tennessee, like the Players Palace. We had a restaurant, we had six hundred and forty capacity in the main ballroom, and we had a smaller V.I.P. room called the Denise LaSalle Celebrity Room. Then, upstairs, there was a big lounge with five gaming rooms, pool tables, and slot machines. They weren't the kind that paid off; if you hit the number, the club itself would pay. The Players Palace was a big place, and it required a lot of maintenance; there was a three-room apartment upstairs, where we had a caretaker who lived there full-time.

We couldn't afford to book superstars like Etta James or somebody like that, but we might have the Bar-Kays, Con Funk Shun, those kinds of people, and of course I'd perform there, too. You know that live recording on my album *Unwrapped*, where I do a medley of "Make Me Yours," "Precious, Precious," and "Trapped By a Thing Called Love"? We recorded that at the Players Palace; you can hear Wolfe as the MC introducing me and everything.

The Players Palace closed in 1981. My career had taken off, and I wasn't going to take my money and keep putting it back into that club; the club had to take care of itself. When I saw that wasn't happening, wasn't nothing left to do but close. Too Tall Jones's brother Cliff was our business partner and we left it with him, but Cliff didn't stay in business two months after we pulled out.

Later, we got another nightclub downtown, in the building where we had the radio station. It was much smaller than the Players Palace, seated maybe about a hundred and fifty people, but we had bands, disco, everything in there. We served a little bit of food, maybe some fried chicken and French fries, that kind of thing, but it wasn't what you'd call a real restaurant. The name of that club was Denise LaSalle's The Spot, and we kept it going for a few years, too.

Another business venture of mine came about because I wanted to have a place where I could get the kind of wigs and accessories I needed for my shows. I'd go to California a lot of times, or New York, and I'd shop there. I'd come back home and try to find similar items, but they wouldn't have anything I wanted; there was nobody trying to be glamorous in Jackson, Tennessee! So after Wolfe purchased some buildings downtown—one building had the radio station KIX 96, and then he bought the building next door—I went in there and started Denise LaSalle's Chique Boutique and Wigs. Basically, I put it there for me, so I could go wholesale, get the stuff cheaper, put it in my shop, and buy what I wanted out of my own shop. I didn't have anything but wigs and jewelry at first, but a lot of the people who came in there had seen the clothes I wore on stage, and they wanted to know where they could find outfits like that, too. So I went back to New York and California, to the wholesale places, and I'd find things and bring them back.

The Chique Boutique started getting pretty successful, but it was just like the nightclub. You really can't run a business like that unless you're there to stay on top of it. People were taking advantage of me. I'd come home off the road, and there's no money. I'd bought all these clothes and things, stocked them up, and now I come home and I don't have anything to show for all the money I'd spent, and the salesgirls are wearing my jackets! They'd pin the sales tag up underneath so it wouldn't show: "Oh, I got the tag on it. It got cold, and I put this on and wore it home last night; the tag is still sticking up under there." Say they're going to put it back in stock when they're through wearing it.

I said, "Don't wear my clothes like that! I got to sell this to somebody else." I thought it was real ugly for them to do that. And then I discovered that the girl I'd hired as my manager was double-keeping the books, you know, just messing me around because I couldn't be there to watch my money. I couldn't be there, so they did anything they wanted to do. So I closed it.

After that, I opened a restaurant called Denise LaSalle's Blues Legend Café. That was sometime later, around 2010 or so. It was in a small building downtown that had been a lawyer's office, and it looked like a little house.

I tried to make it feel as much like home as possible. I can't say for sure what my most popular dish was, but I can tell you my catfish ranked right up there. And as far as soul food was concerned, my oxtails. I made a gravy that was somewhat like a stew, but it wasn't really a stew; it was just oxtails cooked down low, seasoned well with a big, thick gravy on them. And I'd always have rice or mashed potatoes or something like that to go with it. Spoon the gravy on top of the rice and mashed potatoes or whatever the customers wanted. And then I had greens. Turnip greens, mustard greens, sometime I would have collared greens with okra, sometimes I'd have cabbage, and there'd be black-eyed peas and string beans and pinto beans. All soul food, all good, and all directly from the Queen's own kitchen.

Yes, I did all the cooking myself, in my kitchen at home. I didn't mind; it's what I wanted to do. I figured no one could cook my own recipes like I could, so I wasn't thinking about having anyone else do it. I did it night and day, all through the week. It usually didn't interfere with my touring too much, because we were closed on Saturday; there was nobody downtown then. We never opened on Sunday, either; we could have made it big on Sunday, because I served the kind of food that folk would love after coming out of church. But my point was, I go to church on Sunday, too. I'd have to eliminate going to church on Sunday in order to do that, so I just wouldn't do it. When I did have to go on the road, I'd prepare the food before I left and refrigerate it; someone else would have to bring it to the restaurant and get it ready to serve.

So I'm spending all that time standing over my stove, working with all those steaming kettles and pans, then I have to lug them down to the restaurant and bring them inside. It started to put a strain on my back, hoisting those big roast pans day after day. By the time I closed the restaurant I had some pretty serious back problems, and they got a lot worse over the next few year. I'll tell you more about that in a little while, too.

Talking about these different enterprises I've been involved in, though, reminds me of something else that's important to me: giving back to the community. I don't know what made me that way; I guess my mom and dad, the way I was raised, what I was taught in church, but however I got it, I don't mind giving back to the community in one way or another. We need more people giving back. A lot of people, the minute they start making money, they move out and jump and run over to the rich folks' part of town, and the folk in the poor part of town don't ever see them anymore. I never believed in running like that. I'll get me a nice house, but you don't have to give it to me over there where the millionaires stay. Just give me a nice house where I am. I don't feel like I got to run off, just to be me. Because regardless of where I go I'm still me, come from good people, just country folk, farming, eating out of the garden, raising our own hogs and cows and chickens and things like that. That's all I ever had growing up. That's all I knew.

So I've always been a person who tried to help people whenever I could. In Jackson, when I had the wig store, I used to donate some of my wigs to the American Cancer Society. They'd send somebody to the store, or sometimes we'd go to the hospital and take them ourselves, to where the patients were having chemo treatments. They'd be bald, laying up in the hospital, and we'd take those wigs out there and put 'em on their heads. When I closed the store, I gave the Cancer Society about sixteen hundred dollars' worth of wigs.

Of course, to be honest about it, doing things like that helped me, too. I remember when I was still living in Memphis and that "Harboring a Fugitive" episode was going on. Don Dortch and I sat up and thought about, what could I do to cut back the negative publicity? So that Christmas, I started an organization called MOM, Musicians Of Memphis, to help needy families. We did a show at the Muhammad Ali Theater, which was on Beale Street at that time, to raise money for the giveaway. Musicians also donated things I auctioned off. Al Green, Rufus Thomas, the Soul Children and J. Blackfoot, Ann Peebles donated something she used to wear, the Bar-Kays sent records and tapes, and that's how the money was raised for our Christmas baskets. If I recall correctly, we raised about $1,500. We got WDIA to tell people to call in, needy families, and then United Way got involved, and we asked people to mail in the name of a needy family and why they thought that family should be a recipient.

On Christmas Eve, or maybe it was the day before, I don't remember now, my band members and I got out and worked until midnight delivering baskets. We gave away 112 Christmas baskets. We also had baskets waiting for people at the theater. We got in touch with the people who'd been notified they were the recipients, to pick up their baskets by a certain hour in the afternoon. If they couldn't make it to the theater, those were the people we delivered baskets to that night.

MOM was so successful I thought about keeping it going and calling it "Arms of MOM," but after Wolfe and I got married, we just started doing

it on our own. We'd have a rummage sale to raise money, then go out and
buy food in bulk and donate it that way. After KIX 96 came into being, the
station took that over.

Not long after Chique Boutique closed in 1995, Wolfe and I got the idea
to create a park, a recreation and performance area where black folks and
white folks could come and have picnics, see shows, and just enjoy themselves without having to go through all kinds of hassles. So we invested in
some land south of Jackson in a community called Bemis, and we named
it Denise LaSalle's Summer Place Park. Big place, like a football field; the
land was graded, it sloped up almost like a natural amphitheater. We leased
out some spaces along one end, where food vendors could set up trailers
as concessions stands. The performance area started out as being just a
stage, but then I closed it in. I had a dressing room on one end of it, another
dressing room on the other end, ladies' dressing room on this side, men's
over there, with a bathroom in each one. Then I had a little treehouse in
our yard, which I had put there for our son, Ray, to go out with his friends
and camp overnight. He wasn't using it anymore, so I took it down, took it
out to the park, and made it a ticket booth at the gate.

We spent a lot of money out there. Almost $40,000. Anybody could do
something there, concerts, events, it didn't matter. White, black, anybody.
It was something that had not been done in this area. But we only did one
show there, and we almost weren't able to do that. We had it advertised
and everything. Buddy Ace was on the bill, I can't remember who else,
maybe Tyrone Davis, and then they wouldn't give us the license. You see,
they didn't want "us" in the neighborhood—"us" meaning black folk. They
didn't want us there because that was an old aristocrat neighborhood. Didn't
nothing live in Bemis at one time but prejudiced white folk. When I came,
the prejudice was going away; a few blacks were out there. But the whites
still ruled the area, and when we bought that place, they're saying, "We
don't want them out in our neighborhood. They ain't gonna do nothing
but bring a lot of trash out here. They gonna do this, they gonna do that."

So my husband went to the mayor, said, "Look, we have spent all this
money to build this place up, and now you mean to tell me you all are gonna
hold us up from having the one show that we've already advertised?" When
Wolfe got through, the mayor said, "Well, y'all can have this one, but the
City Council will have to meet before y'all do anything else." So we went
ahead and did that one show, and after that, we had to go to court. And

then this racist graffiti started appearing around there, "Niggers go home!" and all this, no one ever found out who did it, and it ended up that we said we don't want any part of this if we can't do what we want. We had to go off and leave all that. Buildings, everything, we even left the little house, and we just went on back to what we were doing. So that was it.

Things like that hurt real bad. You stick your neck out, trying to give Jackson, Tennessee, something to be proud of, and end up getting slammed in the face like that. Because that *was* something to be proud of. But we weren't able to do it.

By that time, though, I had something much deeper and more meaningful to be proud of in my life. Wolfe and I were building a family—although, like almost everything else about us, it didn't happen in quite the way you might expect.

Children

I always loved children. I remember back in the country, when I was a little girl, I'd be running around down there with everybody's baby on my hip.

"Whose baby is that, little girl?"

"That's mine!"

I think about it now, how stupid I looked, people saying, "That little girl who was here yesterday, what was she walkin' around, dragging somebody's baby, talkin' about, 'It's mine'?!" I imagine I looked really stupid. But I did that.

Well, that was one dream that didn't come true. I don't remember how old I was when I realized I couldn't have children. I think I was about twenty-one or twenty-two years old when it came to reality. All my life, when I went into the woman years and started having my cycle, it was always messed up. I was never right from day one. I cramped and pained and had floods and blood clots and things like that. And then, when I started having sex, look like it got worse. I ended up getting pregnant and just miscarrying. Pregnant again, miscarriage. The doctor finally said, "What's wrong with you is you haven't got enough elastic in your womb."

They told me, "We have a new technique now, that we can stretch your womb." I said no, because things were beginning to happen for me by then, and I didn't need a baby to stop me from going out there and making my money. If I had only been working on a normal job and I was told that, it would have killed me, I think. But I had just got enough taste of being an artist, enough to know that was what I wanted to be, and I didn't need no babies stopping me. So when they made that offer, I turned it down.

Because I know what that means. Stay at home, take care of your kids. I was raised like that, and no way in the world would I have gone out there without my kids all the time. They would have meant too much to me. So the only thing to do now was just not have them, go on out there, and have a career. It was a choice.

But I've gotten me some babies. Oh, I got plenty of 'em! I have more now than I would've had then.

The first kids that ever became mine, that I considered mine, were the ones in Chicago. Walter, Donna Lynn, and Cheryll Denise, Mama Weese's grandkids, that's my first babies! Walter really is my godson; I went to church and stood up in church and baptized my godchild. The other ones just took me as their godmother. And they're mine to this day; I'm Mommy Ora to them. Cheryll Denise was actually named after me. When I introduce them to people, I introduce them as my children. People look at me, "I didn't know you had so many kids!" Usually we just smile.

Then, later on, after I moved back south and put together my band, Imagination Unlimited, my guitar player, Kenny Ray Kight, and his wife, Josie, had a son they named Kenneth Ray Jr.; they called him Ray-Ray. At that time, Josie was caught up in a lifestyle that didn't allow her to raise a child properly, and Kenny Ray was on the road most of the time. So I just said, "Y'all give me that baby!" Wolfe and I were married by then; his daughter, Bridgette, whom he'd had by a previous relationship, had moved in with us, and I was raising her as my own, too. She's a little bit different from me. She never went in for all that girly-girl stuff, like makeup and frilly clothes; she was more like what you'd call a tomboy. We got into it about that a little when she was growing up, but that didn't change her. Turns out she's also like me in one very important way: Don't you dare try to tell her to do something if she doesn't want to do it! Bridgette is a schoolteacher now in Tupelo, Mississippi, she's a basketball coach, and she's happily married. She comes out on the road with me, takes care of the merchandise sales and a lot of the details out there. She's got my back twenty-four/seven, and I love her to death. Most people think she's mine, and I let 'em think that, because we're that close and I love her just that much.

So when Ray was about five weeks old, I brought him home with me to Jackson. He's been mine from then on. And just like with Bridgette, a lot of people think I'm actually his mother. They be talkin', saying, "Oooh, Denise LaSalle had a baby by her guitar player!" But I ain't studdin' 'em. To me, he's my own son just as much as if I'd given birth to him, and they can think what they want and say what they want. I don't care.

I never pretended that way, though, to his actual parents. I never wanted Ray not to know his parents. I think it's too bad when kids grow up not knowing who in the family loved them, or being separated from them because of some small-minded people. Here are people who love them and want to be with them and do things for them, but they can't get that love because somebody is too narrow-minded to let it happen. So sometimes, to let Josie know her child and be close to her child, I'd let her babysit Ray, and she actually did better as a babysitter than she did when he was with her. I wanted to make sure Ray knew Kenny was his daddy and Josie was his mama. And so that's the way I did it.

The rest of "my" kids, I didn't ask for any of them. They just took me: "Oh, you my godmama, too!" All my band members, I'm their mama. Jonathan Ellison, the guitarist in Blak Ice, the band I have now, his mother died just a few years ago. When Jonathan's mother died, he said, "Well, my mama gone; you gon' have to be my mama." I said, "Okay, I'm your mama." So I been Mama ever since. All of 'em, just like that.

It's never easy raising children, and I'd be lying if I said it wasn't especially difficult to raise a black boy in this day and age. There was a lady, Ethyl, who lived right down the road a piece, who had two little twin boys who were Ray's playmates, Devin and Kevin. If Josie wasn't babysitting Ray, Ethyl took care of him for me when I was on the road. When Wolfe came home, he'd go over there and pick Ray and her two boys up, take them fishing or whatever they'd do. Then at night he took them back to Ethyl's.

When Ray got older and I had to try to get him in school and do things for him, I got consent to be his guardian. It wasn't adoption; I was his guardian. I could sign any papers for him to get him anything he wanted. Even so, though, I was away a lot, and Wolfe was busy with his career, with the radio stations and all his other activities. Ray ended up going through his own changes, with drugs and other problems, like too many other young men. But I never gave up on him, and I always kept him close to me. He'd been around music all his life, of course, so it wasn't surprising when he began to develop an interest in doing it himself. I had a recording studio built in our basement for him; that was his rap studio. But he started bringing too many guys over. I'd be out of town, and when I got back, Wolfe would be really upset, because instead of Ray bringing the kids in and going into the basement with them, they were all over the house.

So I bought Ray a house. I bought him a house on Forrest Street, not far from where we lived, and we put his studio in there so he and all of them could come over and do what they wanted to do. But Ray was still a little wild and that didn't work out either, so I ended up having to get rid of that house and putting him up in an apartment. Later, when Ray had his daughter Monet, her mother was a little dope-head, alcoholic, and all that kind of stuff. She started dating someone else, some little white boy, and I guess he didn't want children or something. So she told Ray he could have Monet. Ray was still living with us then, so I became Monet's mama, and Ray was Daddy. As time went by, I'd have to go get Ray to sign her papers to go to school and different things, so I finally just said, "You sign her over to me, so I can take care of her and I don't have to look to you for everything." We went to an attorney, signed it all over, and so now she's legally under my thumb. And that's how I got her, raised her up like she was my own daughter, had her own bedroom upstairs and everything.

And then I also kept two of Ray's other kids for a little while, Kenneth Ray III, they call him Tre, and his sister Ray'Ven, because with all those problems Ray was going through with drugs and everything, and their mother was another dope addict, so the child protection people took those kids from them; said they were unfit parents. They were going to put those children in a foster home, and I said, "No way. They got a home. They don't have to go to somebody they don't know." So the authorities investigated Wolfe and me to make sure we were okay, and they turned both grandchildren over to us. I had legal custody of them until their mother could prove she'd gotten clean, she'd straightened up and she was able to take them again, and they went back. They still come by the house a lot. I'm still their grandma, really more like a second mama to them. You see, I can't turn kids away like some people can. It's just not in me. And it doesn't really have anything to do with them being my grandkids, either; I'd be the same way about anybody else's child. I'm just like that about children.

I didn't slow down my own activities very much when Ray was growing up, but I did stop taking long trips to Europe. I used to go to Europe a lot, or I would go out to California and be gone for a few weeks. After Ray came into my life, I wouldn't stay gone that long. I always tried to get him interested in things, get him involved in doing things that might inspire him. At one time we had a yard man working for us. His name was Cornelius Charles. He had been a political cartoonist for the *Metro Forum* newspaper in Jackson, and he was an excellent artist. He started teaching it to Ray, and to keep Ray interested, I also started working with him. To learn more about it, I started watching Bob Ross on TV; he was an artist, too, and he'd give art classes, drawing lessons, on his TV show.

One thing led to another, and pretty soon I decided I'd like to try it myself. Wolfe and I went on a cruise, and one morning we came out early to see the sunrise. Standing on the deck, looking out at that beautiful ocean, we saw the ocean waves on the horizon where the sun was coming up; the ocean looked black and that yellow sun was just rising up out of it. So I painted that. It's on the wall of my kitchen right now. I also have a few other paintings I did, hanging in various places around the house. Most of my paintings are abstracts; Bob Ross always said, when you paint something, you don't have to paint exactly what it looks like, but how it looks in your mind; there's no harm to deviating a little bit. Just do a little extra stroke or something, if you want to. That's what I always tried to do. After Ray grew up and moved out of our house, I didn't have any reason to be wanting to paint anymore, so I just left it alone. Another little chapter in my life that I started, but never bothered to take very far. But those paintings are still there.

When Ray got older, I began taking him on the road. He always was a dancer. Can't sing, but he's a good rapper, and he can dance. He used to get out on the floor and dance with the women, do all kinds of flip-flops and fancy things, and so when I started taking him out with me, he said, "Mama, call me out and let me dance." So I found some songs of mine that were right down his alley, and he been floppin' with me ever since. Oooh, the girls go crazy over him! Sometimes people laugh about it—here's this young man up there, grinding for his mama—but I don't care. That's my boy. He'll dance on my show.

ME

MY DADDY

1. 1953: The young dreamer with her eyes on the future. Within a year or two, I'd be back in Chicago to stay, and the rest is history.

1964
Before it all
started
AT THE TROCCADERA
MY FIRST GIG

2. I don't look as scared as I was! But I made the gig, I got over, and after that there was no looking back.

Bank's Trocadero Lounge
4719 INDIANA AVE.
KEnwood 6-9021

3. With Singing Sam (Chatmon) during my days on the Chicago club circuit. Photo courtesy of James E. Wolfe.

4. "I'll steal your man, little girl . . . !" Publicity photo from 1967, after "A Love Reputation" had made me a local celebrity in Chicago. Photo by Gilles Petard.

5. A great night in my life: E. Rodney Jones presenting me with my Gold Record for "Trapped By a Thing Called Love" after it became a No. 1 hit and sold a million copies in 1971. We're on stage at the High Chaparral, at 77th and Stony Island in Chicago.

6. Performing at the High Chaparral, early 1970s. This picture was taken by a club photographer who went by the name "Hustling" Oscar.

7. The house at 4823 S. Langley in Chicago, where I first moved in with Mama Weese. I stayed in the basement apartment (you can see the windows on the lower right). After I married Bill Jones, this is where we lived. I finally bought the building in 1971. (Photo copyright © 2019, Peter M. Hurley)

8. Partying with Mama Weese and her son Walter, at the house on Langley.

9. Here I am with Bill Jones and his son Lynn. We were in Macon, visiting Bill's family. Lynn is the boy in the middle; the other boys are two of Lynn's cousins.

10. Partying at the Palm Village in Memphis. L-R: Don Bryant, Ann Peebles, our friend Earl Case, me, and Bill Jones. Bill loved the high life in those days!

11. With Bill Withers (far right) and his band, at the house on Langley. My friend Patricia McCord is on the far left.

12. Imagination Unlimited was the band I formed after I moved to Memphis in 1974. L-R, from upper-left corner: David Brewer (sax); Ron Deadrick (trumpet); Charlie Brown (keyboards); Willie Peete (bass); Reggie Brown (sax); Archie Love (drums); Kenny Ray Kight (guitar).

13. "One life, that's all we have to live. . . . Let's live it together." July 16, 1977: my marriage to James Wolfe.

14. My brother Hoppy— John Quincy Allen— giving me away at my wedding.

15. With Lou Rawls in Sweden, taken during a tour in the 1970s.

16. The Chique Boutique, my wig, clothing, and accessories store in Jackson.

17. Here I am with a little friend in Denise LaSalle's Blues Legend Café, my restaurant at 436 E. Main St. in Jackson. Photo courtesy of Bridgette Wolfe-Edwards.

18. "Wake up, Ty!" On the road with Tyrone Davis and Bobby Rush—two of my dearest friends.

19. The Malaco years, with Johnnie Taylor.

20. Ruth Brown was one of my early heroes. Here we are, posing at an outdoor festival in New York, mid-1980s.

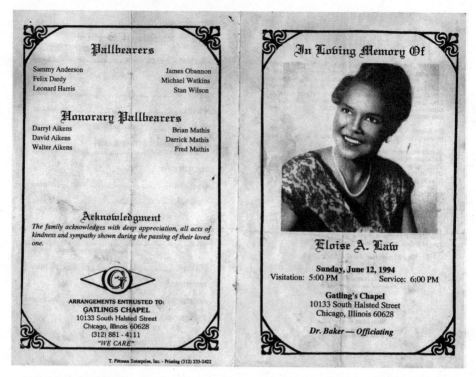

21. My beloved godmother, Mama Weese.

22. Working on my 2000 comeback album *This Real Woman* at Royal Studios in Memphis.
Those sessions were my reunion with the legendary Willie Mitchell.

23. I was crowned Undisputed Queen of the Blues on October 24, 2009, in Belzoni. After the coronation, I did a show at the California Club on Silver City Road, where this photo was taken.

24. That's James Earl Jones with Wolfe and me at the 35th Annual Advisory Board Benefit Dinner at Freed-Hardeman University in Henderson, Tennessee, on December 3, 1999. I wanted James Earl Jones to narrate my poem, "America's Prodigal Son." I'm still sorry we never had the opportunity to work on that together.

25. My parents, relaxing in the yard at the house on Cain Street in Belzoni. Taken either in 1968 or 1969. Photo courtesy of the Rev. Preston Allen Jr.

26. A Gold Record and a golden friendship. Sue Boatright, I love you to the moon and back. Photo courtesy of Bridgette Wolfe-Edwards.

27. I took up art for a while; here's one of my paintings. A lot of people don't know about this side of me. I think I had some talent, but I never took the time to pursue it very seriously. (Photo copyright © 2019, Peter M. Hurley)

28: Loves of my life: my son Ray, his son Kenny Ray Kight III (aka Tre), and Tre's mother Robin.

29. A changed man: The Reverend William Emerson in the pulpit. He founded the Holy Praise Apostolic Church of Jesus in Tarpon Springs, Florida, after committing his life to the Lord in the early 1980s. Photo courtesy of James E. Wolfe.

30. Still the Queen: At Brick's B&B Entertainment Center on West Madison St. in Chicago, the weekend of April 22, 2016. The dress I'm wearing was a gift from Koko Taylor.

31. With two dear friends: Nellie "Tiger" Travis and Cicero Blake. Photo courtesy of Bridgette Wolfe-Edwards.

Thanks to my favorite President and his beautiful family. May God always bless you all. Queen of the Blues Denise La Salle "2016"

THE WHITE HOUSE
WASHINGTON

November 7, 2016

Ms. Denise LaSalle
Jackson, Tennessee

Dear Denise:

I recently learned of the health challenges you have been facing. Michelle and I are keeping you in our thoughts and prayers, and you have our best wishes for your recovery.

At this trying time, may you find courage and strength in the presence of loved ones.

Sincerely,

32. A letter I'll cherish forever.

33. See the love in my eyes! L-R: Latimore and his wife, Yvonne; Theodis Ealey; Charles Mitchell, CEO of the Jus' Blues Music Foundation; Millie Jackson; and Willie Clayton. This was taken at the 2017 Jus' Blues Music Awards in Tunica, Mississippi. Photo credit—Jonathan Mason—Jus' Blues Music Foundation.

34. With Charles Mitchell, my dear friend and tireless advocate for the blues. This was taken at that same gathering in Tunica. Photo credit—Jonathan Mason—Jus' Blues Music Foundation.

35. Sharing a hug in Tunica with my co-writer, David Whiteis. That's
my daughter Bridgette behind us, to the left. Photo credit—Jonathan
Mason—Jus' Blues Music Foundation.

36. More loves of my life: That's Tre again, on my right; his sister Ray'Ven has her
head on my shoulder. Behind me is my other granddaughter, Jamie-Lynn. Her
mother is Bridgette Wolfe-Edwards, Wolfe's daughter from an earlier relationship,
whom I raised—and love—as my own. That's Bridgette's niece Amiah Spears
peeping over Jamie-Lynn's shoulder. This picture was taken at NHC HealthCare in
Milan, Tennessee, where I was recovering from my leg amputation. Photo courtesy
of Bridgette Wolfe-Edwards.

Chapter Ten
A New Label and a New Era

My Country Soul

My last hit for Westbound was "Married, but Not to Each Other" in 1976. That song ended up having a whole new life of its own, when Barbara Mandrell took it to No. 3 on the country music charts the following year. Like I told you, I've loved country music all my life. Even now, when I drive on the highway, my radio stays on country. My band gets a little irritated about it sometimes, say, "Okay, Mama, we're tired of this now!" But I be lovin' me some Dolly Parton and all of 'em. Those boys in Memphis and Muscle Shoals could play them some country, too. If any of the songs I wanted to sing had a country feel, they could ease right in and make it sound that way. I think it was Bowlegs Miller, or it might have been James Mitchell, Willie's brother, who helped arrange "Harper Valley P.T.A." on *On the Loose*, the second album I did for Westbound.

Everybody always accused me of writing country, anyway. My brother Frank, down in Mississippi, that's all he'd talk about: "You need to start trying to sing like it's a blues. That's too country!" And he was right, too. When I'm writing a song, a lot of times I'm hearing it in my head as a country song; when I record it, I'll have to force myself to sing it different from the way I hear it to keep people from saying it sounds country, because it just comes to me that way.

From what I was told, Barbara Mandrell's manager didn't want her to cut "Married, but Not to Each Other" at first. He said it sounded too grown-up, because at the time she was supposed to have been real young; that was her image then. But she insisted on cutting it, and it was a major hit for her. She came to Jackson one time to do a show at the Fairground, and she invited me to come by. She was traveling in a motor home, and when the show was over, she sent for me to come back up there, to sit and talk with her. And when I'd go to Nashville, we used to call each other from time to time. She's a nice, sweet person; she respected me, and I respected her. And I thanked her so much for cutting that song.

From Westbound to ABC

I didn't have any problems with Westbound; Armen Boladian and I are great friends, even today. But somehow they got into some kind of discrepancy with Janus Records, their distributor, and Armen didn't want to go any further with them. My contract was up, and I was ready to renew; I was waiting to go back in the studio, and Armen didn't do it because there was this problem with the distributor. We talked it over, and he said, "I understand, but I can't move 'cause these people got me tied down, and until I get my money I can't do anything." So that's why I left, and I went on to ABC Records.

I didn't just choose ABC, either. I forget now if ABC asked for me or just how I got with them, because I really didn't know much about them. I think it was the connection I had with Al Perkins in Detroit; he'd been working with Al Hudson and the Soul Partners, and they signed with ABC at just about the same time I did. ABC already had Ray Charles, of course; they had B. B. King, and they'd acquired Bobby "Blue" Bland after buying Don Robey's Duke/Peacock catalogue in 1973, but other than that they didn't have a lot of other soul or blues people. But that's why I liked them. They gave me free rein. They said, "We don't know how to really distribute and promote your kind of music, but if you're willing to take a chance on us, we'll take a chance on you." I cut three albums with them, and then MCA bought them out and I did three more for MCA.

My first album with ABC turned out to be null and void. It had been a few years since I'd done an album, so it was like starting over. That's why I named it *Second Breath*. I was cutting like I always cut, and I even brought my guitarist from Imagination Unlimited, Kenny Ray Knight, to play on the session, but I didn't get any major hits off it. I wouldn't blame the musicians at all. Sometimes, you're just not as good as you are at other times. I think it didn't get promoted right either, because like I said, the people there admitted they didn't really know how to promote my kind of music.

There were some good songs on there, though. That was the disco era, and one of the cuts from *Second Breath*, "Freedom to Express Yourself," turned out to be a disco hit in the gay bars and nightclubs in New York. We sold more records in New York than we sold anywhere on that song, even though it only made it to No. 100 on the national charts. A whole new audience for me—those gays were poppin'!

Another song on *Second Breath*, "Sit Down and Hurt Awhile," came to me from Rick Taylor, who used to be with Don Dortch International and was working as my booking agent at the time. I'd let him go out there and front for me. He could get things done, talk to people and get things done, say things that I didn't want to be saying. You know, like, "Hell, no! She ain't gonna do that!" I couldn't act like that. I'd have to always be the sweet li'l gal. Rick Taylor, knowing how to talk the way he talked and being the big man that he was, he'd get more done for me than I'd get done for myself.

Anyway, one day Rick told me he'd been trying to make a deal with somebody, and this person was giving him a hard time. So he said, "I don't know, Denise. I think I oughta sit down and hurt awhile on that." Maybe after he hurt awhile, he could find a way to get around it, he said, but he had to hurt awhile first. So that was my title. I began thinking, "What would make someone think to say this?" So I made it into a situation between a man and a woman, to have to sit down and hurt awhile, and that's where that song came from.

Next after *Second Breath* was *The Bitch Is Bad!* Now that was a *bad* album! I think that was sort of the beginning of singers using the "B-Word" on their records like that. Millie Jackson came right back with *Feelin' Bitchy*, and pretty soon almost everyone was doing it. Richard Pryor was using it all the time, of course, so I really didn't think anything about it. Like I said earlier, I'd been doing kind of raunchy lyrics since the beginning, but I was careful. I shied away from some of the words, but I could've gone there any time. I always wanted to keep the acceptance of people. If I saw one little frown, or see anybody go "ooooooh," I would hold up. I'm a person who watches my audience. I like to see their faces. I can't stand a dark room where I can't see my audience; when I see my audience's faces, I know where to go, when to go there, and when to let up.

There's a funny story behind that album cover, too. That's the one where I'm standing by a swimming pool on a tiger-skin rug, and there's a guy reaching out of the pool to touch my leg. I went out to Los Angeles to do those shots; I already had bought the outfit I was going to wear. So they started me at a bar; this guy was pouring me a drink of liquor in a champagne glass, and I was sitting at the bar with this outfit on, smoking a cigarette. And here I don't smoke, and I don't hardly drink! It was so out of character for me I didn't want to use it, so they took me outside to the swimming pool, and they said, "Why don't you get in and go swimming?"

I said, "Child, I can't swim. I ain't getting in that pool!" The dude could swim. They'd been trying to get us together in a photo, had us layin' all down on the floor, him on top of me and doing everything, and I said, "Shit, no!" So he got in the pool, and I stood up there and posed, and he swam up to me and took his hand and felt up in that split in my pants leg. The tiger-skin rug was their idea. Later on, an artist painted a picture for me based on that album cover, and when he did that, I said I wanted a real tiger, not just that rug, so he painted a real tiger instead. That painting is still hanging on the wall in my living room.

This time, we recorded in Memphis, at Ardent Studio, so the atmosphere was just like home to me. Later on, even though we still did a lot of recording at Ardent, the strings and horns would be added at the Sound Suite in Detroit; gone were the days when a single mastermind like Willie Mitchell would have everything in hand in one place! Lester Snell did a lot of the arranging, old friends like Marvell Thomas and Ben Cauley were on hand, Kenny Ray was with me again, and the strings were played by the Memphis Symphony Orchestra. Michael Toles also played guitar; he was another one of my favorite guitar players, and he worked with me in the studio for a long time. The backup vocals were by Isaac Hayes's singers, Hot Buttered Soul Unlimited, and you can't get much better, or much funkier, than that. "Love Me Right" from that album was a Top Ten hit, the last one of mine to make it that far, and "One Life to Live," the song I wrote for my marriage to James Wolfe, also made the charts, but it didn't get as high.

It seemed like the covers for some of those ABC albums had almost as many stories behind them as the songs did. The same guy who was on the *Bitch Is Bad!* album cover with me also did my next one, *Under the Influence*, but we didn't show him. Actually, my reason was different from what most people think. When I did that first album cover with him, Wolfe and I hadn't quite gotten married yet. Then, after Wolfe and I got married and I was getting ready to do another album, he acted like he was a little bit jealous of the dude; he talked kind of down on it a lot, about my going back out there and shooting with this man again. So I called them and asked them not to put that man on the album cover with me. I'm not gonna break up my marriage over something like that! They used a picture of his body lying under a purple sheet; you can see the outline of his body under there, but you can't see him. Later on, on another one of my albums, *Unwrapped*, there's a guy's hand reaching up, pulling the tape off some wrapping paper with me inside. It's a white guy's hand that's unwrapping me, but for some reason, I never heard anybody say anything about it. No controversy whatsoever.

One other thing that happened to me at ABC, by the way: After they realized I knew what I was doing, producing my own records and everything, they wanted me to produce a record on Bobby Bland. Now Bobby and I became friends later on, but we didn't know each other well at that time. But they wanted me to produce him, and he said he didn't want a woman doing it. He didn't tell that to me, but he told somebody else, "I don't want no woman." Didn't bother me, because I didn't really want to produce someone else, anyway. I'll write 'em some songs, but I don't want to go in the studio for 'em.

A couple songs from *Under the Influence*, "Workin' Overtime" and "P.A.R.T.Y. (Where It Is)," made the charts, but they weren't big hits. "Workin' Overtime" was another song with a strong country feel, but I was feeling a lot of pressure to adapt my style to disco. Everybody was coming up with all this, "Follow the times! You gotta follow the crowd! You gotta do what you gotta do!" So I cut some disco, tried to get it out there. "P.A.R.T.Y." was even more discolike than "Freedom to Express Yourself" had been. But if you listen to that medley I recorded at the Players Palace—it's on *Unwrapped*, which came out after *Under the Influence*—you'll get a good idea of what my shows sounded like in those days. When I had my own band on stage with me I was the same Denise LaSalle I'd always been.

Close Encounters at the Disco—And Time to Move On Again

Actually, some of my disco stuff came out sounding pretty good. I got the idea for "Coma Ta Ya Ha Dance," which was on *I'm So Hot* in 1980, from the movie *The Day the Earth Stood Still*. I just loved that movie. Michael Rennie played an alien space captain named Klaatu, and he had these words he'd say, like a message or a code: "Klaatu! Barada! Nikto!" When I heard all that language, I said, "Okay! I got something here."

So in the song, these aliens come to Earth, and they go to a disco. They try to communicate with the earthlings, and I used that phrase as part of their language, but I gave it a different rhythm:

> *Klaatu barada!*
> *Nikto sonata!*
> *Coma ta ya ha dance!*

I came up with this whole thing from that, where they have these spiny little knees and hips and everything and they get out on the dance floor and make peace with the earthlings by partying with them; turns out they were just saying, "We came to Earth to dance." Dwayne Thomas played some hot funky bass on that song. My storyline was clever, some really funny things, and it should have been a hit. But there were all these high-powered disco divas like Donna Summer and Gloria Gaynor around by then, and my vocal style, my phrasing and my tone, wasn't quite like theirs, so that might be one of the reasons why the song never really took off.

In another song, "E.R.A. (Equal Rights Amendment)," from *Denise LaSalle and Satisfaction: Guaranteed*, the last album I did for MCA, I even rapped a little. ("Satisfaction" was the name of the vocal group on that session.) I'm talking some real shit on there, too, the kind of stuff I'd been putting down on my records and on stage for years:

> *We've been denied; we've been pushed aside and told we can't be free*
> *I ain't gonna be no doormat woman, so don't wipe your feet on me!*
> *. . . Now you fellas try to get everything you can,*
> *But you say it's all right because you're a man;*
> *You call yourself a player when you sleep around,*
> *But you'll call me the biggest whore in town . . .*
> *. . . I don't mind my man runnin' free,*
> *But if it's good for you, then it's good for me!*

And then I had a crowd of women on there with me, chanting "E.R.A.! E.R.A!" Another one that should've been a hit.

By then, though, MCA wasn't happy with me. "I'm So Hot," the title song from my previous album, had made the national charts. The black radio stations were playing the hell out of it, and I knew it was popular. Wolfe heard it, and he asked me to use it to write a theme song for his radio show. So I wrote some lyrics, we went in the studio, and we cut "Super-Wolf Can Do It" with him rapping the new lyrics over the backing track from "I'm So Hot," just like Billy Emerson had laid "Love Reputation" over that Nolan Chance track so many years earlier. We put it out on our own little label, which we called Big Bad Wolf. I never asked MCA's permission; we just did it. I guess I figured this was just for a local radio show. They'd never hear it; they were way out there in California.

But that record took off. Like I said, Wolfe was really big in those days, and a lot of people picked up on it. I should have offered it to MCA, but Joe Robinson from All Platinum Records, Sylvia Robinson's husband, came to me and asked me to lease it to him. So to get that money, I did that. They put it out on Sugar Hill, which was making a name for itself as one of the first big hip-hop labels, and it went nationwide. Today it's considered a kind of underground classic of old-school rap. Wolfe even made a video of it; you can find it on YouTube. Nobody ever said a word to me from MCA, but when I got ready to go back into the studio and called for my budget for another session after *Guaranteed*, they said, "Well, we changed our mind. We think we won't do any more records."

They released me from my contract. They never said one word to me about that track; they just said, "We've decided to pass." Hurt me to my heart, though, because I really thought they hadn't heard it. But when they told me "No," I knew right then. Because "I'm So Hot" had done pretty well, and I knew they wouldn't cast me aside after a record like that. So I said, "Well, they must have heard it." I was just glad they didn't sue me.

By the way, even though a lot of the material on those albums sounded different, I was still calling the shots: I was credited as the producer, and the production company was usually still Ordena. I also had quite a few of my old dependables on board for a lot of those sessions: Kenny Ray and Michael Toles played guitar; Marvell Thomas played keyboards. On *I'm So Hot*, Marvell's sister Vaneese was one of the background singers, and Ollie Nightingale, another great soul singer from Memphis, did a guest vocal on the song "May the Funk Be with You."

Now that I think about it, though, I did have another problem with MCA that came up. When we were cutting *Guaranteed*, a guy from Jackson, Tennessee, named Wayne Douglas gave me a song and said the song was fresh; nobody owned it. I had a contract with MCA that said that we split the publishing; if I did 75 percent of the album, I got a $25,000 deposit against royalties, as a publisher. So I had done most of the songs on this album. This guy told me the song was free and clear, to go 'head and cut the song. It turned out to be a really good tune, "When Love Separates," but then while I was waiting for them to pay me my advance, they got a letter from this other guy, Reginald Eskridge, saying, "This is my tune. I own it, lock, stock, and barrel. I wrote it, I own it."

So when the album came out, splitting the publishing between Duchess, which was MCA's publishing company, and Ordena, and Top Line Music, which was Wayne Douglas's publishing company, Reginald Eskridge wanted to sue MCA. That put me in a really bad light with them because they got angry with me, said I didn't take care of my business right, because I should have had a contract with the songwriter. And technically, they were right, but, you know, you think, most times, gentlemen's agreements work. And Reginald wasn't innocent in this thing, either. He was there in the studio all the time while we were cutting; he should have come forth and talked to me. But he claimed Wayne just told him, "You can't talk to her. She's a star; you don't talk to her. I do all the talking. I'm the in-between man."

I told him, "Well, you should have talked to me anyway. You were there; you were there all the time." I always felt like they did it deliberately, just to get me to cut the tune. And I never did feel good about that. Because it was like one big trick to me. And after that, my contract was up, and MCA wouldn't renew. So I know that probably had a lot to do with it, too.

For a couple years, I just kind of sat there and did nothing. I was still performing, of course; wasn't anything else for me to do. I won't say it didn't slow down, but I was touring, even though after a while I didn't have any new material to put out there. Because, you know, when you have a hot record out it's always faster, then when it starts to slow down a little, that's what lets you know it's time to go back in the studio and cut something new. So that's when I called them to get my money for another session, and that's when they said they were going to pass and not renew my contract.

So here I am all of a sudden, out there trying to keep it alive on the road, wondering, "What's next? Where am I gonna go now?"

And that's when the blues came calling.

Chapter Eleven
Steppin' In on Some Down Home Blues

The Move to Malaco

Dave Clark was a legend. He was an old-school promo man, the kind who used to drive around the countryside looking for radio station antennas and then talk his way in and convince the DJ to play whatever records he was hustling. In fact, he was probably the first one to do that. Dave was a Jackson, Tennessee, boy, born there in 1909, and he just about invented record promotion. He serviced radio stations, jukeboxes, record stores, anywhere they had records he was there, charming folks however he had to, hustling his product and getting it out there. He knew everybody, I mean, *everybody*, in the business, and he was certainly no stranger to me when he called me up from Malaco one day and said, "Denise, can you write a hit for Z.Z. Hill? We need a good song, and we love the way you write, so why don't you write a song for Z.Z.?"

Z.Z. had just scored his big hit, "Down Home Blues." No one expected a blues song like that to be a hit in the early 1980s, but it was, and all of a sudden Z.Z. was just about the hottest thing out there. So Dave called me, asked me to write a follow-up, and I came up with "Someone Else Is Steppin' In." Remember I told you how I used to write songs with a particular singer in mind? Well, that's what I did with Z.Z. I took the melody and the changes of "Down Home Blues" and wrote a new set of lyrics. I changed the bass line around a little, but aside from that it's pretty close to the same song. "Steppin' In" turned out to be one of Z.'s best known records.

So then, when I didn't go back to MCA and I was struggling with no label at all, I was talking back and forth with Dave Clark, and finally Dave asked me, "Whatcha doing?" I said I wasn't with anybody; MCA wouldn't take me back. So he said, "I'm gonna get somebody to call you."

Tommy Couch, one of the Malaco owners, called me and said, "I got things we want to talk to you about. Come on down here and do a little something for us. You want to do that?" They had me come down to Jackson, Mississippi, where their offices and studios were. We sat up there and discussed the business, and I agreed to sign with them and do a record. I made a one-album deal, and if we both agreed after that, it'd be two. I did it on my own terms, too. I've never given away my publishing; I've always had part of the publishing with every company I've ever been with. And if I could split with MCA, what's a little old company like Malaco going to do? So I felt, you know, Malaco better be honored to have me there, so don't go talkin' crap to me about my publishing.

At that time, though, I wasn't thinking of myself as a blues singer. Blues to me meant people like Koko Taylor, Muddy Waters, and them. A lot of black folk didn't even like the word "blues" then. That's one reason "Down Home Blues" was such a surprise; no one knew there was even an audience for that kind of stuff anymore. But it turned into the record that launched a whole new contemporary blues genre. Then, after I wrote "Steppin' In" for Z.Z., it was so successful that Tommy and Stewart Madison, another of the owners there, started talking to me, saying, "Hey, you know, that's a great tune you wrote for Z.Z. You want to cut some blues for us?"

I said, "I don't really sing blues. I don't know."

Stewart said, "Well, I think we ought to try you in here, and I think you can do it."

So I was called a blues singer from the day I signed with Malaco. I was writing and singing pretty much the same kinds of things I'd been doing all along, so actually I don't think I changed that much. It's just that Malaco was being called a blues label, and so as soon as I went there, people started calling me a blues singer.

I didn't like it at first. It made me mad. I was a black audience artist, and I knew there weren't a lot of people called blues singers then who were singing to a black audience. I said, "What I sing doesn't sound like blues to me; it sounds like R&B, same thing I've been doing. But now, here they come up with that jive about 'blues singer'!"

It was Wolfe who talked me into it. Wolfe told me, "Denise, I want to tell you, it's like this. In the R&B field you got Gladys Knight, you got Aretha, you got Stephanie Mills and all them little young girls out there. All these people got way more prestige than you have."

He said, "Ain't nobody singing the blues as a woman but Koko Taylor, Etta James, it ain't but three or four of 'em out there. Take the name 'blues' and go 'head on, and you gonna be Number One. R&B is the music you've been doing. You haven't changed your style. You're singing the same songs that you've been doing. All you got to do is take the name 'blues.' You got hardly any competition! Why don't you just accept it? Why don't you just go on and cut some blues, see what happens?"

He encouraged me to do that. And I said, "Okay, good deal. I'll try it."

Then Wolfe brought me a song title, "You Can Have My Husband but Don't Mess with My Man." He had heard a version of it, I think by Koko or somebody, but really it was Irma Thomas who'd done it first. I told him, "I like that title! But I don't like that song, the way they're doing it. I'll write me another song with the same title, and then I'll cut it my way."

So I wrote my slow version of it, altogether different; the only thing the same was the title. And it turned out to be my first hit with Malaco. One difference, though, was that before then I had never had a guitar solo on my records; my songs always had keyboard solos, so even if they were in the 12-bar structure, they didn't sound like what you'd call real hardcore blues. But when I did "Don't Mess with My Man," I went raw. And it turned out to be a smash, instant smash. And so therefore I said, 'Well, okay. This what y'all want, I'll go for it." So I started cutting using guitar solos, using the style they were calling blues then. Even so, though, I didn't sing it like Muddy Waters or Koko Taylor. I just sang what I felt, a smoother kind of blues, like maybe Ruth Brown or someone would sing. I didn't go to that lump-de-lump, twangy, style. I just sang my way of blues, and that's what I've been doing ever since.

Launching My Blues Career

I ended up staying with Malaco for almost fifteen years, and then I did one more project for them in 2010, after I'd officially left the company. We didn't always see eye-to-eye on everything, but I enjoyed my time there more than anywhere else I ever worked. I always told people it was like family at Malaco, and it really was. Stewart, Tommy Couch and his son Tommy Jr., Wolf Stephenson, and all the rest of them really had your back, and they also had songwriters like George Jackson and Frederick Knight working there, along with people like the late Harrison Calloway, one of the finest arrangers I ever knew.

After I joined Malaco, they began recruiting other artists, mostly veteran soul and R&B singers like me. I think Latimore might have gotten there a little before I did, but the rest, like Little Milton, Johnnie Taylor, Bobby "Blue" Bland, and them, they all came in after me. Some, in fact, came in through me. I was the one who got Johnnie Taylor together with Malaco. That revitalized his career just like it revitalized mine, and it did a lot of good for them, too. Carl Sims didn't sign with Malaco until later, but I had him opening shows for me in the 1980s; he'd worked with the Bar-Kays and Otis Redding, but he didn't have much of a career going by the time he started with me. I encouraged him to get out there and make a career for himself, and he eventually signed with Malaco and did a few things with them. Later on he was with Ecko during the same time I was there, and although he never made it really big, he's still out there, still recording for independent labels, still performing.

My first album on Malaco, *A Lady in the Street*, came out strong. "Don't Mess with My Man" was the first hit off it, and then the next hit was the title song. It actually became something like a signature song for me, one of my anthems. It's another one I got from a conversation. I don't remember who I was talking with, but he said that for him, he wanted a woman who's a lady, but when she come in that bedroom she need to be freaky as a motherfucker! So I wrote the song from that. I also did my own version of "Down Home Blues" on that album. I didn't try to imitate Z.Z.; I added a lot to it, like that narration I came up with at the beginning. That's why it's labeled "X Rated" on the record, so the DJs know what they're getting into when they play it!. It caught fire, too, especially on my shows.

Z.Z., by the way, also became a good friend of mine. One of the nicest fellows you'd ever want to meet. Good performer, too. But he was strange. He didn't clown like the other guys on stage. He'd walk up there, get the microphone, just stand there and rock back and forth, just rockin' in rhythm. Some people used to kind of laugh at him, but it wasn't a laughing matter. He was just a little different, that's all it was.

Z. and I, the two of us being with Malaco, when they booked one of us they usually booked the other one. He was getting ready to start making more money; his price was going up to ten thousand a night, and the booking agent had raised mine to eight thousand, but Z. got killed before we could get there. He never made ten, and I never made eight, at least not at that time. There were occasions where we did a big show somewhere, where we might get that, but as a regular base salary, we never made it to that level. Because he died just at that point, in 1984.

When Z.Z. died, Wolfe and I drove down to Texas for his funeral. On the way, in Arkadelphia, Arkansas, our engine overheated and we had to find a mechanic. A local man recommended someone he knew. He said the man looked like he couldn't do it, he only had one leg, but don't worry, he was a good mechanic. Well, I'll tell you, this guy was sitting there when we came to his garage, and he got up and started hopping around on that one leg, and he did the entire job by himself, carrying his tools, carrying all the parts he needed, doing all the work by himself, hopping all around his garage on that one leg just like it was two. He fixed us up, we got back in the car, and we got back on the road. I have never seen anyone get around like that. Truly an amazing man. Later I learned he'd lost his leg in a motorcycle accident; some KKK guys or something like that had run him off the road. But he didn't let it stop him. In his day, when he was coming up, especially for a black man, you just did whatever you had to in order to survive; wasn't no special "rights" or "accommodations," you just went on and did it. That's the kind of man he was.

After *A Lady in the Street*, my next one was *Right Place, Right Time*. It had another song on it that's become kind of a trademark for me, "Your Husband Is Cheating on Us." I got that idea from a conversation I had with another friend of mine, a disk jockey up in St. Louis. I can't remember his name now, but he said a guy he knew was going with a married woman, and then he found out she'd started messing around with someone else. This guy told my friend, "Man, what hurts me so bad is I found out she had a husband, she had me, and then she had another man on the side! I can't quit her, and I can't hit her! But sometimes I want to call her husband up, say, 'Mister! Your wife is cheatin' on us.' And let *him* whup her ass!"

So this disk jockey called me, said, "Denise, I have a song title for you." And that's how I got that song. Later on, Little Milton did it as "Your Wife Is Cheating on Us," but I did it first.

The title tune on *Right Place, Right Time*, which I sang as a duet with Latimore, was another one I originally wrote as a country song, and it still sounded that way when Lat and I did it. I don't think ballads like that get the recognition they deserve. The record companies don't seem to like my ballads as well as I do. But the ballads are more true to heart, true to what I feel. The fun tunes, where I throw all that bullshit in there, a lot of times those are more made-up stuff. But very few of my ballads have made the radio. Very few. "Married, but Not to Each Other" went up pretty high, but it went further with Barbara Mandrell than it did with me. "Right Place, Right Time" did okay, but only because it was a duet with Latimore, and it didn't do all it should have, either.

Another ballad, "Paper Thin," from *Still Trapped* in 1990, is one of my favorites of all the songs I've written. Or "Why Am I Missing You?" where I talk at the beginning about how sometimes it hurts to be in love, and then I go on and talk about how my old man and I got into it and I threw him out, and then I said it gets lonely in the middle of the night, y'all, you get to needin' somebody, you find yourself asking yourself this question, "Why? Why am I missing you?" I'm telling you, I love that song. That one, or "Goin' through Changes" or "Sit Down and Hurt Awhile," these are songs that touch you in your heart. And I think they're better songs than the ones they choose for the singles. But it's those other songs, the ones with the bullshit in 'em, that end up carrying the album.

Love Talkin', my third album for Malaco, wasn't quite as successful as the first two had been, but I did get to record my own version of "Someone Else Is Steppin' In." When Malaco asked me to cut it, I didn't want to at first. I told them, "I can't top Z.Z. with that record."

They said, "Denise—cut the song. I think you can do it."

So I said, "Only under one condition."

They said, "What?"

I said, "If I do it my way. If you let me do it my way, I'll cut it. But now, don't tell me nothin' 'bout cleaning up no lyrics and stuff. I'm gonna do the song, I'm gonna put in it what I want to put in it, and that's what y'all put on the record, or else I'm not gonna do it."

And that's just what I did. I did a whole lot of talk, my little rap on there, and they didn't cut any of it out. It turned out to be a big hit for me, and to this day it's one of the most popular on my shows.

Just about the time when *Love Talkin'* came out, I lucked into one of my biggest songs, the last record of mine to reach the national charts. It all started when Malaco got upset with a New Orleans record man named Isaac Bolden over a song called "My Toot Toot," which had originally been recorded by a Zydeco singer named Rockin' Sydney. Bolden, who was based in New Orleans, cut Jean Knight doing a cover version, which Tommy Couch heard on the radio. Tommy contacted him, and they agreed that Bolden would lease the record to Malaco for national distribution. But Bolden turned around and leased it to Atlantic instead—another record-industry "gentleman's agreement" bites the dust!

Tommy and them were pretty steamed about it, so they went into the studio and worked up a backing track that sounded as much like the original as possible. I was at a national DJ convention down at Miami Beach. They called me up and said, "We got a copy of it; we want you to learn it and cut it." I went up there, I cut it, and Wolf Stephenson mastered it the same night. I think I cut it on a Sunday or a Monday; we retitled it "My Tu-Tu," and they had it on the street by Thursday. That's how fast they did it, just to try to get ahead of Jean Knight's version. Jean's ended up going a little higher on the charts than mine did, but it was still a pretty big hit for me, the biggest I ever had at Malaco. *Love Talkin'* had just been released when we did "My Tu-Tu"; Malaco made another pressing of the album right away, with "Tu-Tu" on it, and that's the one you'll usually find today. That's the song I always use to close my shows, and it never fails to get the house. The song did even better overseas, reaching the Top Ten in Britain; Epic had the overseas distribution, and they released an album called *My Toot Toot* that included everything on *Love Talkin'* including "Tu-Tu," which they renamed "My Toot Toot" all over again, plus a couple of other tracks. So that whole episode turned out really well for me.

By now, you know I'm pretty strong-willed, especially about my music, and I don't bite my tongue about anything. I ended up getting into it a little with some of the folks at Malaco about the sound we were getting on my records. When I went there, I went as my own producer; that was part of the deal. But then Wolf Stephenson started to interfere. He was the engineer on most of the sessions, and I'd have something the way I wanted it, or maybe I'd fix something on my own, but then he'd wait 'til I left and change it, push up instruments, pull down instruments, change the voice, all different things. I'd say I want the drums to come in and hit real hard here, or I want to do this and do that, but he'd fix it his way.

After I'd made a few albums with Malaco, seemed like the hits weren't coming as fast anymore; "Tu-Tu" was kind of a lucky accident; it wasn't a song that had originally been intended for an album. So Tommy came to me and said, "Denise, when you first came here, boy, you was hot then! But lately you ain't been cuttin' nothing." I got pissed when he told me that. All of a sudden, I'm not getting good product? I said, "That's because you don't allow me the freedom I had when I first came here. When I came here, I came here as my own producer. I could go in the studio and sit with Wolfe to mix my stuff. Now all of a sudden, I leave, and he changes it and puts it his way. And you wonder why I'm not gettin' no hits?"

So that's when they started letting me go to Muscle Shoals. They had bought the Muscle Shoals studio, and they said, "We'll let you go to Muscle Shoals Sound, and you pick whatever engineer you want and whatever musicians you want. And you do your stuff down there without any overseeing."

I went down there, and the first album I did, *Hittin' Where It Hurts*, jumped out like a bullet. I coproduced that one with Marvell Thomas, and he also played keyboards. "I Forgot to Remember" was on there; that's one ballad that did really well. Next out of Muscle Shoals came *Still Trapped*, the one with "Paper Thin" on it, the song I love so much. It also had "Drop That Zero," another one of my signature songs, and "Wet Match," which I just found out Bobby Rush took and made into a song of his own! But another one on *Still Trapped*, "I'm Loved," is special to me because of the story behind it. I wrote it for my husband. One day, he walked out of the house without kissing me goodbye, on his way to the radio station. And I said, "Wait a minute. I didn't get my kiss. You come back here and give me my kiss."

He turned around and came back in the house and kissed me, and he said, "I want you to know one thing. Whether I kiss you or don't kiss you, I want you to know you're loved."

And when he said that—"Oooh! I'm loved! I'm loved! Okay, okay! I'm loved!"—I said, "I'll have it written when you get back." He came back home that night, I made him get in the bed. When he got in the bed, I straddled him in the bed on my knees, and I sang that song to him.

When I cut "I'm Loved" for *Still Trapped*, though, Malaco didn't want to put it on the album. They had some little old George Jackson blues stuff they wanted me to do instead. George was going through some personal problems then, and I felt his writing wasn't very strong at that particular time. So I told them, "Well, I'm gonna tell you one thing. I'm givin' this to you: If this song is not on my album, then don't ask me to cut another record for you. Because I promise you, I will not cut another record." And that's how I got that song on there.

Another one I did for Malaco that I wish more people knew about was "Child of the Ghetto." That one came along later, on *Still Bad* in 1994. It came from a pretty deep place; it wasn't my own personal story, but it came from some of those stories of what black people were going through. I was thinking about a girl, a child of the ghetto, trying to move up from the ghetto to better herself, trying to raise her child right and keep him safe in the world they were living in. That song touches me deeply. I don't perform it, not even in my gospel shows, because I can't get through it. Every time I do it, I cry. I cry so hard every time I try to sing that song. I cried all in the studio when I was trying to cut it. I just bawled; I think the band finally had to lay down the track without me, and I came in and sang it later.

Now this might sound funny to you, but I actually wrote that song with a country singer in mind. I was thinking of Kathleen Mattea when I wrote it. I believe it would have been a bigger hit if a white person sang it. And after listening to Reba McEntire, I think she could do that song, too. But I'm not pushy in that way. I can't just walk up, knock on a door, say, "I'm Denise LaSalle, can you do this?" Still, I really wanted to take that one to Nashville and see could I get Kathleen Mattea to sing it. That's a pretty song, and it has a message I think a lot of people need to hear.

Soul Survivors

By the time I signed with Malaco, performing opportunities—the shows, the venues—had changed a lot. Back when I was having my big chart hits, I'd do a show somewhere, and the only other entertainment they had was maybe a local group who'd come in to open. Nowadays, they don't trust any one artist to pack a house, so most of the things I get are those package shows with at least three or four other people. The shows run all night, and most of them are in auditoriums or civic centers, or maybe show lounges in casinos, or they're at outdoor festivals of some kind. The old nightclub circuit has dwindled, and a lot of the places we used to play are either gone or no longer have live entertainment. I remember the last time I played East of the Ryan, on 79th Street in Chicago; I was shocked to see how that place had deteriorated. They still have shows there every now and then, but it's not the elegant venue it used to be.

But the new way of doing things is cool with me. It keeps me working, and appearing on those package shows lets me renew friendships I've had for years. I've made some new ones, too. I finally got to know Bobby Bland well after both of us signed with Malaco. We went on a European tour together, and we sat together and talked about our families and our homes, and we got to talking about cooking. He told me he'd bet I couldn't beat his wife, Willie Mae, cooking; I said I wouldn't be so sure about that! But I've met her, and she seems to be very nice. I know some musicians kind of resented her when they got married because they thought she was keeping him isolated, keeping him away from them, but really what she was doing was for his own good. There was a documentary about him on *Unsung*, the TV series, and she was very honest about how she had to protect him, help keep him away from drugs and things that were hurting him. One time she even took a shotgun and put a drug dealer off the bus in the middle of the night! She was there for him all the time, and you can't ask any more from a wife than that.

And then, what I like about her is that after Bobby died she didn't stop coming around. You know, most women would have gone on their way; you'd never see them anymore. But she evidently really likes the music. I know she's a good friend of Millie Jackson, and of course she and Bobby Rush are close because Bobby and her husband were the best of friends. So I just think she's a very nice lady. Just a genuine, nice person.

I'd known Johnnie Taylor since he was singing gospel in Chicago. Like I said, he was always a little temperamental, kind of hard to get along with, but we became good friends through the years. He still had his ways, though. He got to acting so bad at one point that he couldn't work. Don Dortch used to book him, and Don quit booking him because people said he was too nasty and too drunk, wouldn't come on stage on time; sometimes he'd get all the way to town, get to the hotel, and then they couldn't pry him out of the hotel to get to the gig. He had to cool it a little before he could get back to working steadily again. One thing I'll say for Johnnie, though, and I always liked this in him: That man made *sure* he got paid! In cash, before the show, or he ain't goin' on. We'd be backstage laughing, because he'd be up there doing his show and his pockets would be bulging, full of that money. I don't think anyone in the audience noticed it, but we all did, and that was one thing about him that tickled us.

Lou Rawls came up singing gospel in Chicago, too, but I didn't know him then. When I met Lou, we were in Switzerland. I had never even shook his hand 'til then. We worked about five or six countries together that year, a big tour. Somebody, I'm trying to think who it was, was acting ugly, being real difficult. You know, you got these egos out there, and this dude, I can't think of who that was, had just pissed me off, and I just said, "Forget it! I ain't got nothing else to say about him!" So Lou had to try to get us together, say, "Come here. Come here! Shake hands!" He was the peacemaker on that tour, and that's what I remember about him.

I already told you about Millie Jackson. That's my ace boon coon! People are afraid of her; they're scared of her, boy, 'cause she'll say anything! But really, she's a doll. Another lady I've known for years, who also got kind of a second career going at Malaco, is Shirley Brown. Malaco released a wonderful live recording of a show Shirley and I did together in Greenwood, Mississippi, called *Divas in the Delta*.

I've always gotten along well with Shirley. She has her little mean streak, too, but it's always been geared toward other people; it's never been toward me. I wrote a song for her one time, which she recorded on her album *Holding My Own* in 2000. I think it's another good example of how I write when I have a certain artist in mind. It started with a song I had, called "I Was Not the Best Woman," on my album *A Lady in the Street*. The woman is saying something about how she wanted this man so bad she took him from another woman, but she didn't realize that she wasn't the best woman when she took him, she was just the biggest fool. Everything that other woman refused him, she'd give it to him free; the other woman would stay at home while this woman worked to pay the bills, and *he* stayed at home while she worked to pay the bills. So she says, "I was not the best woman, I was just the biggest fool."

Shirley wanted me to write her a song based on those words, so I tried to fashion one in her style. Her sound is more Aretha-like than mine, so I had to come up with something different. I wrote, "You said that love was just a gamble when you tried to take my man / But, honey, all is fair in love and war, and may the best woman win." That's a little bit of what I used in my own song, but then I said, "So pull out all your stops, shoot your best shot / I'll be the winner every time / 'Cause it's a natural fact that you ain't no match for this comeback kind of love of mine."

Then I said, "I'll always be the best woman," you know, an Aretha kind of thing, "'Cause you got to play the game to my rule / I'll always be the best woman, and you'll always be the biggest fool." And then the bridge said, "I ain't gonna be no doormat woman," which is from "E.R.A." and also from another song I wrote that Malaco didn't put out; it ended up on *Wanted*, on Ecko, in 2004. "I ain't gonna be no doormat woman / Ain't gonna be played for no fool / So, woman to woman," which is the line from Shirley's big hit, "Woman to woman, come on and take it like a woman," that's from another one of her songs, "You might as well throw your hand in: You lose!"

Latimore is another one I worked a lot of shows with and got to know really well. I know I already told you that Lat is one of my dearest friends in music and one of my dearest friends in life. I love him from the bottom of my heart, and in fact, I'll admit it: I probably liked him enough to break my rule about not having an affair or anything like that with an entertainer. Oooh, I lusted after that man! But never would I go that route with him, and what I like about Lat is that Lat's so cool. Throw hints, throw hints, but we'd laugh 'em off. He'd throw 'em, but I didn't catch 'em! Just let it roll in this ear and go out again. Very shrewd young man, he was. What I liked about him, though, he didn't beg, he didn't try to pressure you. He just let you know he liked you. If you like him well enough, you come on with it. And I was so glad he was like that. We never did anything more than talk a li'l shit and stay friends. He calls me his sister, and we love each other just that way.

Bobby Rush takes gigs where nobody else could go. He'll go and play with just him and his guitar and his harmonica, do it for all the white folks, because he couldn't go in a black club and get away with that. Not many of us can do equally well with both the black and white audiences, but Bobby can do it, and I think it's great.

I'm so proud of Bobby; I love Bobby so much. But you know, he's full of shit, too, and that's another thing I love about him. He had some legal problems a while back, and he had to spend some time away. And when he got back out here, he told everyone he'd been on tour with Tina Turner. "Yeah, I've been on tour with Tina! Tina was real hot!" I started laughing—don't talk that shit! Because I knew where he had been. But Bobby has always been a comeback man. I don't care what they do to him, he's got a method of comeback.

Bobby's show when he plays for a black audience is not the same as when he plays some of those sit-down gigs for the white folks. Honey, Bobby's raunchy when he's with us! Bobby be turnin' it out with them nasty girls up there. They'll be up there dancing, all the men looking real hard at 'em, and Bobby just say, "You can look, but you can't have nothin' up here on this stage! Your eyes may shine, your teeth may grit, but ain't shit up here you gon' git!"

Some of the younger artists who were just getting started when I signed with Malaco have also become good friends of mine. I think they kind of look up to me as someone with experience who might be able to teach them something. One thing I've always been aware of, which I've always tried to do: There are some artists, good artists, could have been superstars, maybe. But they can't get along with anyone. They have attitudes, they're cocky or arrogant, they don't know how to treat people. And you can't have that, especially in this business. Word gets around, don't nobody want to deal with you. And you know something? They're lonely. They get old, they get lonely because hardly anyone wants to have anything to do with them. They don't have friends. And that's just pitiful.

The entertainers of my generation, most of us, know how to treat people. It's a lot of the younger ones coming up, I don't know why, a lot of them came up under someone who was already established who should have taught them something, taught them how to act, you'd think. But I've seen some of them use people, misuse people, try to take advantage—here's a guy been in the music business fifty years, he's an agent or a promoter, he owns a record label, he owns a nightclub, and some little one-hit singer come up and think he can hustle this guy! Take advantage of him, beat him on a deal or something. And he doesn't think word is going to get around about this?

I remember when Sir Charles Jones started out. He was touring with Marvin Sease first, but then he came out with his own records like *It's Friday* and *Is There Anybody Lonely?*—looked like he was really going somewhere. But when I first saw him, he just turned me away from him, up there telling the audience about how much money he got, and "I want to thank y'all for buying me my Cadillac!" and all this. Oooh! That made me so mad! I didn't want to have anything to do with him. But later on, I sat down with him and told him exactly what I thought, how he needed to treat the people with more respect, be more welcoming, a little more humble, not act like he's some kind of gift to them. And since then he's cooled some of that stuff down, and we've become very good friends. He calls me his godmother, says he's my godson. We're the best of friends now.

Floyd Taylor, Johnnie's son, was another one I knew from the time he got started. I remember I had to pull Floyd's coat, too. When he first came out on the road, he came out there demanding seven to ten thousand dollars a night. Floyd was not easy to get along with. Like I said, Johnnie Taylor used to have a bad attitude, and I think Floyd kind of thought he had to show off like Daddy.

But that's so ugly, when artists act that way. I told Floyd, "You are not Johnnie Taylor, and you ain't gonna get paid like Johnnie Taylor, so you might as well come on in here and do this thing right. Your daddy had a nasty personality. Most of the time everybody talk about it, but they always forgave him because of who he was. I'd hear people say, 'I ain't never going back to Johnnie Taylor's show no more; he did this, he said this, he talked about the women so bad'—and next time you look up, they'd be right back in there."

"But Floyd," I said, "You're not Johnnie. You can't do that. What people like about you is that you sound like your daddy. If you want to get some gigs, and want to get paid, you better start doing Johnnie Taylor's songs. Don't neglect yours, keep on being consistent with yours, come out with the best records you can come out with as yourself, but don't ever think you can walk out there singing without doing your daddy."

He didn't like it; he's talking about how he wants to be different, and "Everybody thinks I want to be just like my dad, but I'm gonna do this, and I'm gonna do that." But after I told him that, he started doing it, and he started getting more work. So he came in one day, he said, "You know, you told me something one time that really made a difference in my life. I've started to sing more of Daddy's songs now." He kept on doing it, and he also had a few little hits of his own, and he kept working until the day he died.

I also got to know Marvin Sease very well. He had kind of a raunchy show like I did, so I liked that. I was just glad to see the audience accept him for what he was, because once he got his full band and everything together, he put on a hell of a show. My husband used to bring Marvin to Jackson before he got famous. He had just put out his first record, before "Candy Licker," and Wolfe used to bring him in. He didn't even have a band then; he was singing to tracks. But even then, he was the best I had ever seen with tracks. His tracks were real music, they weren't synthesized, and it was only his voice out front. So that meant he had to put on a show, or else. I liked him for that. He was the best I'd ever seen out there with the tracks. Then, when he began to have his hits and he could afford to carry a whole band with him, he became one of the biggest artists out here on this circuit, and I loved him dearly.

Preserving the Blues

I need to explain a little more about my feelings about the blues. I always loved blues, but for a long time I didn't want to be a blues singer because everybody talked down on blues so much. Because actually, when you think about John Lee Hooker, Lightnin' Hopkins, and all those guys back in their day, this was blues, right? Well, when I was getting started, young people, young black people, didn't want to be identified with that kind of music. All of it was singing the truth, of course, and about life and the way life is, but what we didn't like about it was that guitar-harmonica thing. We wanted *music* on our albums like everybody else. It wasn't necessarily the words that were bothering us, it was the "do-dang, do-dang, do-dang." Everything sounded the same on those records. No horns, no background, just a singer singing a song, guitars, and harmonicas.

Now I respect these people for what they did, and who they were in their time; they helped create this music. I respect that, but I don't want to hear it today, except to sit around and reminisce. It's just like the dresses women wore in 1911; you couldn't catch me in one now.

I never will forget. Wolfe brought a show to Jackson one time; I think it was at the Fairgrounds. And I guess he was trying to attract a white audience, because he brought in this old guy from Leland, Mississippi, playing some "Dump-da-dump-da-dump" shit on an old guitar. Boy, I stood out there and listened to him, I wouldn't have paid him fifty dollars to do a show for me. But those white folks were out there fallin' out, jumpin', and jammin', just going crazy over him, while all of us black folk were standing around saying, "What the hell is this?"

It kind of stunned me, how that could be. But that's the way it was. I always felt like a lot of white folks still love to see us lookin' like country slave niggers, anyway. We came here as slaves, and "slave" was where they wanted to keep us, okay? So let's be honest. Some of 'em still want to keep us slaves, want us to go out there like some ignorant mutha, don't know nothing, country as we wanna be. But when black folk come out there and start dressing up and looking good, making music that has more to it than "twang-de-twang-de-twang-twang-twang"—oh, no! "That's not really the blues!" Like they can tell us what our own music is supposed to be! But that's how a lot of them think.

I could have gotten up there, too, and become one of them ol' snaggle-toothed, snuff-dippin' women, try to get them white folk to like me, but I ain't studdin' 'em. I'm going to go up there pretty as I can. I'm going up there and if it comes to that, I'm gonna look good enough for them white men to hit on me! Now I don't fall for any of that kind of thing, because that's not what I'm out here for, but I always wanted to be liked for the way I looked and dressed.

Even Bobby Rush. He'll go and sit down with them white folks, playing solo guitar, wearing some overalls and a hat. How much money you think Bobby could make sitting in a club, playing that guitar and that harmonica, for black folk? Black folk want musicians! They don't want no one-man band. They'd walk out on his ass in a minute! He can go to an awards show, and black people sit there and laugh and go along with it, because most of those shows are geared mostly to the white audience anyway. But ain't a black club in town gon' hire his ass doing that.

Now Bobby knows what he's doing. He's keeping his gig, and no matter how he does it, it's always the real Bobby Rush, just a different side of him. He won't bow, and he won't shuffle. And there's nothing wrong with that, either. I don't mind it. I don't mind it because when he does that, we're singing two different kinds of blues. I do not sing Muddy Waters–style blues. I do not sing Koko-style blues. I sing soul-blues my way, half-R&B, half-blues. Maybe I'm just different, but I got to please me. Denise got to have her soul satisfaction. I don't give a darn what anybody else has to say about me. I'm not going out there, singing songs that I don't feel fit my personality, to please anybody.

In fact, I'm the one who coined that phrase "soul-blues." Because at first, when they started calling me a blues singer, blues singers weren't getting a lot of recognition; they were all being put in Koko Taylor's and Muddy Waters's category, and that's not where I was known. *Cashbox* and *Billboard*, where I had always been in the same line with Millie Jackson and Betty Wright and everybody else, now all of a sudden they took my name out of there and put me in the "blues" line, which hardly any black folks even cared about.

Then all the white folks, the blues people, said, "Well, we can't call you that because you don't sing blues!"

"Well, what do I sing?"

"You sing R&B."

"Well, what does 'R' stand for?"

"Rhythm."

"And what does 'B' stand for?"

"Uh . . . blues?"

Used to piss me off.

So I said, "If you're going to name me, I think you should have another category called soul-blues. If the blues people don't want us, and the R&B people don't want us—the Grammy people, people who make those decisions, *Cashbox*, *Billboard*, *Record World*—call us soul-blues, or name us 'new blues' or something." I started sending that out there. And "soul-blues" was the name that stuck.

Everywhere I stood on the stage, I talked about it. I asked people, "Would you do me a favor? I have an application to join a new organization, NAPOB, the National Association for the Preservation of the Blues." And people would come down, I'd sign autographs for them and they would join. We started bombarding all those people with letters. I wrote to NARAS, to all the big radio stations, every program director, the big radio DJs like Frankie Crocker in New York, they all got one of those letters. I started getting a response back, and they began saying, okay, we're gonna give y'all two hours on Saturday, or something like that. It went on from there, and "soul-blues" was what they picked up on.

I have to say, though, I didn't get much support from other entertainers. I remember talking with Z.Z. about it, and he wasn't interested. A lot of them were like that. You'd be surprised. Johnnie Taylor, I know he didn't like to be called a blues singer anyway, but that's not what his problem was. He just didn't want to be a part of my organization. It's kind of like, "If I didn't think of it, it wasn't my idea, and I don't want no part of it." Not only Johnnie; I got that feeling from several of them. So I went ahead, and most of the people I got were regular folks from everywhere, all over the United States, and in foreign countries, too.

I made it my business to keep a regular newsletter going to all the fans, make them aware of where we were playing, what was going on in this world of music. I got letterheads printed up, sent my stuff out looking professional; I had a young lady come to my house and type and do things for me. Then later, she worked out of an office in the back of my wig store. I didn't care if it put me in the hole a little bit; I did what I wanted to do, and I felt real good being president of it. But after a few years, when the blues started being heard so much all over the country, it seemed like people kind of lost interest; I guess they no longer thought NAPOB was necessary. When it got so I'd have to pay totally out of my pocket to do it, I quit.

But even today, people always ask why black folks came to hate that word "blues" so much in the first place. I know why. Because blues represented hard times, being downtrodden. I wrote a poem about it. It's called "America's Prodigal Son." It has the blues telling its own story, how it was born in America, a product of slavery, and then, when they got down on the blues in this country, it went to Europe and became the toast of the European countries. But now, when it comes back home, we're ashamed of it, and it's being kicked around. So for me to come up with those kinds of thoughts about how everybody's walking away, leaving the blues singers sittin' there, trying to say they're nobody, but they're actually the ones who got this stuff started, something just kicked in my head and said, "Write that. You need to tell that story." I always wanted to get James Earl Jones to narrate that poem in that big, deep, beautiful voice of his. It could have been a wonderful thing!

My biggest dream now is to open up a school, Denise LaSalle's Blues Academy, to teach this heritage to our young folk and help them carry it on. I'll tell you all about that in a little while. For the time being, though, I'll just say it the way I said it in the poem:

> Yes, America, I've been in your corner all the way, yet you seek to destroy me . . . but America is my home. I'll always love her. Some of the greatest people I know are Americans. While they may have forgotten that I'm the one that helped them through their hard times, shared their failure and their triumphs, I'll always be grateful to America for making me the great music that I am, and for accepting my children, Jazz, Pop, Rock and Roll, and my Grandchild, Rap.

Only in America could I have been born, nurtured, and flourished as I have.
But until America wakes up and accepts me again and gives me the respect that I
rightfully deserve, I will be a nomad, a prodigal son, immortal and indestructible.
But, whenever you want me, America, I am just a musical note away.

Chapter Twelve
Cry of the Black Soul

Living in America

I've been blessed in so many ways. I honestly believe I have lived, for most of my life, during the best years this country has known. There were problems, of course, serious ones; I already told you about the things I saw and experienced in Mississippi, things that made me realize I could never go back there to live. And a lot of those things are still going on. But during my life there was also hope in the air, optimism, the belief that we could see a better day if we only worked hard to make it happen. And we did believe it. Black folk, and a lot of white folks too, we believed it, and we tried to live and carry ourselves in just that way. So I always say that I lived—and I thank God for this—I lived during the best years that America has ever seen.

I know a lot of people won't believe this, but I've been out here on this road for almost fifty years, and I honestly don't remember but one or two times when I ever had to confront any kind of outright racism or segregation. A lot of others will tell you different, but I'm just talking about what happened to me. One time was when I had done a show in Atlanta, Georgia. I was still married to Bill Jones then, and we were getting ready to go down to Macon to visit his people. I forget exactly where we were staying, but it was a little town outside of Atlanta, kind of like a suburb. I called for a taxi, and when the cab came, I went to get in, and that man took off. I'm holding onto the door handle and he's taking off, fixin' to drag me, and I'm hollering, "Ho! Whoa! What's wrong?!"

He said, "I can't ride you in this cab!"

"Why not?"

"Mister J. W. Harris would kill me if I ride you in this cab!"

And when he said that, I went back into the hotel where we were staying, and the white woman standing behind the counter just said, "Well, Mister J. W. Harris doesn't drive black people in his cab."

I said, "Well, why did you call him when I called downstairs and asked you to call me a cab? Why did you call him? You knew I was black."

She said, "You black people, comin' down here, y'all try to do this and this and that." I just told her, "You won't have to worry about me any more coming here."

So I called somebody I knew, and Bill and I just rode to the airport and rented us a car and drove on down to Macon.

Then in Memphis one time, this must have been in the late '60s or early '70s, when I first started going down to Willie Mitchell cutting records on Bill Coday and them, there was a Holiday Inn downtown. We had tried to get into the Holiday Inn Rivermont, where we usually stayed, but that one was full, so we booked downtown. But when we got over there, they told us they were full.

How you got a full house, and you just gave me reservations when I called you? So I just picked up the phone and called Rivermont and told them that this other Holiday Inn wouldn't let us in, said they were full. The lady said, "They are not full! What I'm gonna do, I'm gonna call down there myself and reserve your room. I'm gonna give you the reservation number and everything."

So I went back over there, and that woman looked at me, "Didn't I tell you we were full?"

"Yes, you told me that. But Holiday Inn Rivermont just gave me this. This is our reservation number."

Oooh, she was hot. She was hot! But she gave me the room.

I wasn't comfortable with it, though. I told Bill, "Next time we run into this kinda shit, I don't wanna stay. 'Cause, you know, these people's so lowdown and dirty, ain't no tellin' what they'd do. Might send somebody up there to the room and do something to you. I ain't studdin' 'em."

So I didn't try to stay down there any more until things got better. By the time I moved to Memphis, though, I didn't have any problems. No use of me lying; I never ran into any problems at all. In fact, believe it or not, during that time, the white people treated you better than the blacks. Because they didn't want it said they were prejudiced. They would go out of their way to please you and do what you wanted. I'm not lying on them; believe me, I wouldn't have a good word to say about 'em if they were still evil and mean like they had been. But by that time, around 1974 or 1975, they would go out of their way to be nice to you, because they didn't want to have it said they were prejudiced. They might not have felt it inside; inside, they might've been hating your guts, but they didn't show it.

I know I told you about some of the problems Wolfe ran into later, trying to acquire his radio stations, and then we had that episode with the Summer Place Park. But I'm talking about just dealing with everyday folks, and for that, I can truly say I encountered very few problems. Very, very few.

I look around me now, and where the troubles have gone to, and it breaks my heart. There was a period in this country when twenty-five people wouldn't get shot on weekends, especially black folk. When I first moved to Memphis, I wasn't scared staying in my apartment by myself. But before I married Wolfe and left there, I had gotten so I bolted every door, locked every lock. I'd gotten scared of Memphis.

Now you got more young black men in jail for smoking pot—*pot!*—than you have murderers. And that's what hurts. Here's somebody over here who killed somebody. They give him a little time, and he's walkin'. Now here's a guy, nothing but some marijuana on him, and they put him in jail. Everybody's smoking reefer, white, black, green, and gray, but they can't stand to see a black guy with some of it. You smokin'? You black? You goin' to jail, Jack.

It's the same way with the harder drugs, heroin and cocaine. We all know more white folks are doing that stuff than anyone else, but who's doing the time? And where did that shit come from, and who's bringing it into our communities in the first place? That, and all the guns? I can remember when I didn't even know about any kind of drug but pot, and all the people I knew didn't know about anything but pot. But all of a sudden, here comes heroin. Heroin was the shock of the century, when black folk heard about heroin. You had some people jumped out there trying to do it but they saw right away that it's nothing but committing suicide, so they left it alone. A lot of people I know just moved away from that. But too many of 'em didn't. Heroin was deadly; it was a deadly thing. And then when this crack came out, when they started with this crack cocaine, people went for that because it was cheap. They had a lot of folks on crack.

I told an interviewer one time, I said, "I hurt for my people." That's just the way it is when I look around at my community and see what's going on. I wrote a poem called "Cry of the Black Soul"; Wolfe recorded a rap version of it. He put it to kind of a reggae beat and renamed it "40 Acres and a Mule." I honestly don't think it turned out too good; I want to get those words to a real rapper who can get it out there and get the kids to listen to it, because I think it's one of the most important messages I've ever expressed. It's talking about history, *our* history, after everything we've come through, all those years they tried to beat us down and break us, but they couldn't do it. And now that we begin to move up just a little bit, they have us killing our own selves. Send this drug to the ghetto! You don't even have to give 'em no hangin' rope. He'll hang himself!

I don't see any way to stop it unless black people take it upon themselves, and stop it ourselves. We can't keep looking somewhere else, to white folks or anyone, to do it for us. A few years ago, Wolfe came up with an idea that led to what we were going to call the Unity Project. To help launch it, I released an EP by that name on Ordena in 2015. I wrote an inspirational song, "Unity (Back in Community)," which I sang, and my son Ray, using his rapper's handle R-KI, did a rap version of it. It all came about because things were happening around here in Jackson that were very disturbing. The kids had gotten just out of line in the city, everybody trying to kill each other, trying to hurt each other. Every time you look around, seemed like there were more disgraceful things going on. My husband started saying, "What we need is to put unity back in this community. Denise, why don't you write a song on unity?" He sat down and put things that he wanted to say in the song down, and I went ahead and put it all together, and that's how we came up with that song.

We had big plans for the Unity Project. We were going to conduct educational programs and workshops in the high crime areas around Jackson and West Tennessee; we were going to call this the Unity Tour. We'd go from neighborhood to neighborhood, sponsoring family festivals and other events to get people out of their houses, bring them together for a common cause, try to bring some trust and cooperation back where it used to be strong and was so lacking now.

Well, it's difficult to get that kind of thing going, and it wasn't much later that I began to have some pretty serious health problems, so that slowed us down. And, I hate to say it like this, but my husband has a lot of good ideas, but he tends to drop a thing and move on to the next one if it doesn't pan out right away. A lot of good projects have been started, but they just end up on the shelf undone. So the Unity Project kind of got put on hold like that, and that's where it stands now.

But there's another way I want to reach out to our young people, and it's even closer to my heart than the Unity Project. I believe the best way I can do it is through music, this music that's given me so much and that I love so much. That's what I want to do now, more than anything else.

That's Why I Call It *Our* Blues

I believe you have to have a willing mind, a strong mind, to be what you want to be in life, instead of what someone else wants to make you into. I believe if we do the best we can, somebody will make it through. You're always going to have some failures out here; there's always somebody who's not going to adhere to the good part of who they are, or who they can be. There are some believers, there are some doubters. The ones who want to be somebody will struggle to be somebody, and the ones that don't give a darn, they won't. That's the way it is. Those who care will struggle; these are people who really want to see change.

And then, too, some people who have made it don't care about paying back, passing it on to others. They're doing all right themselves, so they'll say, "Hey, I ain't gonna worry about it; I'm doing fine." Or someone like my father. He didn't know any better, so he thought he was "doing all right," even though he was just about as poor as you could imagine. But that's all a lot of people knew in those days, so I had to go against his wishes to encourage my brother to stay in school, go to college, and graduate. Only thing I ever disagreed with my daddy on. But there are some people still like that today. All they know is what they see around them, and they don't try to think about doing what it takes to make something better for themselves.

I believe our young people need to hear this message, now more than ever. And I believe the message of the blues is one of the best ways to bring it to them. Now, I like rap, too. I can appreciate it. It just depends on what it is. It's got to be about something. I don't like anything when you're writing about nothing, and you're just out there making a lot of noise and saying something that doesn't mean anything to anybody. I don't like anything that denigrates people. I like to talk about real things, the natural goings-on between a man and a woman. We have our ups and downs; we fight about things, we have our differences about sex, we have our differences about everything. But I believe in writing about what's real, and I don't believe in writing and singing things that will make people feel bad about themselves, or make them feel they can't be anything but disrespectful and low-down.

My dream now is to establish a music school, the Denise LaSalle Blues Academy, for young people to learn about the music and its heritage. It's *our* music, it's *our* heritage, and that's what we want to talk about, that's what we want to teach, keep this music in our community, keep our kids focused, see if we can make it better. You see, a lot of kids don't know music because their mom and dad can't afford to give it to them. They can't get instruments, they can't get lessons. It wasn't always like that. Even in Belzoni when I was young, my parents managed to get me some piano lessons from Miss Sharpe, and they even helped me get a little old piano to practice on. Today, a lot of kids don't have that opportunity.

I want to get instruments donated and be able to hire music teachers and educators, teach the kids to make music on real instruments, not just computers and synthesizers. That's so important. When people ask me what advice I have for young artists just starting out, I say, "Learn music!" I've been saying this for years. Stop going to a machine, letting the machine make all the sounds. Learn how to play instruments. There's a keyboard, learn how to play it. Guitar, bass, learn how to play it. All the horns, learn how to play them. My reason for that is simple, and it also goes deep: We don't know what tomorrow is going to bring. We don't have any guarantee that electricity will be available in this world much longer. Some fool drop a bomb or something, cut all the electricity off in this country, all the terrible things people are doing to the Earth, we have no idea what the future is going to look like. But if it happens, how long do you think it'll be before we get our electricity back? And meanwhile, who's going to play the music? What are they going to use? So sure, use the electronic things since they're here, but learn to play without them. Because you never know.

And then, if we can get these kids into music, say, "I know what I can do!," we let them know that music is something they can succeed at. And by learning about the blues, and where the blues came from, these kids will learn where *they* came from. Right now a lot of them just think, like I said before, the blues is all about being sad and downtrodden and all that. They've been taught to think that way, but it's not true. By teaching these kids the blues, and by teaching them the history of the blues, we're teaching them the history of their own people. We come from strong people, and that's what this music is all about. So no matter what kind of music they know, every recital that I have, they're going to have to play a blues song or a gospel song. Those are the only two musics that will be allowed to be played there. Anybody else wants to go with the rock & roll and the hip-hop and everything, fine. Do your thing! When you leave my school, you can do whatever you want. But when you're in my school, you're going to learn to play blues and gospel. I'm doing it my way, and that's the way it's going to be.

You see, if we don't work to hold on to what's ours, we're going to lose it. A lot of times you'll hear, "Oh, white folks tryin' to steal our blues. White folks stealin' our blues!" And I see what they mean. All these big blues organizations, the awards ceremonies and all that, who gets the awards? Who gets the recognition? All these black blues singers out here, been struggling and going on for years, and they get kicked to the side. Now, don't get me wrong. I don't have anything against the white artists getting something if they're playing the blues the right way; they deserve something. A lot of the white blues singers are my friends. Janiva Magness has done a couple of my songs; I haven't talked to her in a while, but when I go to the conventions and things like that, we always mingle, get together, and we talk. And Bonnie Raitt, that's one of my good girls, too. Go to a meeting or an awards ceremony, she makes her way to me; I don't have to go to her. She has a lot of respect for the artists who came before her, and she really tries to honor them any way she can.

So, of course, give these artists what they deserve. But don't just do it because they're white, especially when you have these other black artists out here still being overlooked. I don't think that's cool at all. A lot of my people don't even go to those awards things anymore because everything always goes to all these white people, and they feel really hurt. Here are these black artists who've been giving you, all their lives, music, music, music; and now comes Johnny-Come-Lately out of nowhere, gets the award, runs off. Of course we think that's wrong, and we think it's racial. Or someone finds some old cotton-patch blues singer, hasn't had a hit record in fifty years, ain't no black folk even know who he is anymore, and they give him some kind of "Lifetime Achievement" award or something, after everything he did when he was really putting it out there got taken from him or ignored.

But it's like I said about the problems in our community. We have to take our own responsibility, too. Sometimes I hear that stuff about "white folks stealin' our blues," and I have to say, "Why would you say they're stealing it? You gave it away! You don't want it, you didn't want to have nothing to do with it. We turned our backs on our own music." I tell 'em in a minute: "You talkin' 'bout white folks stealing the blues? White folks ain't stole nothin'! You gave it to 'em!"

Now I know that may sound harsh, but why aren't more black folks on the boards of these organizations, where they could keep the score even? Why don't you join something and try to live for it and make it be something? No, too many of you just walk around and want to be "Mr. It," want to sing, want to make the music, but nobody wants to be on the board to help govern things. So if you don't do it, don't knock the other people because they're doing it. White folks are just like anyone else; they're going to vote for who they know. I can't blame them for that.

So if we want to keep the music, we'd better act like it, because it's sure gonna be gone. It's our music; we ought to be the first ones to be trying to work with it. That's what I like about Charles Mitchell. He's got that Jus' Blues Music Foundation down in Atlanta; they have a convention every year where they present awards, and they have shows where they feature artists in all different styles of blues. They also do educational programs. They're just about the only black-owned and black-run blues organization in the country doing that kind of thing. Charles may not be rich, he may not have a lot of money, he may not be able to do everything he wants to, but at least he's trying to do it from a black man's perspective instead of just sitting there, poor-mouthin', saying, "Ain't nothin' we can do, I'll just let the white folks do it." So I like Charles, I admire him, and I'll do anything I can to support him, even it's not that much I can really do.

You see, I believe if it's done right, there will always be black folk who'll love the blues and want to hear it, because it speaks to us in our own language. Not just the historical things I've been talking about, but the way we talk today, our everyday conversation and ways of saying things. Because we love life stories. We like bullshittin', and we like to tell it like it is. We don't like any "you got to sweet-talk it and make it sound so perfect," because we're not that kind of people. We believe in calling a spade a spade. And you ain't got to be using all this "proper" language; we like colloquial language for our songs. Just like we talk, just like the way I'm talkin' now. And we also don't mind a little dirt and a little smut, 'cause it tells it like it is. This is the way our lives are, you know?

Somebody piss me off, I'm not gonna try to say, "Well, that lady did this, that lady did that—" No, that *bitch* did that to me! You see what I'm saying? I'm not talkin' 'bout that "lady!" What kind of a lady are you, treatin' me like this? You're a *bitch*, that's what you are! And that's the way we like our songs done. We like our songs done like we feel. And if you're a motherfucker, we'll call you that. That's the way I feel, and that's why I feel I'll always have an audience. And if I done got too old, then somebody else doing the same thing I'm doing gonna come along and have that audience. Long as they keep that motivation that I had, they'll do it.

So that's why I want to get this Blues Academy going. Get these kids off the street, get them learning something. Get them to see that the blues is their music. Get them to *claim* the blues as their music. Get them to see the blues is something they can be proud of. And then, if they can be proud of their music, they can be proud of themselves.

Cry of the Black Soul

All of my life I've been stuck in this crack
If you're white you're right; if you're Black get back
Although your face may be White of shade
One drop of Black blood and they call you spade

An innocent victim brought to this place
Torn from my country and my race
I was King, I was Queen, way back then
Now never to know what I might have been

Lashes on my back, sweat on my face
Dehumanized, to the point of disgrace
Slaving and toiling to clear a land
Only to be treated as less than a man

But then one day the South lost the battle
The smoke had cleared, the dust had settled
Give 'em forty acres, give 'em a mule
Let the Niggar go, you're free, you fool

You got you mule, you got your land
But stay right here, we'll give you a hand
Just make an x on the dotted line
You just sold out, the mule and land is mine

So freedom was not yet realized
Still victimized by the White man's lies
No forty acres, no mule in sight
Filled with anger and the will to fight

Robbed of my heritage and pushed to the side
Stripped of my honors but never my pride
Yeah sir, no sir, smile and fake it
Knowing someway, somehow I'd make it

Civil rights and equal opportunity
Maybe for some, but not for me
The jobs for which I'm often denied
Passed down to men less qualified

Today America's a different place
And Jim Crow now has a different face
Lynch mobs are still in hot pursuit
Dressed up as men in business suits

No hoods, no ropes, no hanging tree
Let the Niggar think we set him free
Put a gun in his hand and fill him with dope
He'll kill himself; we don't need no rope

I fought wars by your side, to save your ass
Yet you thumb your nose, call me second class
There's no denying, I fought my way out of hell
Did pretty good, with a nickel and a nail

Like Harriet Tubman, Nat Turner and all
Martin and Malcolm all heeded the call
Willing to die for what they knew was right
To win the battle if they did lose the fight

There are those who stood and never bowed
Leaving a legacy of which to be proud
Kinky hair, broad nose, thick lips and black skin
A moral victory I just had to win

I've got my place in the history books
Through Banneker, Douglass and Gwendolyn Brooks
Rosa Parks, Oprah, and Colin Powell
Have all laid milestones of which to be proud

Now if I had my forty acres and my mule
Considering the years that I've been abused
Multiply the interest and then compare
I'll bet you I, too, would be a millionaire

But I wouldn't change one single hair on my head
My nose, my skin, I'd rather be dead
I'm black and I'm proud, and I don't give a damn
As long as you respect me for who I am

Chapter Thirteen
Still the Queen

Smokin'—and Moving On Again

My last album for Malaco was *Smokin' in Bed*, in 1997. Like I said before, I mostly enjoyed my time there. But there were a few things we didn't see eye-to-eye on. I already told you about the argument I'd had with them about the production and the mix on some of my songs. And then with *Smokin' in Bed*, even though I liked the way it came out, I didn't really appreciate how they promoted and marketed it. I had some songs on there, like "Never Been Touched Like This" and "If I Don't Holler," that I thought could have been really big with the younger listeners. After I recorded those songs, my husband started playing them on KIX 96 in Jackson, and I'm telling you, people were calling in from all over, asking where they could buy those records. The album wasn't even in the stores yet; I ran down to Jackson, Mississippi, picked up some copies at Malaco, brought them back, and we sold them right there at the station. We must have sold at least a thousand before the record stores even had any.

But even after that, Malaco didn't want to put any of those songs out as singles. The last real hit I'd had with them was "My Tu-Tu," and that was an all-ages smash. But they weren't promoting me into that market. It felt to me like they didn't have confidence in me, that they didn't believe any of the songs on that album were strong enough to stand alone. But I knew that wasn't true.

I must say, though, in terms of the money, I felt that Malaco dealt with me fairly. They're pretty honest, as far as I'm concerned. I've always gotten a royalty statement from them, and I never felt like I got shafted. So I could recommend them, tell people I've been fairly dealt with over there. Even so, though, after *Smokin' in Bed*, I felt that it was time for me to go. I wrote them a letter, told them I wasn't going to renew my contract, that I was going on my way. And they wished me well.

By the way: You know that bed I'm reclining on, on the cover of *Smokin' in Bed*? That's my real bed, in the bedroom of my house in Jackson. I bought a furniture set with that design, and I liked it so much I decided to use it for the cover of that album. Friends of mine come by, they look in my bedroom, their eyes get wide. "Oooh, I've seen somethin' famous now!" Some people even tell me that's their favorite of all my album covers.

When I left Malaco, though, I also had another reason, an even bigger one, that had nothing to do with the company. *Smokin' in Bed* was a hot album, even if they never put out any singles from it, but then, right around that time, my husband suddenly decided he'd been called to preach. He told me he'd been called to the ministry, and he wanted me to cut a gospel album and go with him on his walk with God.

"God's Got My Back"

I always loved spirituals and gospel music; I sang in the gospel group in Chicago, and I had always sung in church. But since I turned professional, I never thought of myself as a gospel singer. I had sung background in the gospel group; I could do the tenor voice, but I never wanted to lead. I knew I didn't have that kind of spectacular voice like Shirley Caesar or Aretha or someone like that. So I'd never seriously considered making gospel my career. But I also knew that the kind of blues singer I was, I would hurt my husband's career if he became a minister. And so I decided to change for him.

I won't say it was easy. Wolfe and I had some conversations about it, and I remember I told him how I was feeling. What bothered me so bad, I told him, he marries me and I'm me, and now he wants to change me to be something else? That bothered me terribly. It got so I didn't even feel right about doing my shows anymore. It took all the feeling out of it, him contradicting me, talking about me, saying, "You're embarrassing me!" and things like that. I was just being honest, telling him how I really felt.

"You say you've been called to preach," I told him. "Well, I ain't been called for nothin'! I'm just doing this to help you, to support you in this. So I'll write me a gospel album, and I'll record it, and we'll try to do this thing together."

Don't misunderstand me. I'm a Christian woman, and when I sing gospel, I'm singing what I truly mean and truly believe. But I always felt comfortable singing the blues, too. Like I've told many people, that's how I make my living; it's not how I serve God. It's like if I was picking cotton out in the field somewhere. That's not serving God; it's how I make my living. I didn't think I necessarily had to change what I did for a living to serve God.

But I didn't want to embarrass my husband, so I was going to go gospel to give him my support. And when I made the album *God's Got My Back* in 1999, I found it was as easy as choosing and writing songs for the blues. When you know what you want said, you just think of how you want to say it. As a writer, you create a reality in words. You're writing about life, the life you see going on around you. You write what you know and what you see.

Like the gospel version of "Goin' through Changes." That came to me as I was coming out of Arkansas, between Little Rock and Memphis. There had been something on the news, some child had gone to school with his daddy's gun, went in there and shot up a teacher or something like that. And I said, "That hurts me to my heart, to see things going like this. God is going to destroy this world, ain't gonna be too much longer, if people don't change. God is tired of going through changes with us." And that's what made me write that song.

"God Don't Make Mistakes" was given to me by my sister-in-law Kay Wolfe. They had a family gospel group in Marianna, Arkansas, back when Kay and them were children, and their mother always had a dream of recording a gospel record. When their father was dying, their mother wrote that song for him. She died about three months after that, so she never got to record it, but when I made *God's Got My Back*, I put it on there to honor her.

So I made my announcement that I was retiring from the R&B field, and I was going to cut gospel from there on. But then my husband didn't follow through with what he said he was going to do. He didn't get a church he was trying to get; he wanted to purchase this church building and start his own church but he didn't get it, so he just went back to radio and started doing whatever else he wanted. He'd still preach; he'd wait for somebody to call, somebody might call and say, "Mr. Wolfe, would you come and speak in our church?" But then he'd go to our own church and wouldn't even get in the pulpit with the other preachers.

And meanwhile, I couldn't get any gigs. I had turned my thumbs down on the blues, so they weren't trying to book me, saying, "She's gone gospel." But then I found the gospel people wouldn't book me either, because I was the woman that gets up on stage and talks all that mess; they're afraid I might cuss or something. So I'm sittin' here starving to death! So after a year, sitting up waiting on him—"Come on! Let's go to work on this gospel thing!"—well, he wasn't going anywhere with it, and if he's not going to do anything to enhance himself, then why should I be stuck out here? I can't live like this. I got to have some work. So when that turned out the way it did, I told him I'm goin' back singing the blues.

It took a minute, but word got around that I was doing it again, and I began getting bookings. I still included the song "God's Got My Back" in my shows, too. I wrote that song from the heart. I've been blessed, I know I have, it's something I wanted to say, and the blues people always appreciate it when I do it. I know a lot of other people, some church people, really don't like it when a singer goes back and forth like that. But I don't care how I be criticized. I ain't studdin' 'em.

And you know something? Only black people do that. Willie Nelson, all those country singers, Patsy Cline, Naomi and Wynonna Judd, Hank Williams, even Elvis. You name 'em. All of them had gospel records, and they all did gospel songs in their shows, too. Nobody said it was wrong for them, so why is it wrong for me? So if that's the way you feel about it, that's you. This is the way I feel about it. And I'm going to do it my way or no way. That's what got me all those whuppins from my mama, remember? I'm not gonna fall into your trap, tellin' me what I can and cannot do. I've got the Holy Bible for my instructions, and I can go as far into that Bible as anyone, as far as I can go with it. So for these other people, I don't care what they say. I'm not trying to please them. They can love me or leave me. 'Cause ain't none of 'em givin' me nothing.

I'd wait until the end of my show, and I would do a little talk about it: "One thing that I always know, I've been through a lot. I've been here for many years, been through a lot of trouble and pain, a lot of 'em dead and gone on that started after I did. It's not because I'm such a great singer that I'm still here. It's because God's got my back."

And then I'd sing the song, and that was my testimony.

This Real Woman Rides Again

I had made up my mind that I wasn't going back to Malaco. I didn't know where I was going, but I decided that before I went to anybody, I was going to cut a record on my own, in the style I wanted. See, I still had a problem with everybody trying to make me be what they wanted me to be. So in 2000, I cut my double album, *This Real Woman*, and put it on my own Ordena label. We recorded in two different studios in Memphis: Sounds Unreel on Nelson Avenue, and Royal on Lauderdale. It was my first time back with Willie Mitchell since I'd been on Westbound, and I must say it was wonderful to see him and work with him again.

Not that he was actually doing much work at that point, though. I picked my own musicians, and William Brown was the engineer, the same engineer I'd used over at Ardent during my time at ABC/MCA. He came down and did *Smokin' in Bed* at Malaco, too. But Willie, he was a Libra; he was always there! He just didn't do much; just sat back and let William Brown do all the work. Sometimes it might get to sounding good and he'd come in there, "Hey! Do that thing! Do that thing!" Come in and put two cents in, you know, but mostly he just sat back, drinking whatever he was drinking, calling himself running the studio while everyone else took care of whatever had to be done.

I dug back into some of my history for *This Real Woman*. I put the original version of "Trapped" on there, and I also remade "A Love Reputation," gave it a whole new sound with that great band I'd put together, with Michael Toles on guitar, Lester Snell on keyboards, Al Wilder on bass, James Robertson on drums. Lester did the horn arrangements, too. I mean to tell you, that band was cookin'!

One funny thing about *This Real Woman*: My best-known song from that album I don't even sing anymore. That ol' big-foot man from Alabama, Poonanny, he was kind of a joker, a comedian-type entertainer, and he was the one who told me, "Gotta lick it 'fore you stick it!" Yeah, Poonanny with his nasty self. And I went ahead and wrote it.

But then I found the audience didn't like it. I could feel it. I told you, I pay attention to my audience; I can tell what they're feeling. Back in those days, white folks accepted the idea of oral sex; you could tell. They accepted it. But a black man would say, "Uhh, uhh! Yecch! Hell no! I ain't stickin' my head down there!" He wouldn't admit to even doing stuff like that. I mean, this is what you heard all the time. So when I sang that, I'd see people in the audience rolling their eyes, looking disgusted, touching each other across the table and not look back up. I actually saw people get up and walk out!

So I learned not to sing that. By the time I did "Snap, Crackle and Pop" on Ecko in 2004, everyone was singing shit like that, so my song fit perfectly by then. But just a few years earlier, when I tried to do "Lick It" in my shows, I found out I couldn't get away with it. A man like Marvin Sease, with "Candy Licker," he was singing to the women, and they loved it. But didn't no man want some woman up there tellin' him to do that mess. So I just said I'm not singing it no more. And I quit.

It's funny, too. Another one on *This Real Woman* was kind of about oral sex, I guess you could say, even though I never mentioned it in the song. I'm talking about "Down on Clinton." Boy, they gave Bill Clinton such a hard time about that little piece of stuff he got from that white girl! They just gave him such a hard time, and I was saying, "Why are these people down on Clinton so? All of 'em done had some! I don't give a damn which one of them grown-ass motherfuckers out there, they done got some pussy from somebody!" And that's how I started talking. I said, "Leave that man alone. So he got him a little piece! So what?"

> Ain't no need of gettin' down on Clinton
> Every man got a little devil in him
> Some like to drink, some like drugs—
> But everybody likes to get a little bit of love!

We gave it kind of a Zydeco/country feel, and it got played some on the radio; you got some radio stations won't play something because they're afraid of the controversy, then you got some radio stations that don't care. That's the way that record got played. And when it did get played, it got bought.

"If I'm Only for Myself"—A Summons from Bob Dylan

I got a call one day from Malaco Records, and Malaco said Bob Dylan was trying to get in touch with me.

"Who in the hell is Bob Dylan?" The name was familiar, but I couldn't think who Bob Dylan was. So they told me, and I asked them what he wanted with me. They said he wanted to talk to me, wanted me to write a song for him or collaborate on a song, told me, "He said he wants to call you."

I said, "Give him my number."

So they gave him my number, and his manager called and put Bob Dylan himself on the phone. We started talking, and he kept telling me how much he admired my writing. I mean, he could name every record I'd ever cut, so I knew I had a man here that kept up with my career. He knew more about me than I did! He'd be telling me stuff that I'd even forgotten I'd done. And I'm just sitting here with my mouth hanging open.

He was a famous songwriter, I knew that, but said he wanted my writing. He wanted me to write a song called "If I'm Only for Myself, Who's Going to Be for Me?" I said, "Okay, "I'll write it." He gave me an address and everything, said, "I want you to write this for me."

So I did my little research, bought a couple of his records. And when I heard that voice of his—Horrible! He ain't got no voice! Remember when all those folks got on TV and did "We Are the World"? They had forty people up there singing, and he had the worst voice on there. But that voice, that's what made him. So when I wrote that song, I wrote it just like I felt Bob Dylan would do it. I sat down and listened to the way he sang, the way he phrased his songs, and I said I know I can't do it just like him, but I can do just enough for the people to know this is Bob Dylan's style. And on the end of it, when I sang, "Who's gonna be for me-e-e-e-e," that was just like he would to it. He would do that song just like that.

So I wrote it, sent him a demo, but by the time it got there, Bob had gone to Europe. I didn't hear anything from him, and it came back.

He called me again, said, "Where's my song?"

I said, "I sent it to you, the address you gave me. It came back in the mail."

He said he had moved. "Well, I'm gonna give you this address. Send it to this address."

I sent it to him; it came back again, "Addressee Unknown."

Well, by that time I'd asked some people about him, and they were telling me he was kind of eccentric, so I was beginning to wonder what was going on. Then something really strange happened. I did an interview with the *Jackson Sun*, where I told them I was writing this song for Bob Dylan. Somehow he found out about that and he called me up, acting like he's mad at me. Said, why did I have to tell somebody that I was writing a song for him? Like he was so furious about me telling the world that I wrote the song.

I said, "Well, why not? What difference does it make, unless you wanted to take the song for yourself? Why shouldn't I have said I wrote it for you? I was proud that you asked."

You know, I thought that was something to be proud of. I'm writing a song for the great rock star Bob Dylan! Giving him nothing but praises and stuff. And now he gon' call me up, mad! Well, when he did that, I was through with him. I honestly believe, to this day, that Bob Dylan wanted to steal my song. He didn't want it known that I wrote that song, and the world knows I wrote it now, so now he can't steal it. Call me and ask me to write you a song, and I write the song, and now you get mad 'cause I tell the newspaper? I'll say that 'til I die. He wanted to steal my song.

So I ended up putting it on *This Real Woman*, and at the beginning of the song, I told the story:

A few years ago, the great rock star Bob Dylan called me and gave me this title, and asked me to write this song for him. Well, I wrote this song especially for you, Bob, but when I mailed it to you, it came back to me "Addressee Unknown." Well, this is the only way I know how to get this song to you. And I hope you like it, Bob.

Well, he eventually came to Jackson to play at the Jackson Coliseum; they call it the Oman Arena now. Wolfe and I went down there, and they sent word to him, Denise LaSalle is here to see you, and he went off: "Send her back! Send her back! Come on back!"

We went back, and we talked to him. He acted like he was so glad to see me, and he talked so nice and long, talking about how much he's admired me through the years, and how he loves all my songs and what I write, and blah-blah-blah-blah-blah-blah. He's very cordial, very nice person.

I wanted to know why the records came back; he said, "I had moved on to another place, and they sent 'em back."

And I said, "Well, I lost contact with you. So I just cut the song myself."

He never mentioned about me writing any more songs for him or anything like that, and I'm sure he must have heard the version of "If I'm Only for Myself" I did on *This Real Woman*, so I just went on about my business and didn't let it bother me anymore.

"Kickin' Ass and Takin' Names!"

This Real Woman did pretty good for me, but I was still thinking about trying to get back on a label, and that's when Ecko Records called. It wasn't John Ward, the owner, who called; it was Larry Chambers. He does the market- ing and promotion for them, and he's an old hand in the record business, has connections and knowledge going back years. By this time, in the early 2000s, Ecko was an up-and-coming label in this music, which now all of a sudden everyone was calling "southern soul."

I didn't like that "southern soul" when I first heard it, and I still don't. Far as I'm concerned, southern soul is nothing but rhythm and blues, the same rhythm and blues we did yesterday. You see, a lot of artists and a lot of labels, they still don't want to be kept in that "blues" category. Even at Malaco, they say they can't sell anything with that name "blues" on it, unless maybe it's Bobby "Blue" Bland, and he's not even alive anymore. "Soul-blues" worked for me; some other singers, like Willie Clayton, sometimes he'll go by that, too. But now, what they're doing, they're sending this "southern soul" thing out there to young minds that aren't solid in the music, creating a new category for these young artists they're trying to market.

They saw these younger singers couldn't get the prestige the older ones in this business were getting. We were the big R&B singers, so they had to jump up and make up a whole new category so they could get a leg in. But all they're doing is the same music we've been doing all these years, singing the same lyrics, copying their music off us, maybe make it sound a little different with the synthesizers and the beats and all that stuff, but it's still basically the same music, but now they're going to name it something and say, "That's it! That's southern soul! That's new! That's big!" Shit! Ain't nothing but the same thing. Don't tell me I'm singing "southern soul." I'm singing R&B like I always sang. You're not gonna push this "southern soul" off on me.

But anyway, Ecko got in touch with me. When I first met John Ward, he didn't even have a studio; he was doing everything out of his house in Memphis. I was kind of shocked by that, but I knew he'd had some success with his label by then; he'd had a hit on Ollie Nightingale, "I'll Drink Your Bath Water, Baby," back in the '90s; Bill Coday had done a few things for him, he had people like Barbara Carr and Sheba Potts-Wright, who used to be one of my backup singers, so I wasn't too worried. John moved into his studio on North Hollywood not long after I met him. But I recorded *Still the Queen*, my first Ecko CD, back at Royal Studios, where I still felt at home. It included four tracks I'd originally used on *This Real Woman*, but all the rest were new. My other Ecko CDs I recorded at John's studio on Hollywood.

I wrote the song "I'm Still the Queen" because everybody was trying to take that title from me. All these young girls coming up were saying, "I'm Queen of the Blues now, now that Denise LaSalle's gone." So I wrote a song, put it to a funky beat, and delivered a message straight to 'em:

All of you soul-blues mamas that thought the Queen was gone
Well, I'm back—check me out, y'all—sittin' high on my throne.
Girls, when I was away, you might've got a little bit of fame,
But look out! The Queen is back—kickin' ass and takin' names!

I'd also decided I was going to keep recording my inspirational numbers and gospel songs. "God Is Absolutely Mad About You" was on *God's Got My Back*, and I put it on *This Real Woman*, too; on *Still the Queen*, I had a newer song, one I'd written after the 9/11 terrorist attacks and released as a single, called "There's No Separation."

A lot of people misunderstood that song. That song doesn't mean anything like, "Your religion is wrong and mine is right," or "I'm gonna take you to jail 'cause you're a Baptist, I'm gonna take you to jail 'cause you're a Methodist, 'cause you're Catholic," or anything like that. You're not supposed to prosecute anybody. I wrote that song when 9/11 happened, when they took down those buildings, and everybody, I don't care who they were, if they had any say-so, on TV, radio, or anything, what were they saying? They're telling everybody to pray. Even President Bush was on television, asking America to join him in prayer for the victims and their families. And I said, "Oh, so now it's okay to pray? All of a sudden, after they took prayer out of our schools and everything, now all of a sudden it's okay to pray again!"

And that's what I was thinking about when I wrote that song. See, they took prayer out of school, which I think is wrong as two left shoes. Ever since we've been going to school, at the beginning of every school day everybody had a prayer. They'd play the National Anthem, and they would pray. And we still need that; we need it now more than ever. We need prayer, our country needs prayer, our children need prayer. Don't take prayer out of my school. Don't tell me we can't pray in school. Let my children pray! That's what that song was about.

I was my own producer at Ecko, just like I'd been all along. When I was there, Ecko still had a real rhythm section, but I could pick my own musicians if I wanted to. I used Michael Toles on guitar, or maybe Kenny Ray or Bobby Manuel; Lester Snell played keyboards sometimes, and he also did some of the horn arrangements. Sometimes I'd use Jay Jackson on keys, or maybe Gary Wolfe, my brother-in-law, who's also my keyboardist in Blak Ice, the band I have now. I had Al Wilder on bass, and my drummer was Willie Hall; if he wasn't there, I'd use James Robertson. John Ward is a good musician, too; he's a guitar player, and he played guitar on some of my songs. John, or maybe Jay, might go back to the keyboard later and add some strings and maybe a few more horn lines, but I kept everything as real as possible. And people could tell, too; that's what everybody said about my music. They said, "You're the only one at Ecko sounds different." They liked that "live" sound.

A lot of the songs I recorded at Ecko became really popular with my fans. I always begin my shows with "I'm Still the Queen." You might say that's my anthem now, and when I get to the part where I call out "What's my name?" the audience shouts back "Denise LaSalle!" and sings "Still the Queen!" right along with me. In "Snap, Crackle, and Pop," I went back to what I was saying in "Lick It Before You Stick It" and updated it for a new time. Like I said, back when I did "Lick It," folks weren't ready to hear that kind of thing from a woman. But by 2004, when I put "Snap, Crackle and Pop" on *Wanted*, my second Ecko CD, there were all kinds of songs like that out there, and everyone was ready to hear what the Queen had to say.

I had a lot of fun calling out my friends like Bobby Rush, Marvin Sease, Clarence Carter, and Theodis Ealey in "Snap, Crackle and Pop." All the extra stuff I do on it now, that's just things I came up with on stage. Something will come to me while I'm doing a song, and I'll try it, and when it works, I keep it. When I started doing those sound effects, talking about what a satisfied coochie sounds like when it goes snap, crackle, and pop, people would fall out laughing. Do it again, they fall out laughing again. Do it again, they laugh. So I said, "Hey! This works!" So I went into it, and into it, and into it, and I ended up with the whole thing.

I have to give John Ward and them credit for "Mississippi Woman." That song was originally called "Mississippi Boy," and it was written by Floyd Hamberlin Jr., a songwriter and producer from Chicago. A singer named Will T. recorded it, and then Charles Wilson picked up on it and did a version. The folks at Ecko heard it and thought it would be a good song for me. I changed the words around a little, we put it on *Pay Before You Pump* in 2007, and people began to associate it with me. A lot of them, in fact, actually think I wrote it.

I left Ecko after I did *Pay Before You Pump*. It wasn't any kind of big falling-out or anything; John and I are still friends, and I've been friends with Larry Chambers for years, but I just thought they weren't doing anything for me. The first couple years I was there, I got royalty checks. But then it felt like they got comfortable with me or something, like they figured I'd go along with anything. Put my records out, the records get played, they get sold; I know people are hearing them, because they sing along with them at my shows. But then when royalty time comes, it's so pitiful, so little. Ecko said, "Well, they stealin' all the records, Denise; ain't nobody buying records."

Bootlegging is a problem, yes, I know that. But why is it I'm still getting royalties from everybody else? I never had any quarrels about royalty statements from Malaco or anyone. And when I put something out on my own label, I keep track of it, and I know people are buying it. Bootleggers are stealing some, but they're not stealing it all. So those little royalty statements I was getting from Ecko just didn't jell. I can get more money selling out of the trunk of my car than Ecko was paying me. So when my contract was over, I said I wasn't coming back.

I was still active, though. I was touring, playing mostly festivals and those big package shows, and I could tell my fans still loved me and were eager for whatever I was putting down. In June of 2009, my dear friend Koko Taylor passed away. She'd been known for years as "Queen of the Blues," but I didn't feel any competition, and I don't think she did, either. One time when I played at East of the Ryan in Chicago, she came to see me; I introduced her, and I told the audience that while Koko was Queen of the Blues, I was Queen of Soul-Blues. Then I sang "I'm Still the Queen," and when I got through, she was on her feet, applauding and cheering along with everybody else.

After Koko died, this Queen received her crown. On October 24, 2009, just a little over three months after Koko passed, I was crowned the Undisputed Queen of the Blues in my hometown of Belzoni by the president of the Mississippi Delta Blues Society, Ms. Helen Sims. Helen is a historian; she has a Civil Rights museum in Belzoni dedicated to Fannie Lou Hamer and Rev. George Lee, and she does a lot to honor our history and our culture. For my coronation, she sent out a press release: "The void left by Koko Taylor's death can only be filled by Denise LaSalle." To honor the occasion, I did a show with my band, Blak Ice, at the California Club on Silver City Road. That's just down the street from Rev. Lee's church, and it's not far from where the Charlie Holmes incident took place. So there was a lot of history, rich history, painful history, *our* history, being commemorated and remembered that day. I've been blessed to receive quite a few awards and commendations in my life, but none have meant more to me than to be recognized in this way, by my own people and my own community.

I have to say, though, this is one thing that really surprised me about Koko Taylor's daughter, Cookie. Seemed like the next thing I know, Cookie went to the Chicago Blues Festival and gave a crown to Shemekia Copeland and declared her Queen of the Blues, saying she was passing it down from her mama. I'm telling you now, that shocked me, because Cookie knew me well. She knew me, and she knew me and her mama were tight. After her mama died, she said to me as her friend, as her mama's friend, she said, "You the closest thing I have to my mama, now." And I never thought she would do that. Shemekia Copeland's daddy was Johnny Copeland. He was a blues singer, used to be with Alligator Records. Black folk don't hardly know anything about him, or about Shemekia either, really. She's just like him; he was on all those white blues festivals everywhere. All over the world he's known for that, and so is she. If I hadn't been out here on some of those festivals, I wouldn't have known who either one of them was. So it really got to me when Cookie went up there and gave that to her. Kind of hurt my feelings, I'll be honest with you; no use to me lying.

Well, I was going to go back and start releasing material on Ordena again, but in 2010, Tommy Couch Jr. talked me into going back to Malaco for one more project. It was great to be back, but I have to say I wasn't too happy with 24 Hour Woman, the CD we made. I think the song they decided to release as the single, "Cheat Receipt," wasn't the best choice. Luther Lackey wrote it, and I thought it was an okay song for the album, but it should not have been released as a single. It didn't have enough punch. But then, I really didn't like the whole album that well. I think I could have done better, but I used all I had available at the time.

There were changes coming in my life, though, big ones. Within a few years, I would find myself facing challenges such as I had never known. My very faith would be tested, and there would be times when things got so dark and painful I wondered whether I had it in me to carry on. But I never lost that faith, and the affirmations I received during those difficult times, the affirmations I continue to receive as things have gotten better but the road ahead remains challenging and uncertain, have uplifted and encouraged me in ways I might never have thought possible. As I sang in "God's Got My Back," and as I reaffirm every time I pray, and every time I think about all the things I've been through:

> *I'm so glad, yes, I am*
> *God is so merciful that*
> *He looked beyond my faults*
> *and He saw my needs*

Chapter Fourteen
God Don't Make Mistakes

Faith

People ask me what I believe, and I tell them right away: I'm a believer in the Lord and Savior Jesus Christ. I'm a believer. That's what the Bible says. Believe in Him with all your heart. I know I've asked Him to forgive me for my sins. Those sins I've been forgiven for, they're not coming against me in the Judgment. Never to be brought against me again.

I am a religious person, and you can take that any way you want to. I don't care what anybody says about it; I believe in the Lord and Savior Jesus Christ, and I know, if there's any such thing as a Heaven and a Hell, it's going to get me Heaven. I don't let anybody tell me different, because I truly believe in God. There's nobody in the world can tell me there's not a God. Because I've tried Him too many times, and He's been with me, to my rescue. All the trouble I've been in, everything I've been through, He's always been there to give me the helping hand, to keep my head above water.

He's Always On Time

I've seen some things that went down, just looked like I was drowning in quicksand, but God stepped in, right in the nick of time. There was a time when my finances got so bad it looked like I was going to lose my home. I know I told you about the radio stations and the buildings my husband and I owned, and that for a while we were among the most successful black entrepreneurs in Jackson. But, things began to go wrong with some of those investments. Wolfe eventually sold the radio stations for several million dollars, but he never got the money. He still owed five hundred thousand for the purchase of one of those stations, and he also had a lot of debts to clear. All those buildings were hard to keep up; sometimes he had people in there paying rent, sometimes he didn't. I helped pay for a lot of it, too; he always paid some, we had an agreement that I wasn't going to carry the whole load like I'd done with Bill Jones, but I paid a lot of the bills.

But then he was still buying buildings. When he'd buy them, they were auction properties, meaning we had to end up repairing them to bring them up to code, put a roof on, put floors in, go under and put pipes in, and all that kind of thing. So that's how the money got bad. Bad decisions.

And then, I always have been generous with my family, and not just my own family, but Wolfe's family, too. His mama and daddy got money from me all the time 'til they died. I helped my sisters and brothers if they needed help, and until my mom and dad died, I was there for them, too. And all the things I like for myself: I like my house looking nice, I like plenty of good things in my house, I like nice clothes, and I like to travel and do things. I would've been able to do all those things, too, if I hadn't had to pick up slack for a lot of that other stuff. But I did, and that's why our finances got behind. And then these children started growing up. Neither Ray nor any of my grandchildren ever had to want for anything. I was always there to help, whatever they needed. Ray grew up, I bought him a car—it's all just a bunch of stuff was happening.

Things got so bad we had to declare bankruptcy. The Music Maker Relief Foundation, the organization in North Carolina that does so many things to help blues musicians who are struggling, stepped in to help us with our mortgage so we wouldn't lose the house. And I thank God for Tim Duffy and his wonderful group, too, because He brought them to me in my hour of need. Like I said, He's always on time. Not necessarily when you want it, but He's always on time.

But my time for needing Him more than ever was just beginning.

Problems with My Heart

I'd had a few physical issues over the years, but they never slowed me down much. As I grew older, though, some worrisome things started to happen. Five or six years ago I discovered I had a ninety percent blockage in my carotid artery. I was on the verge of having a stroke or an aneurysm, and I didn't even know it. What happened was, I woke up one day and I could hardly see. My vision wasn't fuzzy or anything like that, but I couldn't see out of the top half of my eyes; it was like there was a curtain or a shade drawn down, blocking my sight. I went to my eye doctor, and he knew what it was immediately; he sent me right to the hospital. They removed the blockage and put a stent in there to get my blood flowing again.

Even so, my health seemed pretty good until I started having back problems from lugging those heavy pots and pans around. I ended up with sciatica, problems with my sciatic nerve. Very painful, and it began to cut down on my mobility. It got so it started affecting my shows, too; sometimes, if my back was really bothering me, or if I was exhausted from staying on the road in all that pain, I might be hoarse, struggling with my voice. Looking back, that was probably also the beginning of my heart problems, even though I didn't know that yet. I began sitting in a chair to sing, which I had never done. But the Queen still did her show. Sometimes those chairs had castors on them, and if the bandstand was level with the floor, I might end up rolling myself all through the room, talkin' shit and clowning. I'd have those folks up on their feet cheering before it was over. That's the kind of thing I would do.

By the time I closed the restaurant, in about 2015 or so, I was in pain almost all the time. I began using a rollator to get around, which is like a walker that unfolds into a chair so you can sit in it. But it's a little tricky, because those wheels might scoot out from under you and you can fall. I think that's what happened in 2017 at the Memphis Blues Awards; I fell down in the ladies' room. I knew I'd hurt my hip pretty badly, but I had a gig the next night and I didn't want to cancel, so I just gritted my teeth and made it through. When I got back to Jackson, I went to the hospital, and they diagnosed it as a dislocation, not a fracture. It still hurt something terrible, and as the weeks went by it didn't get better, but they insisted it was just dislocated. I struggled on with my rollator, but it got harder and harder, especially for someone like me, who doesn't like to be stopped from doing anything I want to do. Some of the shows I did, I struggled to get through; I'd take painkillers, and by me not being used to drugs of any kind, it fogged up my mind. I'd forget lyrics or lose my place, and sometimes the medicine would dry out my system so bad my throat felt parched and

I could barely croak, let alone sing. I always made it through, but it was a horrible feeling, not being able to be at my best for my fans.

By then, though, there were other things going on with me that I hadn't known about, but I found out about them soon enough. About a year before I had that fall, in July of 2016, just a week or two before my birthday, I was scheduled to go up to New York to do a show. I remember I had a lot on my mind at that time; my granddaughter Monet was going through a crisis in her life, and we were all extremely worried about her. So just as I was getting ready to leave, I suddenly found myself gasping for breath, like my chest was closing in on me and I couldn't breathe. I made it back into the house and upstairs to my bedroom, but it just got worse, and I ended up going to the emergency room.

Before I knew it, I'd been rushed into surgery for a triple bypass. I had congestive heart failure, and it was only through the grace of God that I was stricken when I was instead of just a little later, when I would have been on the road. The surgery was successful, and for a few days after that I felt fine, looking forward to going to Tunica for the Jus' Blues conference in August. But then things started going wrong. I honestly believe, to this day, that I was sent home too early and my medications weren't balanced right. I went into something like a daze, or worse—basically, I was out of my mind for a couple weeks. I could barely talk; I hardly knew where I was. And then my heart began to palpitate, and I had to go back into the hospital.

And that's when God came through for me again.

They couldn't get my heart to beat right. They took me back in there, said they're going to administer an electric shock to my heart to steady it, and they lost me. When they put me under, before they could shock my heart into rhythm, my vital signs went blank and they had to bring me back out. But they might not even have done that, because before I went in for that surgery, someone had put a purple bracelet on me. I didn't notice it until Wolfe pointed it out. He recognized it immediately. It was DNR, "Do Not Resuscitate." Wolfe knew what it was because my sister-in-law Marsha, Gary Wolfe's wife, the woman Gary married after he and Karen got divorced, had just died, and she'd had one. She was a lupus patient and was having a real rough time, so she didn't want to be resuscitated if that happened to her. But I hadn't asked for one, and Wolfe said he hadn't either.

So when Wolfe saw it—"What they doin' with that bracelet on you?"

I said, "What bracelet?"

"That purple bracelet. Let me see that. I know what that is! Let me call the nurse."

He called and asked who had said to put it on me, and everyone just said, "I don't know." We never did find out. But Wolfe just told them, "Get that shit off my wife!" And we were lucky he did, because if they hadn't removed that bracelet, I wouldn't be here now.

More Trials—My Amputation and Its Aftermath

I got my strength back slowly, but it was still rough going. Something happened to my appetite after the heart surgery. My sense of taste went funny, and I could hardly eat anything. All I really wanted to eat, for some reason, was peanut butter and Ritz crackers; I always had a box of crackers on the nightstand next to my bed. Sometimes in the morning I'd drink a fruit slurry, and if we went out to dinner I might have some fish, and occasionally Wolfe might bring home some Chinese food or something, and I could eat a little bit of that. But over the next year or so, I lost a lot of weight. I just couldn't find it in me to eat much of anything. I might cook a meal for Wolfe and nibble at the food a little, but that was about it.

I went back to performing as soon as I could. The gigs weren't too plentiful anymore; in this business, if you don't have a new record out or something on the radio, those job offers can dry up in a hurry. And I guess people knew I'd been having health problems, so that didn't help, either.

I did get some recognition, though, and it came from the very top: President Obama included "Trapped by a Thing Called Love" in his "Summer Playlist" for 2016. So I wrote him a letter, thanking him for that. That's not the first letter that went to the Obamas' house from our house. The first letter, I wrote for my granddaughter. When they first made it to the White House, Monet was a little girl. I wrote this letter and had her copy it over. We sent it to Sasha and Malia, Barack and Michelle Obama's daughters, and they wrote back. I used to have that letter in the kitchen along with the other letters and things in that V.I.P. collection I told you about; I don't know whether Monet saved it after she moved out of the house, but I haven't seen it for a long time. But anyway, that was the first letter. And then, when the news about his summer playlist came out, I wrote to thank him, saying how much

I admired him, and then the next thing I knew, I got a letter back from him! He thanked me, said he'd heard I was going through some health problems, and wished me well. That is something I will cherish until the day I die. A personal thank-you from our greatest president, after he himself had named my song as one of his favorites! What an honor, and what a thrill.

I also recorded a few more things during this time. A producer got me to do a couple of songs that only appeared on YouTube, "Grown Folks Business" and "Tiptoeing through the Bedroom," but I hardly paid them any mind; he offered me the money, I did 'em, and that was it. Bigg Robb, one of the up-and-coming singers in this modern "southern soul" style, featured me in his video "Blues and BBQ" in 2015, and that one came out a lot better; I think it probably did both of us some good. I already told you about the EP I did along with my son, to kick off the Unity Project tours that unfortunately never happened; I also put out another inspirational CD, *The Gospel Truth*, in 2017; it was a compilation of spiritual songs I'd recorded on earlier albums. I included "If I'm Only for Myself" on there, too. So Bob, if you're listening, this one's for you!

It was slow going for a while, though. I have to give my old friend Lee Kirksy in Chicago, Mr. Lee, a lot of credit. He kept me working, even if some of the jobs he got me were pretty small, in little nightclubs or lounges of the kind I hadn't played in since I was just starting out. Sometimes, because of the congestive heart failure and the medications I was on, my voice got pretty clogged up and hoarse, but I always made the gig, and I always worked to do as good a show as possible. But I won't lie to you. I did start getting weaker, and it became harder to get through a performance. Sometimes, though, things went okay. Another show I did in Chicago, at the 2017 Chicago Blues Festival, was one of my best during this time. I felt good, I looked good, and I sounded good. A lot of my friends and relatives from Chicago came to see me; other artists who were on the festival that year, old friends of mine, came to talk backstage. Willie Mitchell's granddaughter Oona was there, too, and it was wonderful to see her again.

I'm afraid, though, that I have to say things went downhill pretty fast from there. On August 5, 2017, after coming home from attending the Jus' Blues conference in Tunica, I did a show at the Carl Perkins Civic Center in Jackson along with Sheba Potts-Wright and Karen Wolfe, my two former backup singers who've gone on to careers of their own, and Willie Clayton.

My voice was so bad that night I had to do something I'd never done: I apologized to the audience, told them I couldn't go any further, and cut my show short.

Oh, I felt terrible! I spent most of the next day curled up in the bed, feeling as lonely and depressed as I think I've ever felt in my life. Was it really over? Did I have to face the unthinkable, that my life as a singer was coming to an end? I'd written a lot of songs while I was recovering from surgery; I had a notepad full of new lyrics, and I thought I'd get together with my guitarist Jonathan Ellison, cut a demo, and try to get them to other singers. Maybe I could keep going as a songwriter, even if my own singing days were numbered.

But oh, no. I didn't want that. I'm still the Queen! Denise LaSalle is my name! I don't want that to be over! On September 16, I was booked to play the Mississippi Delta Blues & Heritage Festival in Greenville, Mississippi. I wasn't feeling well at all; the drive from Jackson to Greenville was extremely difficult, and I got there just before I was scheduled to go on. I remember sitting there backstage, and I guess I must have looked as bad as I felt, because the event's coordinator, Mable Starks, came to me and said that if I couldn't go on, it would be okay. I'd get paid anyway, and there would be no hard feelings. "No," I said. "I've never done that in my life, and I'm not going to do it now. I'm going on."

There was no lift or anything to get a wheelchair onto the stage, so everyone kind of held their breath as they rolled me up that steel ramp in my chair and placed me in front of the microphone. I only made it through two songs. I handed the mic to Karen Wolfe, who was singing backup for me that night. Karen took over and finished out the show.

I went right back to Jackson and into the hospital. I was on the verge of kidney failure, my heart problems had gotten worse, I had neuropathy, it seemed like everything that could go wrong was happening at once. It wasn't too long after that, that someone noticed what they thought was a mosquito bite on my leg. The nurses dressed it and wrapped it up, but it turned out they'd misdiagnosed it. I know you've probably read that I had my leg amputated due to complications following a fall, but that is not true. My leg was amputated because I had a staph infection that went untreated for too long. By the time they got around to realizing what it was, the gangrene had already set in.

My foot turned black; the skin got all crusty. Black, like shoe polish; blisters like a sac of water, and the water was black. Every time I moved, that water was shaking around in there. Scared me to death. So I started questioning what it was. I'm sitting there, telling the doctor to please stick a hole in it and let the water out. He said, "No way"—and of course I wondered why. When he told me I had gangrene, I could not believe that. Because I don't have diabetes. So what could this possibly be?

It was a staph infection. They said it was cellulitis, but my daughter asked, and she found out that's what a staph infection is. If I had diabetes, in the hospital they wouldn't be sending me big old pieces of corn bread, cake with frosting, fried chicken, and all that stuff; they wouldn't be sending me sugar. As many tests as they've run, I've never heard a doctor say I had diabetes, and they kept sending me all this sugar and stuff in my meals.

So when they told me I'd have to have an amputation, it was a terrible shock. First they thought it might be just a few toes, and then the whole foot. When they told me the danger I was in, I said, "Well, y'all cut that sucker off, throw it out in the river. I don't want it eating its way up my legs." But before it was over, they were telling me they were going to have to take the entire leg, from the knee on down. I had a sore that came all the way from my foot, up to my knee almost. All the skin was peeling off of my leg. So that's when they made the decision to take off the whole thing.

All my life I'd been hearing about gangrene and all kinds of things like that. Whoever would have thought I'd have it? I never would have dreamed something like this. All I know is, it's still a scary something to talk about. Because once that one leg is gone, that still doesn't mean they got it all. I've known some people to have gangrene in their leg, from diabetes; take the leg off, then two or three months later they got to go get the other leg. So it's still frightening to think what the future might have in store.

I went to Vanderbilt in Nashville to have the amputation. That's when I received another shock. When they looked at my X-rays, they asked me, "When did you break your hip?" I told them I hadn't. They said, "Oh, yes, you did!" Turns out I'd fractured my hip, probably down there in Memphis when I fell, and somehow the doctors in Jackson had missed that, too; they'd diagnosed it as being just dislocated. I'd been hobbling around all this time on a broken hip. No wonder I was in so much pain!

A lot of things happened after the amputation that I don't remember. Wolfe told me about some of them, and other people, like my daughter Bridgette and my good friend Jazzii A., who used to live right down the

street from me—she's a promoter, a label owner, a radio DJ, and a lot of
other wonderful things—filled me in on others. At one point I contracted
an infection that spread through my body so fast they had to put me into
a medically induced coma to let the medicine work. They used that drug,
Propofol, that killed Michael Jackson; when you go under that, it's hard
sometimes to come out of it, and that's what happened to me. They tell me
I was in that coma for about nine days; every time they tried to bring me
out, I'd panic and start thrashing around, my blood pressure would shoot
up, I'd be trying to yank all the tubes out of my throat and everything, so
they had to re-administer the drug and put me under again.

It was during this time that I experienced a miracle. Again, I don't
remember it, but my husband says that Betty Wright had started calling
from her home in Florida to see how I was doing. I knew Betty somewhat,
but we had never been anything more than just cordial friends. For some
reason, though, when she found out what was going on, she began check-
ing up on me, calling to ask Wolfe about me, always staying in touch. So
there I was, in a coma, and Betty called my room and asked Wolfe, "Can I
sing to her?"

Wolfe put the phone to my ear, and Betty sang the gospel song, "Your
Grace and Mercy Brought Me Through." She sang the whole song to me over
the phone, and my husband said that as she was singing, my eyes started
moving, and I started trying to move my lips a little; it was like I was coming back from somewhere far away. As she came to the end of the song, he
says, I smiled and I started whispering the words: "Brought me through."

He says he got so excited he could barely contain himself. He grabbed
the phone back and told her, "Betty! She's coming alive! She's coming alive
again!" And from that point, I started talking. That was the beginning of
my recovering from that.

Betty had been through a lot. She'd had a son who was shot to death in
2005; she wrote her song "Dry Well" in his memory. Then her career had
kind of fallen off, and she was trying to build it back up again. But she was
there for me. It was like she'd been called to me; someone I didn't even
know that well, who came into my life and showed by her prayers and her
spirit what the power of God can do.

Still, I had some dark moments. For a long time, I kept feeling phantom
pain, like the leg that wasn't there was screaming in agony. It felt like a tree
or something was lying on it, a heavy weight that hurt so much I couldn't

stand it. There were times when I'd be lying in pain, all alone in the middle of the night, searching my heart trying to think of what I might have done to be punished like this. I'd ask God, "Why? Why are You making me suffer so? I know I've done some wrong in my life. I know I haven't always been as good as I should have been. But what have I done that could have been *this* bad, *this* terrible, for You to want to make me suffer like this? To have to go through this pain? To have to go through what I'm going though now?" There were times when I almost prayed to die.

It was the love of my husband and my family, and the love and support of good friends like Jazzii, that helped me pull through. And of course, it was my faith in God. I may have teetered on the brink of doubt a few times, but I never fell over. I never stopped praising Him, and I never will. Sometimes we need to go through trials to remind ourselves how blessed we are. That's what happened to me.

Living on Mother's Prayers

I'm in rehab now. Most of the pain is gone; the swelling in my stump is going down, and the doctors say it shouldn't be too long before they can fit me up with a prosthesis. I'm looking forward to going home. Wolfe says he's going to have our house fixed up so we can move our bedroom downstairs, where the den is now, and then we can have motorized stair lifts put on the stairways so I can get around.

I spend a lot of time thinking back on my life, realizing how fortunate I've been. You know that saying, "Living on Mother's prayers"? I think I'm living on my mom and dad's prayers, and I think they were living on their mamas' prayers before them. Our whole family has been blessed. They're all good people. There are no jailbirds in our family, there's nobody that I know of who's been incarcerated, nobody who ever killed anybody; there were no Saturday night fights between men and their wives or any things like that. My folks were good Christian people. They prayed for their children, and God answered their prayers.

All my siblings have been successful. All of them. They were successful in whatever they wanted to do, and they all raised good families. Nate, of course, became a singer for a while, and then he went back to his first love, which was education. My sister Doll didn't get any further than about the fifth or sixth grade. But she raised nine children, and I think every one of

them has a college education. They're all schoolteachers and things like
that, raising their own kids, got good jobs. Then Sutter, my oldest sister,
she never birthed but one child. His name is Christopher Pruitt, and he's in
Wisconsin, working with an agency that assists troubled young men with
counseling, helping them get jobs, get an education, that kind of thing.
He was involved in a gun accident when he was a boy living in Chicago.
He and his friend found a gun that someone had thrown away, and I guess
they thought it was a toy; when his buddy pretended to shoot it at him, it
went off and shot him in the back. He could have been killed or paralyzed,
but he wasn't. He still walks with a limp, but he's doing fine. He's a highly
respected member of his community, a role model to a lot of young men,
about as fine a gentleman as you could ever want to meet. So all the Allen
kids came out okay, and their children are doing fine, too.

As for me, I know there's no way I would have made it this far without
my mom and dad's prayers. I've always been a good person, I truly believe
that, but I just don't know how to be anything but what I am, and I'm sure
I might have done things that would have gotten me in a lot of trouble, but
I think their prayers have kept me on the right level. A lot of people don't
know this, but I might have become an alcoholic. I don't drink now, and I
haven't for years, but when I was a lot younger, back when I was living in
Chicago, beer was my drink. I used to drink six-packs of beer every day God
sent. King-size Budweiser, every day.

But God was watching out for me. What happened was, I forgot to buy
my beer one Saturday night. That next morning, when I got up, the only
place to get beer that early on a Sunday was down under the "L" track on
47th Street. I went flying down there. I wanted to be the first in line to get
my beer. So I'm standing there, and they handed me a six-pack, and I paid
for that six-pack of Bud and pulled the top off one of the cans and threw it
up to my mouth and started drinking. I looked in that big mirror behind
the counter, the shoplifting mirror, and when I looked up in that mirror
and saw the desperate look in my eyes, and that beer running all down the
side of my mouth, on my chest and everywhere, I took that beer down. I
couldn't give the six-pack back to them because I'd opened one of the cans,
so I took it home and left it in the refrigerator for someone else to drink.
I was through with beer.

Then I used to try to drink liquor, too. You know, to fit in with the "in"
crowd, all those party people who like to hang around music and musicians.

I didn't like the way alcohol made me feel. I'd get sick, I'd get dizzy, and I finally just said, "I don't need that," and I left it alone. I don't think I was smart enough or good enough to do all that on my own. I think that was God's will.

And any other kind of drug, you can forget it. You can dump this room full of cocaine, you can dump me a roomful of crack, you can dump me a roomful of heroin. I'll walk by; I wouldn't touch it. I wouldn't even try it. I wouldn't even be curious to see how it felt. How many folks could do that? I'm a stubborn person. I just thank God I've been strong enough to say "No." All these years I've been in show business, all the mess and nonsense I've seen and been around—that's God's hand on me, and that's the power of my mom and dad's prayers.

I could tell you so many other times when I might have been in danger, but I came through it, and I know that's because He was looking out for me. You can't spend as much time on the road as I have, traveled so many miles in all kinds of conditions, and not have a few close calls. Once we were driving down the highway and a wheel ran right off the bus. Another time, we were coming out of Greenwood, Mississippi, and I got sick to my stomach; I said, "Pull over. I have to throw up." They pulled over to the side of the road, and I sat down in the door of the bus, getting ready to get sick, throw up between my legs. And my mind said, "Don't throw up there; walk down in the ditch and do it." I got up, hadn't even gotten to the ditch, and I heard "BAM!" A car had smashed into the rear of the bus. The bus got bent up so bad they couldn't drive it; it had to be towed. If I'd been sitting in that door, I wouldn't be alive today. And the guys who were on either side of me holding me, my band members, they wouldn't be here either.

Another time we were coming out of Texas, heading over to Louisiana, and a drunk driver came from the other side of the road and ran right into us. Nobody got hurt, not a scar on anybody. I think about all those miles we've put in, driving day and night from one gig to another, and no one's ever gotten seriously injured. That was a blessing. Because I know a lot of people, people like Bobby Rush, my old friend Jimmy Johnson, Koko Taylor, so many more, they've all had accidents out here where someone got seriously injured or even killed. And look how far I've traveled. I've been all over the U.S., in Europe, Asia, Africa, everywhere, and the Good Lord has kept us safe through all of it. That's called living on Mama's prayers.

So yes, I tell the world this all the time. God has been truly, truly good to me and has blessed me. If I had to do it over again, I can't think of anything

I would do different. Marrying early, leaving home, I'd do that again to get out of Mississippi if everything was like it was down there then. I would do it all over again, knowing what I know. Some people might think I should regret messing around at the beginning of my career with Billy Emerson, the way he treated me, but why should I have regrets about something like that? He taught me, he got me started, he cut my first record. Don't be for him, I wouldn't be who I am today.

Only one thing I might change. I think I should have kept my music lessons going. When I moved to Chicago, I left my music teacher down south, and I never would get involved with anybody up there teaching me. If had kept doing my music, I could have done a lot more for myself. If I could read and write music, I think maybe I could have been another Quincy Jones or something. Because I sure had the knack for it. I'm a heck of a writer, I know that, but I'd have to use other people to get my arrangers to know what I'm talking about; sometimes they'd get it, sometimes they got close to it, sometimes they missed. That's why my stuff didn't always turn out the way I wanted it to. If I'd had more control over that, I think I could have done a lot better for myself, and I could probably have had more success writing for other people, too.

But I like who I am, and I like the way I am. I'm a rounded performer, whereas a lot of other people aren't. You talk about songwriter, artist, producer, publisher, manager—I'm all those things. I don't know anyone who has done all the things I've done, especially a woman. Even someone like Carole King: She's a writer, producer, artist, but as far as her being a manager of other people and guiding other people's careers like I did for Coday and the Sequins and them, back when Bill Jones and I had our labels, I don't know that she's done anything like that. But I've done it all. I book my own shows a lot of the time, I've made my own career, I made other people stars before I even made myself one, I've owned record labels, published my own songs, produced my own sessions in the studio, all those things combined. So I certainly have no business with regrets, or wishing things had turned out different from the way they have.

And also, people might find this hard to believe, but I never really cared about becoming a superstar, making it that big. I'm happy doing the work. I like what I do. I've enjoyed it. I like writing songs; I like getting them over to people. Just give me a decent living, that's all I care about. I believe that had I made it to superstar status, it would've changed me. And I never wanted to change. When I'm home, I go shopping at Kroger's just like everyone else. A lot of the people who come in there know who I am, but I'm still just Miss Denise, their neighbor who happens to be a singer and have some records out. I'm not out there like, "Oh, I'm Denise LaSalle, I'm this, and I'm that." We chat, we spend the time of day. That's just the way I am, and I like being that way.

And then, too, I never wanted to be away from my family so much. I love my family. I like being close to them. I don't want to have to say I haven't seen my family since last Christmas or last year sometime, or have to come home and find that my children or grandchildren hardly know me, and I'm like a stranger to them. I've seen that happen, and it's sad. My children and my family are some of the greatest blessings in my life, and I want to love them and cherish them every way I can. And then, Wolfe and me, yes, we've been through some changes, I won't deny that. Financial problems and everything else. We've stuck together through a lot; we're still going, and you can't ask for much more than that. So I'm not having any business with regrets.

Return of the One-Legged Diva

Yes, you read that right. We're gonna get it started. The One-Legged Diva! You know, some people just give up; they just get mad at the world and quit. Well, the world ain't done nothing to me for me to be mad at it. The world gave me all I have, all I know, and I'm very grateful. I'd like to contribute a little bit more to it.

There are a lot of ways I think I can do that. I told you I have all those new songs I've written, just waiting to be put to music. I have to get a demo made of those. And my Blues Academy is still my biggest unfulfilled dream. Keep our children interested in our heritage, get our kids off the ground. It's something I've been talking about for years, and it's still the way I'd like to keep my name and my legacy alive. And, of course, as I just said, my family. My husband, our daughter Bridgette, Ray, my grandchildren, my sister Sutter, who's living in Wisconsin, all my nieces and nephews, they love me, and I love them and need them just as much. So there's a lot for me to live for, a lot of things I'd still like to do.

But then, I think about it this way, too. Tomorrow's not promised to any of us, and I know it's not promised to me. I don't feel up to doing too much a lot of the time. My body is too weak to do the things I used to do. No use staying on this earth forever if I can't do anything. What am I going to do, just sit here all curled up? I look at some of the people here where I'm staying, these elderly people in rehab with me, how bad they look, sitting in their wheelchairs all hunched over, twisted up, drooling, can't hardly move, can't say a word, their eyes staring out—I don't want to be like that. No, not for me.

The school can still be in my name, even if I'm not here. It's my name that's important to me. If I can get in there and help, fine. But if I can't get in there and be able to contribute something, then just give the school my name. Name it after me, tell my history of what I was and what I did, and let Wolfe and the rest of them handle it.

So yes, I'm determined to come back out of this. Just a few days ago, a friend of mine said I need to write a song: "How can I kick my man's butt if I only got one foot?" We both got a laugh out of that one. Imagine the One-Legged Diva saying something like that! But my point is, I'm saying if I can't do it, don't worry about it. I've done plenty. My advice to young people—this is what I want to tell them in my school, and it's what I'm saying now—don't let the things out there in the world turn you around, and always keep your prayers going up to Him. Because I'm telling you I know—*I know*—what it means to be in good state with God. He does hear and answer prayers, and I know that, because I'm here by the grace of God. Whether I make it all the way back or not, however much time He has in His plan to give me, I've lived my life, I've enjoyed it, I've accomplished something, and if the Lord says it's time for me to go, then that's the way I feel about it.

God's got my back.

Coda

"Speak to God on My Behalf"

DAVID WHITEIS

When Denise LaSalle passed away on January 8, 2018, the music world lost a beloved, life-affirming presence, a woman who had left her imprint on musical generations and eras ranging from mainstream '60s/'70s-era R&B through the modernist hybrid known variously as soul-blues and southern soul. Hers was a voice of contemporary immediacy irrespective of decade or style. She might have been a little ambivalent about the term "feminist," but from the beginning, her songs conveyed a bold, often provocative message of womanly assertiveness and pride. Even in her early days, long before she began to think of herself as a "blues" singer, her lyrics and delivery both reflected and updated the classic blueswoman's stance of power and independence, a stance that linked her to such legendary blues singers as Bessie Smith, Ma Rainey, and Ida Cox.

For those of us who were privileged to know her personally, though, it's her loving and indomitable spirit that we will miss most. She certainly took pride in the sobriquet Queen of the Blues, even if it came to her relatively late in life, but I will always remember her, first and foremost, as the Queen of Hearts. I have known very few people in life with a heart as deep and as giving as the heart of Denise LaSalle. The love she shared with James Wolfe for the last four decades her life; her dedication to her family, as well as the countless "adopted children" she collected over the years;

her kindness and generosity as a mentor, especially to young women like Karen Wolfe and Sheba Potts-Wright, who left from under her tutelage to forge musical careers of their own, and who continue to honor her as their musical godmother; the blessings she bestowed as a loyal and true-hearted friend—these, as much as the music she made, represent the living legacy of Denise LaSalle.

There were so many things I still wanted to ask her. She received numerous awards, citations, and commendations during her life; for instance, in 2009, she was honored by the Mississippi State Legislature for her "lasting impact" on rhythm and blues and for her role as "an unofficial ambassador for the State of Mississippi." It's still my regret that we never got around to discussing these accolades, as rife with paradox and irony as some of them undoubtedly were, what they meant to her, and what they represented as further realizations of her childhood dreams.

Years earlier, in 1976, Denise had been the first African American entertainer to perform for the inmates at Parchman Penitentiary, Mississippi's notorious prison farm. "It's kind of a strange feeling," she told *Jet* magazine at the time. "It has sort of a sadness about it." With her profound compassion, especially for young people caught up in the vicissitudes of a system still sullied by racism and inequity—read "Cry of the Black Soul" again to see how deep those feelings truly ran—I'm sure she would have had some valuable and poignant thoughts to share about this experience. She was also a good friend of Kolleen Gipson Wright—Ms. Queenie—the mother of R&B superstar Erykah Badu, certainly yet another link between generations and genres, and another representation of the universality of this music and its message.

After I wrote a chapter on her for my 2013 book *Southern Soul-Blues* (to which she also contributed her prose poem "America's Prodigal Son" as the Foreword), Denise contacted me and told me she wanted us to work together on her autobiography. We had been working on it for over a year when she passed. We last spoke in her room at NHC HealthCare in Milan, Tennessee, where she had been staying since being discharged from Vanderbilt following her amputation. Although there were still plenty of things we wanted to cover, we had enough done for the book. I promised her that her life story would be in good hands.

She called me on January 6, about a week after we'd spent those final precious days together in Milan. She thanked me again for having spent that time with her, and we made plans to see each other again as soon as I could make it back south. The last words we said to each other were, "I love you."

On the evening of January 8, Jazzii A., the polymath journalist/producer/radio DJ/promoter whom Denise refers to here as one of her closest friends, was putting together a radio show in honor of soul singer Otis Clay, who had died two years earlier. In his memory, she compiled a tribute to artists who had passed away—a "Soul Heaven" theme—culminating with a segment featuring Clay himself. The final song she played was "When the Gates Swing Open," Clay's trademark gospel song, the one he had sung at so many people's funerals over the years. When it was coming to an end, as the final notes were fading out and Jazzii was wrapping up her taping—at that precise second—she got the call from Denise's daughter, Bridgette: "Jazzii, come to the hospital. My mother is dying."

The Queen left us, two years to the day after Otis Clay—and Otis Clay sang her home.

A Note on the Text

The reader will notice that several important dates—Denise LaSalle's year of birth; the precise timelines of her move from the country to Belzoni, her departure from Belzoni and her subsequent marriage, her return home, and then her second and final move back to Chicago—have been omitted from this narrative. Through the years, conflicting information has been given concerning some of these details of Denise LaSalle's early life, often by Ms. LaSalle herself. Her date of birth has usually been cited as either 1939 or 1941. The conventional narrative has suggested that she eloped to Chicago when she was thirteen. She was usually chary about mentioning the name of her first husband, but the assumption has almost always been that his surname was Craig—the Artic Craig she first mentions here in Chapter Five.

Subsequent research shows that this chronology requires some emendation. Data from the U.S. Census and the Humphreys County Clerk's Office in Belzoni, Mississippi, along with the oral recollections of family members including James Wolfe, Bridgette Wolfe-Edwards, Naomi "Sutter" Pruitt, the Rev. Preston Allen Jr., and the Rev. Morris Allen, confirm that Ora Dee (or Ora D.) Allen was born in LeFlore County, Mississippi, outside of Sidon, on July 16, 1934. The area then known as The Island, nestled between the Yazoo River and Fish Lake (recalled here as "Catfish Lake"), is still visible on maps, and there is also a Phillipston Road, perhaps one of the boundaries of the old Phillipston Plantation.

According to her sister, the family moved to Belzoni in 1947. Records show that Ora D.'s [*sic*] first marriage was in 1949, when she was fifteen (she misrepresented her age as eighteen), and that the man's name was Joseph Johnson. Her sister confirms that she met Johnson, who was also known as "Jack," while visiting in Chicago. They went down to Belzoni to get married but soon returned north; she went home again after the marriage failed, but she came back to Chicago in about 1954 or possibly 1955, after the murder of Rev. George Lee. She married Artic Craig in 1956, when she was twenty-two. Craig was a coworker with her brother A.J. at Campbell Soup, as she relates here. For reasons that aren't entirely clear, she again went back to Belzoni to marry him, but she seems to have come back to Chicago immediately, where she'd stay until moving to Memphis in 1974.

For a young black girl growing up in early- to mid-twentieth-century Mississippi, life could be daunting. It was a world without safety or sanctuary, in which the yoke of Jim Crow oppression maintained a relentless, suffocating stranglehold. "God help us if we tried to cross the line," as Denise relates here. Day-to-day life necessitated constant vigilance; many people found themselves compelled to shape-shift and obfuscate with the dexterity of a Yoruba trickster just to survive. Not even church could guarantee a haven against treachery. We will probably never know exactly why Denise LaSalle seemed so determined to telescope approximately seven years of her early life into one.

I have related her story here as she told it. She was open and honest in her recollections, and I'm confident that her memories of events, if not their precise chronology, were accurate. Some of her anecdotes, such as her story about David Ruffin at the Cobo Arena in Detroit, may have been somewhat distorted by faulty memory; Ruffin left the Temptations in 1968, several years before this event occurred. Again, I do not doubt that the incident took place as she remembered it, but perhaps it involved some other entertainer. It's also possible, of course, that Ruffin was there that day, probably to visit with his former colleagues, as he was known to do; this might explain why he was sitting out in the auditorium during the sound check, rather than being on stage or backstage with the group. Either way, I have included these notes for the sake of historical accuracy concerning the timeline and chronology of some of the events in Ms. LaSalle's life.

The line "Speak to God on my behalf" is from the song "You and I," written by "Light" Henry Huff (Henry Lincoln Huff, ASCAP), as performed by Dee Alexander on the album *Wild Is the Wind* (2008: Blujazz BJ3369).

Index

Denise LaSalle (1934–2018) was a soul and blues singer-songwriter and businesswoman. Her songs include "Trapped by a Thing Called Love," "Married, but Not to Each Other," and the modern-day soul-blues standards "A Lady in the Street," "Don't Jump My Pony," and "Someone Else Is Steppin' In." LaSalle entered the Blues Hall of Fame in 2011 and the Rhythm & Blues Hall of Fame in 2015.

David Whiteis is a journalist, writer, and educator living in Chicago. His books include *Blues Legacy: Tradition and Innovation in Chicago* and *Southern Soul-Blues*.

Music in American Life

The Crooked Stovepipe: Athapaskan Fiddle Music and Square Dancing in Northeast Alaska and Northwest Canada   *Craig Mishler*

Traveling the High Way Home: Ralph Stanley and the World of Traditional Bluegrass Music   *John Wright*

Carl Ruggles: Composer, Painter, and Storyteller   *Marilyn Ziffrin*

Never without a Song: The Years and Songs of Jennie Devlin, 1865–1952   *Katharine D. Newman*

The Hank Snow Story   *Hank Snow, with Jack Ownbey and Bob Burris*

Milton Brown and the Founding of Western Swing   *Cary Ginell, with special assistance from Roy Lee Brown*

Santiago de Murcia's "Códice Saldívar No. 4": A Treasury of Secular Guitar Music from Baroque Mexico   *Craig H. Russell*

The Sound of the Dove: Singing in Appalachian Primitive Baptist Churches   *Beverly Bush Patterson*

Heartland Excursions: Ethnomusicological Reflections on Schools of Music   *Bruno Nettl*

Doowop: The Chicago Scene   *Robert Pruter*

Blue Rhythms: Six Lives in Rhythm and Blues   *Chip Deffaa*

Shoshone Ghost Dance Religion: Poetry Songs and Great Basin Context   *Judith Vander*

Go Cat Go! Rockabilly Music and Its Makers   *Craig Morrison*

'Twas Only an Irishman's Dream: The Image of Ireland and the Irish in American Popular Song Lyrics, 1800–1920   *William H. A. Williams*

Democracy at the Opera: Music, Theater, and Culture in New York City, 1815–60   *Karen Ahlquist*

Fred Waring and the Pennsylvanians   *Virginia Waring*

Woody, Cisco, and Me: Seamen Three in the Merchant Marine   *Jim Longhi*

Behind the Burnt Cork Mask: Early Blackface Minstrelsy and Antebellum American Popular Culture   *William J. Mahar*

Going to Cincinnati: A History of the Blues in the Queen City   *Steven C. Tracy*

Pistol Packin' Mama: Aunt Molly Jackson and the Politics of Folksong   *Shelly Romalis*

Sixties Rock: Garage, Psychedelic, and Other Satisfactions   *Michael Hicks*

The Late Great Johnny Ace and the Transition from R&B to Rock 'n' Roll   *James M. Salem*

Tito Puente and the Making of Latin Music   *Steven Loza*

Juilliard: A History   *Andrea Olmstead*

Understanding Charles Seeger, Pioneer in American Musicology   *Edited by Bell Yung and Helen Rees*

Mountains of Music: West Virginia Traditional Music from *Goldenseal*   *Edited by John Lilly*

Alice Tully: An Intimate Portrait   *Albert Fuller*

A Blues Life   *Henry Townsend, as told to Bill Greensmith*

Long Steel Rail: The Railroad in American Folksong (2d ed.)   *Norm Cohen*

Dewey and Elvis: The Life and Times of a Rock 'n' Roll Deejay   *Louis Cantor*
Come Hither to Go Yonder: Playing Bluegrass with Bill Monroe   *Bob Black*
Chicago Blues: Portraits and Stories   *David Whiteis*
The Incredible Band of John Philip Sousa   *Paul E. Bierley*
"Maximum Clarity" and Other Writings on Music   *Ben Johnston,
    edited by Bob Gilmore*
Staging Tradition: John Lair and Sarah Gertrude Knott   *Michael Ann Williams*
Homegrown Music: Discovering Bluegrass   *Stephanie P. Ledgin*
Tales of a Theatrical Guru   *Danny Newman*
The Music of Bill Monroe   *Neil V. Rosenberg and Charles K. Wolfe*
Pressing On: The Roni Stoneman Story   *Roni Stoneman, as told to Ellen Wright*
Together Let Us Sweetly Live   *Jonathan C. David, with photographs by Richard
    Holloway*
Live Fast, Love Hard: The Faron Young Story   *Diane Diekman*
Air Castle of the South: WSM Radio and the Making of Music City
    Craig P. Havighurst
Traveling Home: Sacred Harp Singing and American Pluralism   *Kiri Miller*
Where Did Our Love Go? The Rise and Fall of the Motown Sound   *Nelson George*
Lonesome Cowgirls and Honky-Tonk Angels: The Women of Barn Dance
    Radio   *Kristine M. McCusker*
California Polyphony: Ethnic Voices, Musical Crossroads   *Mina Yang*
The Never-Ending Revival: Rounder Records and the Folk Alliance
    Michael F. Scully
Sing It Pretty: A Memoir   *Bess Lomax Hawes*
Working Girl Blues: The Life and Music of Hazel Dickens   *Hazel Dickens
    and Bill C. Malone*
Charles Ives Reconsidered   *Gayle Sherwood Magee*
The Hayloft Gang: The Story of the National Barn Dance   *Edited by Chad Berry*
Country Music Humorists and Comedians   *Loyal Jones*
Record Makers and Breakers: Voices of the Independent Rock 'n' Roll
    Pioneers   *John Broven*
Music of the First Nations: Tradition and Innovation in Native North
    America   *Edited by Tara Browner*
Cafe Society: The Wrong Place for the Right People   *Barney Josephson,
    with Terry Trilling-Josephson*
George Gershwin: An Intimate Portrait   *Walter Rimler*
Life Flows On in Endless Song: Folk Songs and American History   *Robert V. Wells*
I Feel a Song Coming On: The Life of Jimmy McHugh   *Alyn Shipton*
King of the Queen City: The Story of King Records   *Jon Hartley Fox*
Long Lost Blues: Popular Blues in America, 1850–1920   *Peter C. Muir*
Hard Luck Blues: Roots Music Photographs from the Great Depression
    Rich Remsberg
Restless Giant: The Life and Times of Jean Aberbach and Hill and Range
    Songs   *Bar Biszick-Lockwood*

The University of Illinois Press
is a founding member of the
Association of University Presses.

University of Illinois Press
1325 South Oak Street
Champaign, IL 61820-6903
www.press.uillinois.edu